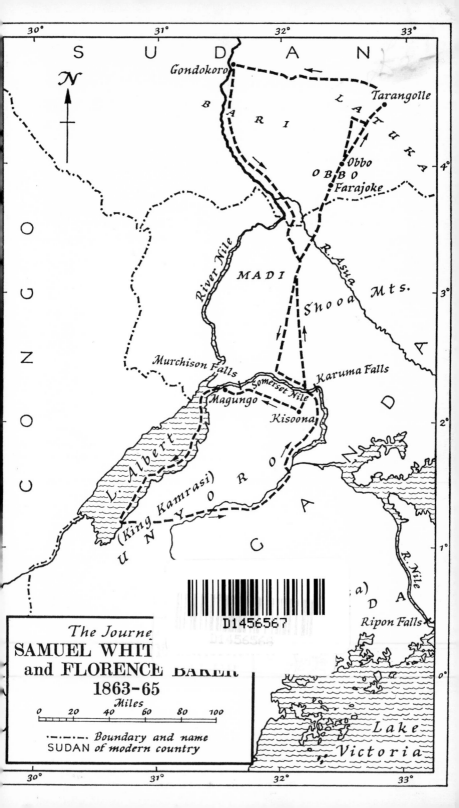

The Journe
SAMUEL WHIT
and FLORENCE BAKER
1863-65

Miles
0   20   40   60   80   100

—·—·—·— Boundary and name
SUDAN of modern country

THE LONG WALKS

THE LONG WALKS

Journeys to the sources of the
White Nile

FREDERICK BRADNUM

READERS UNION
VICTOR GOLLANCZ LTD
London 1970

Journeys to the sources of the
White Nile between 1857 and 1865

THE FIRST EXPEDITION

RICHARD FRANCIS BURTON   JOHN HANNING SPEKE
(1821–1890)   (1827–1864)

From Zanzibar to Ujiji on
Lake Tanganyika, and back

June 1857–March 1859

THE SECOND EXPEDITION

JOHN HANNING SPEKE   JAMES AUGUSTUS GRANT
(1827–1864)   (1827–1892)

From Zanzibar to Lake Victoria; through
Karague, Uganda and Unyoro to Gondokoro

September 1860–February 1863

THE THIRD EXPEDITION

SAMUEL WHITE BAKER   FLORENCE BAKER
(1821–1893)   (1835?–1908)

From Gondokoro to Lake Albert and back;
via Latuka, Obbo, Unyoro and Bari

March 1863–March 1865

Contents

Foreword 13

Introduction 17

THE FIRST EXPEDITION 33

Richard Burton: from *The Lake Regions of Central Africa* 48

John Hanning Speke: from *What led to the Discovery of the Source of the Nile* 84

THE SECOND EXPEDITION 87

John Hanning Speke: from *Journal of the Discovery of the Source of the Nile* 123

James Augustus Grant: from *A Walk across Africa* 150

THE THIRD EXPEDITION 181

Samuel White Baker: from *The Albert N'yanza, Great basin of the Nile* 234

Index 267

List of Illustrations

Between pages 128 *and* 129

Sir Richard Burton by Lord Leighton
Canoeing on Lake Tanganyika
Ladies' Smoking Party
Speke and Burton (backview) in "The Valley of Death and the Home of Hunger"
Speke in his "exploration outfit"
Grant in his "traveller's uniform"
Grant joins in the dance
Mtesa, with some of his wives, reviews his soldiers. Speke looks on.
Grant being introduced by Speke to the Queen Mother of Uganda
Mtesa, King of Uganda, "Walking like a lion"
Speke's and Grant's "Faithfuls" photographed in Cairo. (Seedy Bombay, with hat, in foreground)
Florence Baker
Baker in his travelling costume
Baker the hunter, hunted
The storm on the Albert lake
Baker's first view of the Murchison Falls
The Obbo war dance

FOREWORD

Foreword

A FEW YEARS ago my good friend Willoughby Gray wrote an exciting television programme about the quarrel between Richard Burton and John Hanning Speke, which culminated in the latter's sensational death. This programme fired the imagination, as they say, and I drafted an idea for a radio play based on the events in central Africa during the Burton–Speke expedition. It was to be an imaginative reconstruction of the clash between two violently opposed personalities, thrown together in isolation, whilst travelling half-way across Africa and back. Third Programme would have none of it however, and the B.B.C. Features Producer, Maurice Brown, wisely diverted me to write a programme about the odd goings on surrounding the discoveries of the sources of the White Nile. My programme was called "A Storm in the Nile Basin", and was duly broadcast on the Third. From it grew this book.

The research I did for the radio programme opened my eyes to the enormous amount of material published, at the time, by the Nile explorers on their explorations. Books which, with the exception of Baker's two volumes, had not been reprinted this century, which covered, in great detail, three of the most eventful explorations ever made into Africa, or anywhere else. They were also books that told one a great deal about their authors, and which surprised in their revelation of the strange and chaotic circumstances in which the expeditions took place.

They were remarkable journeys by remarkable people and in their casual, wayward fashion they set in motion the acquisition of vast tracts of Africa for the British Empire. They are now largely forgotten: placed in an historical limbo, and their achievements seemingly no longer of much account since the sun has finally set on the empire they helped to establish. And yet, perhaps because what they accomplished is not any more shaded red upon the map, their journeys should be appreciated again for what they were at the time—courageous endeavours to extend the boundaries of geographical knowledge.

In this book I have attempted to do three things. First, to set the explorations briefly into their historical background. Secondly, to retrace each expedition over the whole of its route, and to consider the behaviour, and the motives, of the men (and one woman) who made the journeys. This last task has not been undertaken from a wish to sit in judgement upon the explorers; but only in admiration, and wonder and sheer curiosity. Their journeys will seem amateur and inefficient—which they often were—in this, our time of carefully organised, scientifically orientated exploration. Their achievements, however, were solid enough. Also I found, when writing the story of these journeys, that I was, at times, confronted with a record of irrational and even mysterious situations. I have tried on these occasions to advance an explanation, or explanations, for what happened. Otherwise I have kept to the recorded facts—the plain, unvarnished truth—although these facts often seem bizarre, and the plain, unvarnished truth wildly improbable.

Lastly, from the eight hundred thousand or so words written by the explorers on their journeys, I have selected some forty-five thousand words, and by this selection I have tried to illuminate the essence of the explorations and the imminence of the explorers' personalities. This selecting was not an enviable task and obviously a considerable volume of interesting material could not be included; but perhaps what I have included will give some idea of the sort of books that were written, so hurriedly, just over a hundred years ago, and have since been so neglected.

F. B.

THE LONG WALKS

Introduction

You have had a long walk, Captain Grant!
—*Palmerston when meeting Grant*

THE DESCRIPTION IS apt: they were a series of long walks of
the sort taken by Grant in Scotland at weekends; by Speke in
Somerset when on leave, gun in hand; by Baker as a boy around
the purlieus of Enfield; and by Burton wherever he found himself,
if the whim was strong. They were part and parcel of the spirit
of restlessness which set the British gentlemen of their time
walking about the world as if they owned it.

They did, of course, own quite a lot of it, and because of these
journeys into Central Africa they would own a lot more. Not
that territorial annexation was the purpose of these journeys; that
happened almost casually, then and afterwards. Lake Victoria
and Lake Albert were the obvious names to spring to mind when
Speke and Baker became the first Europeans to gaze upon those
vast stretches of water. It is only surprising that Lake Tanganyika
was not rechristened, likewise; but Burton, who came to it first,
thought differently from the others. The long walks themselves
were undertaken, not for gain and hardly for glory, in the quint-
essence of sheer adventure.

At the beginning of the nineteenth century there was a gentle
stirring of interest in Europe about the dark blankness of Central
Africa, the sources of the White Nile, and the size and position
of the lakes from which, in all probability, the Nile rose. It was a
vast land into which no European had ventured for some eighteen
hundred years; and that journey, north and west from Zanzibar
by the Greek merchant Diogenes, had been transformed by time
and word into a legend. The best-known maps were those of the

Alexandrian, Claudius Ptolemaeus, from the second century, and the Arab cartographer Al-Idrisi, from the twelfth. Both these maps suggested that the White Nile rose from an area dominated by lakes and mountains, which at least could be said to be an intelligent guess. Nobody really knew, however, and it was obviously high time that somebody British found out. High time because the interior was beginning to be opened up by German and Austrian missionaries on the one hand, and Arab ivory and slave traders on the other.

By the time Burton and Speke made the first journey, there were missions at Mombasa, on the east coast, and on the Nile itself at Gondokoro, some six hundred miles south of Khartoum. Indeed, two Germans from the Mombasa mission, Rebmann and Krapf, had already visited Kilimanjaro and returned with the news of a snow-covered peak a few degrees south of the equator. The British geographers, who had not been within a thousand miles of Africa, found the idea deliciously ridiculous.

The missions did not flourish. The African proved stubbornly indifferent to the message of Christianity, whilst the climate, with its attendant fevers and diseases, wrecked the health of the missionaries all too quickly. Baker records thirteen missionaries "destroyed" in six months at one Nile Mission near Khartoum. Speke mentions that "want of employment" was the main reason for the death of so many at Gondokoro, and that to kill time ". . . they spent their days eating, drinking, smoking, and sleeping, till they broke down their constitutions by living too fast".

The missionaries' loss became the slave traders' gain. Their expeditions flourished, marching from Zanzibar to the shores of Lake Tanganyika, from Gondokoro south for two hundred miles to Shooa and the borders of the brutal Chopi country. They set up trading stations on their routes; Gondokoro was nothing else but one such station, succinctly described by Baker as "a perfect hell". They ran their business under the guise of trading for ivory, which indeed they did, but it was the human animal they were after. Their methods were a mixture of brute force and cunning play upon the primitive greed of tribal chiefs. If they could not take their victims by sudden raids on the miserable collections of huts, driving and cornering the inhabitants like cattle, then they bought them for coloured beads, brass wire, and checked cotton cloth.

It could not have been simpler, and in the course of the first fifty years of the nineteenth century it did as much harm to the tribes of east and central Africa as plague, pestilence and genocide would have done. These first British explorers were confronted by peoples whose innocence had been ravaged and their nature debased. They were also to meet other tribes, secure from the slave traders, who lived in a nightmare of superstition, cruelty, and sudden death.

Great Britain was strongly opposed to slavery, and its ambassadors and consuls applied pressure against it where they could. There was little else they could do until the soldiers of the Queen were in control of the slave-trading territory. That time was soon to come, but in the eighteen-fifties, with the connivance of Egypt and Turkey, and the "blind eye" policy of Portugal and France, the slave trader did just what he wished, more or less openly. (The ivory trading was a cover which nobody took seriously.)

Baker spoke out, most emphatically, against the whole grisly business. Because of this he was himself threatened, his porters made to mutiny, and his expedition almost brought to grief in the early stages through the hostility of a powerful group trading from Gondokoro. Only his immense courage (and his wife's steadfastness), his complete belief in the moral infallibility of his person and purpose, made it possible for him to brush his enemies aside at first, and then win them to his side later.

The other three suffered minor irritations but nothing else. Speke and Grant made all the right noises of disapproval when they mentioned slavery in their books. Burton seemed hardly to notice it, except that he grew cross about the way the traders abused the protection of the British flag at Zanzibar. His concern is with the abuse of the flag, not the nature of the trade. The truth was that all four men had no option but to travel some of their way with slave caravans over the well-used slave-trading routes. Even Baker had to compromise: it was impossible not to cooperate with the Arab slaver. To travel otherwise would have been impractical, and would probably have led to disaster.

That is, travelling in the manner which these British expeditions adopted, or had forced on them by necessity. Burton makes the point well when he writes: "It was indeed my firm conviction from first to last, that in case of attack or surprise I had not a soul except my companion [Speke] to stand by me: all those who accompanied us could, and consequently would, have saved their lives; *we* must have perished." He is writing specifically about the distrust he always felt for both his own bodyguard and the Arab guns, and he knew the answer. "For though sixty guns do not suffice to prevent attack in Ugogo, six hundred stout fellows armed with the 'hot mouthed weapon' might march through the length and breadth of Central Africa." Burton and his kind never had so much as six stout fellows they could entirely trust, let alone six hundred.

It was an awkward predicament, but one there was no escape from; Baker, Burton, Grant and Speke were explorers first and last, not missionaries, colonisers or traders. Although they saw the possibilities of colonisation and trade—Baker alone thought of Christianisation as beneficial in a practical way—such things would follow once the first long walks had established Britain's presence in the regions. So they used the slave trade, and managed to remain alive, although their journeys would undoubtedly hasten the end of the slave-trader's day.

Why they were not murdered is an interesting speculation. Other Europeans had been, including in 1845 a young Frenchman, Maizan, whose really horrible death is written up in detail by Burton and also mentioned by Speke and Grant. When men live against the odds, it is usually because they deliberately choose to ignore those odds. Which means having a cool head, and an unshakeable belief in one's superiority over element or man opposing you. All of this was true of these four men, as it was true of a majority of their fellow-countrymen.

They despised the half-caste Arab traders they were forced to deal with. Burton writes, without qualification, that such men were "degenerate in body and mind; the third generation becomes as truly negroid as the inner heathen". And as for the poor "inner heathen", he was a being one stage only above the animal kingdom, who could not be considered seriously as friend or foe. The African was a poor devil indeed, but also an exasperating one. Over and over again our four travellers complain about him. To them he was not the noble savage, but the ignoble brute of an antediluvian continent, who still existed sunk in torpid barbarism. Baker's comparison with the dog is typical of what all four men wrote down frequently. "1863, 10th April, Latooka. I wish the black sympathisers in England could see Africa's inmost heart as I do, much of their sympathy would subside. Human nature viewed in its crude state as pictured amongst African savages is quite on a level with that of the brute, and not to be compared with the noble character of the dog. There is neither gratitude, pity, love, nor self-denial; no idea of duty; no religion; but covetousness, ingratitude, selfishness and cruelty."

The English is tortuous, the sentiment is clear. They did have a lot to put up with and often stood in real danger, not so much from the slave-trader's machinations as from the thoughtless, senseless cruelty of the tribal African.

Their travels took years. Burton and Speke were away from home for almost three years; Grant and Speke for three years and almost two months, or, as the meticulous Grant put it, "eleven hundred and forty-six days"; Baker and his remarkable wife for about four years, although for a year they wandered in Abyssinia, exploring the Nile tributaries.

Although the paths they took into the interior were not untrodden, the land they went through was dissociated from any previous experience, as remote as a journey on another planet, a world where time and custom had little or no meaning—the only Africans they came across who measured time were the Ugandians—and above all they were walking through a waste land that seemed to have no history, was still part of the prehistoric world.

It was an unnerving experience, the vast plains, labyrinthine forests, barren plateaus all empty of the evidence of man's past.

Not a single building that was older than a few years, and, except for Uganda, nowhere a town that was not instantly destructible, nowhere even a trace of a reasonable system of behaviour, not a murmur of anything approaching a civilisation, past or present. Not a religion to be found; not a deity, however false, that was worshipped; and not the merest thread of belief, anywhere, that man had an immortal soul, or that there was a choice between good and evil.

Only a little over a hundred years ago these explorers were, like Gulliver, travelling amongst what must have seemed a race of pitiful Yahoos. Yet they were never arrogant or vicious in their attitude to the African, nor were they particularly concerned with his welfare in any paternal way. The benevolent but rigid demarcation of black from white, the lesser from the greater, the child from the man, from which apartheid grew, was quite alien to them. Burton noted that the native "intelligence is surprising when compared with that of an uneducated English peasant". He was not so sure about education, however. "But it [the intelligence] has a narrow bound beyond which apparently no man may pass." We can content ourselves in the knowledge that although Burton was extremely good at many things he was a terribly bad prophet; his books are full of heady prophecies most of which have been proved either irrelevant or totally opposite to what did happen.

Baker advanced the theory that Central African man was *pre-Adamite*, a rather eccentric Biblical supposition springing from the already known fact that, geologically, central Africa was the oldest unchanged land-mass in the world. (In recent years, of course, the evidence of earliest man has been found in this part of Africa.) This explained something of the great darkness, although the more they tried to explain away the more confused they became. Thus, with the exception of Burton, they placed their hopes upon the African being a fit subject for first education and then civilisation, once the threat of the slave-trader was removed.

It seemed the only answer, a completely new beginning. For the old ways, and the bewildering void of the dark, pointless present, were incomprehensible, and frightening. This frequently, if implicitly, crops up in their writing of the African and his country, a sense of wonder at the inconceivable depths from which the naked heathen sprang. There is even a touch of fear behind their questions and their views, as if the animality, the mindless barbarity which surrounded them, might awaken the pre-Adamite man in themselves.

This is the only fear they can be accused of showing. However desperate their own condition or the situations in which they found themselves, it was accepted, in a matter of fact way, as part of the bargain a man made for a life of adventure—which makes Mrs Baker's courage and strength of mind, in the really terrifying circumstances she was always finding herself faced with, all the more heroic (and extraordinary, considering she was a twenty-five-year-old Hungarian girl).

Sometimes the cool, detached attitude gives way in Baker's narrative to scenes that are mighty near parodies of a Henty adventure story for boys.

It was not fiction, however, but fact; and if Baker had not stood his ground and bellowed like an enraged bull he might well have been shot down. But it was not only the endless battle against sullen hostility which could always explode like gunpowder that wore on the reserves of strength and resolution; there was also the wretched climate and its attendant illnesses and diseases.

On the whole there was an excess of everything. When it was hot it was unbearably so, and as dry as dust. When it was wet it was like a steam-bath most of the time, with sudden plunges under a cold shower. On the high ground cold, dry winds blew steadily. Going through the forests was like crawling through a series of damp, dark cellars, embraced by monstrous vegetable growths. All extremes could be encountered within forty-eight hours of travelling. Burton describes the effect brilliantly. "About noon the fair scene vanished as if by enchantment. We suddenly turned northwards into a tangled mass of tall fetid reeds, rank jungle and forest. . . . After the fiery sun and the dry atmosphere of the plains, the sudden effect of the dank and clammy chill . . . under the impervious shades that line the river banks, was overpowering. In such places one feels as if poisoned by miasma. . . ."

The toll in manpower of this sort of progression was devastating. Speke gives detailed lists of the men he engaged, showing where they dropped out. From Zanzibar he took on 76 men; seventeen only of these stayed through to the bitter end. The others are shown as having deserted, died, been murdered or sent back en route. After that it was a matter of recruiting from local tribes as Grant and he went along, the recruits deserting and being replaced every few weeks.

None of our travellers admits to more than the odd moment's lapse in his determination to press on; there must have been times, surely, when the temptation to turn back was very strong. And later, when to turn back would be quite as difficult as to go forward, he must have sometimes wished not to move at all ever again. Lying in some foul hut, he must often have prayed for a quick death.

The recital of their sicknesses is horrifying. Collective and various fevers whose effects ranged from hallucinations of dual identity to toes that curled up and looked one in the face. Troubles with insects that bit and burrowed into flesh and bone. Cuts and scratches which instead of healing normally remained inflamed for weeks, or brought on ridiculous, gruesome swellings of the joints. Coughs and colds, outdoing anything suffered when at home in the land of such afflictions. Dysentery-like visitations which lasted for months and left each traveller exhausted, and often too weak to move. Speke suffered from a blindness which prevented him from actually seeing Lake Tanganyika, and he was unlucky enough to get a particularly drastic local disease called Kichyomachyoma, "the little irons", the name speaking for itself.

Often they were laid up for weeks on end. Throughout the narratives of their journeys, descriptions like this of Speke's abound: "On arriving here we were disabled by sickness—Captain Burton utterly, and I suffering from Ophthalmia, and a weakness in the lower extremities resembling paralysis."

Again it was all taken in their stride, although Burton complains at one time that he really was convinced he would die, and Baker, after a couple of months of illness thinking of home, a beefsteak and a bottle of pale ale, considered ". . . death would have been a release that I would have courted but I should have liked that one English beefsteak and pale ale before I died".

Against these diseases their medicine chests contained a pitiful inadequacy. Grant gives the contents of his as being "Brown's blistering tissue, plaster, quinine, lunar caustic, citric acid, julap, calomel, rhubarb, blue pill, colocynth, laudanum, Dover's powders, emetic essence of ginger". The whole weighed thirty pounds, and before Grant was half-way through the expedition it was all gone; lost, stolen or used up. Each medicine chest came to a similar fate and contained roughly the same group of remedies Grant's probably being more comprehensive than most.

Burton put his faith in a patent medicine, "Dr Warburg's Drops", which seems to have been a pretty powerful, anti-emetic painkiller, and, if Burton is not over-exaggerating in the aftermath, saved him from the grave once or twice. Possibly "Dover's powders" did the same for Grant or for some thieving tribesman; he doesn't say. Baker found himself taken for a great medicine man through his administration of tartar emetic to the Obbo slave traders, not so much because of what it did as the fact that it did exactly what Baker said it would. "He told me I should be sick, and, by Allah, there was no mistake about it!"

Beyond these medicines was the brandy, six dozen, ten dozen. It was never enough and, as usual, much vanished during the nightly halts. Undoubtedly it was a life-saver, whereas the native beer, pombe, had little to recommend it, being very much an African drink, rather unsuited to the white man's head and stomach.

At one time Baker, unable to move on because the King of Unyoro was being more difficult than usual, made himself and Mrs Baker comfortable on high ground surrounded by sweet potatoes. Baker was an ingenious, enterprising man, and he was soon making a gallon or so of potato-whisky a day. He called his still "King Kamrasi's Central African Unyoro Potato-Whisky

Company, Unlimited", and claimed "I found an extraordinary change in my health from the time that I commenced drinking the potato-whisky. I became strong, and from that time to the present day my fever left me. . . ." King Kamrasi also found the whisky most agreeable, and, as large areas of his kingdom were given over to the cultivation of sweet potatoes, he took to producing whisky as Baker had showed him how in vast quantities. The only known result of his enthusiasm was that he lost his throne, and his life, to one of the neighbouring kings a few years later.

All the expeditions spent long periods of time as the unwilling guests of kings and tribal chieftains. Burton used these halts to discover all he could about native customs, ceremonies, and social behaviour. He was a brilliant observer; his short, explicit study of the Wanyamwezi people, to be found later in this book, is typical of his remarkable, natural talent for anthropology. It is also typical of Burton that he should have neglected the quest for the source of the Nile—and let Speke march alone to his glory —in favour of such unfashionable, unregarded pursuits.

The rest of our travellers found these times of enforced immobility quite maddening. Either they sat on the sidelines and breathed heavy discontent with their situation or, like Speke and Grant in Uganda, they became much too involved. It was a lot easier for Burton, for he alone had the ability to get under the African's skin, and to remain apart at the same time. The truth was, perhaps, that Burton was always the outsider looking in. His solitary, eccentric genius meant that he lived and appreciated life in a way that was alien to the majority. What he observed, he illuminated powerfully and excitingly, and he could disguise himself in any role; but he could never belong.

They triumphed, finally, over every adversity, and like characters from some allegorical story got home. By the time they did so, nobody knew any more what the allegory meant; they had been lost for so long. It was only later, after Baker's return, that the pattern started to re-form and be understood.

For the men themselves, the return to civilisation at Gondokoro or Zanzibar was an anti-climax. It could not be anything else.

The brass bands, or at least the red carpets of the Royal Geographical Society, and other august, learned bodies, came later. The meeting of Baker with Grant and Speke at Gondokoro, as we shall see, is a classic scenario, and it was at least some sort of homecoming, whereas the welcome received by Burton and Speke at Zanzibar was worth no more than a couple of lines' mention by either man. All we know is that Burton received letters from India that he didn't care for, and was snubbed by the new British Consul on the island, whilst Speke set about organising his journey home to England with such fury that he hardly seemed to notice where he was.

The Bakers arrived back at awful Gondokoro in style, Union Jack held high and three cheers for old England and the Sources of the Nile ringing out—to which was added a remarkably dangerous display of firing away with every weapon the expedition still possessed. It all turned to ashes. All the welcoming Turks —as Baker would call the Egyptian irregulars—had to tell them was that they had long since been given up for dead by the authorities at Khartoum. There were no letters, supplies or news waiting for them, and, what was the bitterest bite, no boat available to take them on up the Nile. The Bakers had to wait until they arrived at Suez for their dreamed-of glass of "Allsopp's Pale Ale". They found it on draught with "an ice accompaniment", a tantalising description.

*   *   *

They all kept extensive journals whilst on their expeditions, and once back home they wrote extensive books. Mrs Baker was the exception, unless she kept a journal in her own language. It is nice to think that she did, committing to paper exactly what she thought of the stark naked tribesmen who danced around her hut at the sight of her long blonde hair, and metaphorically letting that beautiful hair down about the ebullient Englishman she loved and the lunatic quest he had vowed to make. She was a woman of great spirit, but historically a silent one.

The books are idiosyncratically representative of their authors. Grant's *A Walk Across Africa* (Blackwood, 1864) is at times as pedestrian as its title. But it is also pleasingly modest and very accurate, and contains some really first-rate descriptive writing as well as some elegant, inornate reporting.

The journey which Speke made with Burton resulted in his curiously titled *Journal of a Cruise on the Tanganyika Lake*, a short book which was published with his journal of the earlier trip with Burton in Somaliland, the whole volume being given the impressive overall title of *What Led to the Discovery of the Source of the Nile* (Blackwood, 1863). The Tanganyika journal gives us the historical moment when Speke first saw the lake he was to christen Victoria, and, gazing down on it, knew that he was looking at the Nile Source. Otherwise the book is a very subdued account of a journey which caused Speke great physical and mental anguish. He is guarded—and at times a little snide—in his references to Burton, which is not exactly surprising.

On the expedition with Grant, Speke made up for the soft tone of the other book. The *Journal of the Discovery of the Source of the Nile* (Blackwood, 1864) is a massive egotistical outpouring often abominably written but never letting up on the narrative interest. In it the strange, elusive personality of John Hanning Speke wanders, with a slightly ravaged air, through some of the most bizarre adventures ever to befall a man.

Burton was the most experienced traveller, and author, of the four. His *The Lake Regions of Central Africa* (Longmans, Green, 1860) is subtitled "A Picture of Exploration", has a Shakespearian quotation prefacing it, "Some to discover islands far away", and is in two fat volumes. Burton was a compulsive writer, and the book is as much a dissertation on exploration as the narrative of one particular exploration. Sometimes the prose becomes overblown, and overladen with Greek, Arabic, French and Latin quotations and phrases, for Burton was intent upon flying his scholarship for all to see. But of course, as is to be expected, when the book is good it is very, very good, and its author's leaps of thought are fascinating.

Finally, Baker wrote his wild adventure story. He ought to have given it a romantic title: *The Albert N'yanza, Great Basin of the Nile and Explorations of the Nile Sources* (Macmillan, 1886) is misleadingly stuffy. The book teems with incident, is written with enthusiasm, and reads like a first-rate, fictional tale of adventure. Perhaps Baker exaggerated at times, but it does not matter. This was the way he approached his journey, this was the sort of situation he exposed himself (and his wife) to because he was the sort of man he was. Open, lionhearted, honest, as strong as an oak, impulsive, and yet nobody's fool. There is a clear-minded intelligence working behind this record of an exploration to which so many unreasonable things happened.

THE FIRST EXPEDITION

From Zanzibar to Ujiji on Lake Tanganyika, and back

June 1857 to March 1859

RICHARD FRANCIS BURTON (1821–1890)
JOHN HANNING SPEKE (1827–1864)

In 1854 Burton had organised a party to explore the Somali country, including the walled city of Harar. The expedition consisted of Burton, Lieutenants Stroyan and Herne, and Assistant Surgeon Stocks. The last-named died suddenly before they reached Aden. Once in Aden, Burton found a replacement in Speke, who was on his way to Africa for two years to shoot, explore, even, perhaps, to seek the Nile source. This was the first meeting of the two men. As things turned out, only Burton was able to get into the interior; going from Berbera—on the East African coast across the Gulf from Aden—he reached Harar, and came out alive. The other three men visited the African coast, and waited for Burton.

When he arrived back Burton put a new plan in action—to go from Berbera, almost due west, to the Nile, presumably where it flowed through Khartoum. They never got there. On 19 April their camp at Berbera was attacked by Somali Nomads, Stroyan was killed, and Speke went through a pretty shattering experience when he was captured by the Nomads. "In another instant I was on the ground with a dozen Somali on the top of me. The man I had endeavoured to shoot wrenched the pistol out of my hand, and the way the scoundrel handled me sent a creeping shudder all over me. I felt as if my hair stood on end; and, not knowing who my opponents were, I feared that they belonged to a tribe called Eesa, who are notorious, not only for their ferocity in fighting, but for the unmanly mutilations they delight in. Indescribable was my relief when I found that my most dreadful fears were without foundation. The men were in reality feeling whether, after an Arab fashion, I was carrying a dagger between my legs. . . ."

After this shock Speke was bound and led away, became involved in a raid on his captors by another tribe, was threatened with being cut in half, downwards, and finally suffered a murderous attack from his guard. This man stabbed Speke over and over again with a spear, and undoubtedly would have finished him off if Speke had not suddenly attacked first, giving the man a sharp back-hander, and then managing to run the gauntlet of the camp and find his way back to his own camp, nearly dead from loss of blood and exhaustion.

This was not all. During the fight, before Speke was captured, Burton had accused him of cowardice. Or rather he had said, when Speke went back into the tent to see what was going on behind them, "Don't step back or they will think we are retiring". It might have been sound advice, but it was tactless, and Speke could not forget it. Then came the rest of the disaster, Stroyan's death and Speke's own capture. In his own words, it was ".... a signal failure from inexperience, and with a loss of £510 worth of my own private property, which I never recovered. I had nothing to show but eleven artificial holes in my body." He criticised Burton for his handling of the abortive expedition, and he could not forgive Burton his remarks made in the heat of battle.

The battle at Berbera was a nasty business, but it was part of the risk any expedition had to face on that wild coast. It should have united Speke and Burton, but it did the opposite. They did not quarrel—it is doubtful if Burton had the slightest idea that there was anything to quarrel about—but Speke began carefully to preserve a grievance, carefully to build up an antagonism against Burton. Again it is doubtful if Burton realised any of this —which was part of the trouble.

It would have been difficult to find two men who were temperamentally further apart. Burton didn't care, Speke cared too much. Burton was not ambitious: already, when they met, he had thrown away the chance of fame by not exploiting to personal advantage his sensational journey to Mecca, in 1853, disguised as a believer. Speke was coolly, deliberately ambitious; a calculating exploiter of his personal triumphs of exploration. Burton was all things to all men; Speke was only his prickly self, guarded, as

conventional as a rural dean. Burton did not make moral judge-
ments on men and their predicaments, although he often gave
practical advice (and that was more often than not pretty un-
sound). Speke was a great adjudicator of men and their actions,
when he got the chance. Burton was the fox, Speke was the
hedgehog.

Yet these two men chose to go on a long and dangerous expedition together knowing full well that they would be shut off from
their own kind, and shut up together as they went through a vast,
unfriendly wilderness for a couple of years. In the light of what we
know now it seems a gross piece of miscasting, a blundering self-
deception by both of them. At the time, however, it must have
appeared as a sensible, logical course of action for them to take.

According to Speke the Royal Geographical Society had
directed Burton to find the Lake of Nyassa, survey it, and explore
the country around it. When he had done this they ordered him
to head north to find the source of the Nile. (They thought it
would be found in Ptolemy's Mountains of the Moon.) Burton
accepted these orders: he was keen to explore Central Africa; he
was cynical about discovering the sources of the Nile in general.
Speke had been dreaming of finding the Source—he thought of it
in the singular—for years: now he was intent on making his
dream come true. Thus Burton asked Speke to join him, and
Speke gladly accepted. It was all very predictable.

What was not predictable was that this course of action had in
it the seeds of a bitter quarrel, and that the quarrel would grow
into a spiteful—and ludicrous—feud. Typical of the way in
which things developed are these two shorts extracts published
after the expedition was over. The first from Burton. "I could
not expect much of his [Speke's] assistance, he was not a linguist
... nor a man of science, nor an accurate astronomical observer.
During the exploration he acted in a subordinate capacity [and
because of his lack of languages] ... he was unfit for any other but
a subordinate capacity." And from Speke: "Captain Burton,
however, knew nothing of astronomical surveying, of physical
geography, or of collecting specimens of natural history, so he
pressed me again to go with him."

When they left Bombay for Zanzibar in December 1856, Burton was thirty-five and Speke was twenty-nine. They both held commissions in the Indian Army, had seen active service in the Crimean War, and had indulged in some exotic exploration before this African trip. Burton, as has been mentioned, had visited Arabia on his journey to Mecca, and travelled through Somaliland to the ancient walled city of Harar (where Rimbaud was to live some thirty years later), to become the first European to enter that sinister place and come out alive. Speke, who had been in the Indian Army since he was seventeen, had been on shooting and collecting expeditions to unexplored parts of the Himalayas, and on a couple of occasions had actually crossed into Tibet.

Now, for the first time, they both had what might be termed an official exploration on their hands; something to be done and accounted for. Burton had been given the money, and the introductions to those in power at Zanzibar; once on the island it would be necessary to organise the expedition from scratch. To recruit guards, porters and guides, pack-animals, domestic staff—slaves, mostly, from Zanzibar. To settle the route, and to arrange the manner in which stores, supplies and beads, wire and cloth for barter, ammunition, instruments would be carried. It was a formidable task.

They arrived at Zanzibar in the middle of December 1856, and in January of 1857 went on a series of voyages along the east coast, north as far as Mombas, south to Quitoa. The excuse was that it was the dry season, and that they needed some experience in East African travelling. It was a typical piece of digressive wandering in the true Burtonian fashion; it had nothing to do with the proper aims of the main expedition, and it achieved nothing.

They visited various coast towns, shot a number of wild animals, and thoroughly enjoyed themselves. But, as Speke mentions in his journal, it gave the merchants and traders of Zanzibar, and those travelling into and out of the interior the chance to organise themselves against the expedition. This they did so well that it is doubtful if Burton and Speke would have managed even to begin their journey if it had not been for the help and influence of the British Consul, Lt.-Col. Hamerton. And they were extremely lucky to have had the Consul's help, for he was a very sick man and died a few weeks after the expedition finally got away.

Neither man wrote very much about the expedition's organisation in their books, and what they did write is more confusing than clarifying. (It doesn't help that they spell native names differently: Baloch, Said bin Salim, Kaole, for instance, in Burton, become Beluch, Sheikh Said Silim, Kaolleh in Speke.) Burton was probably writing ambiguously on purpose, with the deliberate intention of being obscure: it is easier to discover something of the lack of organisation by noting what he leaves out of the record than by working from what he puts in. He mentions that 170 porters were needed, and that only thirty-six had been recruited. There is mention later that with Hamerton's help other men were found, but how many remains a secret. Speke remarks that "the amount of information gathered by the expedition concerning the interior of Africa at Zanzibar, I may say, was *nil* . . ." And later that the information they did glean was worse than none.

Every trick in the game was played against them by the Arabs on Zanzibar and by the Sultan's army of half-caste irregulars, the Balochs, at Kaole, the little coast town across from the island where the expedition started its journey. To make matters worse, Burton had left everything to the last moment, although he had been six months on or around Zanzibar.

They finally left Kaole for the interior not so much an ordered, marshalled expedition as an improvised column, a shambles of a mixed outing. Burton only lets the truth be guessed at when he reflects upon the "indifference" of his expedition compared to the well armed, disciplined and carefully organised expeditions of the Egyptians that he had inspected in Cairo.

They straggled on almost due west, following the trade routes made by the slave and ivory traders' caravans; an ill-disciplined, bad-tempered column. "It was like driving a herd of wild cattle," Burton wrote. Their ultimate goal was Ujiji, a thousand miles away on the shores of Lake Tanganyika. The idea of finding Lake

Nyassa, which Speke mentions in his version of the R.G.S.s orders to the expedition, had been finally dropped. Indeed, Burton had made his intentions quite clear to the Council of the Society, from Zanzibar, that the purpose of the expedition should be to ascertain the limits of the "Sea of Ujiji or Ungamwezi Lake".

He had two good reasons for wishing to amend his orders. First, the route to the Nyassa Lake was a thoroughly dangerous one; the half-caste Arabs and Wasawahili who bestraddled the route were known to be extremely hostile to strangers. Secondly, Burton had discovered one thing at least from the traders at Zanzibar, which was that the Nyassa Lake was of far less importance than the Sea of Ujiji. The R.G.S. had given their consent to this change of objective; Hamerton was very much for it; now all that was required of the expedition was that it should get there, and get back to tell the story.

They travelled very slowly through the valley of the Kingani River, called by the Arabs "The Valley of Death and the Home of Hunger". Both men suffered from malaria and marsh fever, and Speke had a violent fainting fit which was probably a sunstroke. At the end of July they came to halt at Zungomero, a miserable slave-traders' town; ahead of them were the Usagara Hills, and the chance of some better air. This was the end of the First Region, as Burton called the main stages to the Lake. There were three more to go, and roughly the same pattern of progress would mark each stage.

There were the exceptional happenings also. At the beginning of the journey through the Second Region, whilst in the hills—or, as Burton called them, the Delectable Mountains—the expedition came across porters with women and children, dying of smallpox, left to their fate by the side of the route. A few days further on they found themselves entering the territory of two types of ant. The larger was about an inch in length with a bull-dog-like head and mandibles powerful enough to enable it to destroy rats, lizards and snakes.

And the Delectable Mountains ceased to seem so delectable: range upon range covered with rock, a sandy red soil, or a dense bush; the trees bare and the grassland a hard, white stubble. It was the winter season still, which meant that the temperature sank to 48°F. during the night and rose to as high as 90°F. in the day, accompanied by strong south winds. Eventually, after fighting their way through "The Pass Terrible" and the haunted "Devil's Glen", they reached the plains of Ugogo and the end of the Second Region.

They halted at a place called Ugogi, which Burton found very pleasant. The wretched porters were more troublesome than ever, and one ran off with a load consisting of the *Nautical Almanac* for 1858, their surveying books, and the bulk of their paper, ink and pens; a cruel blow to their hopes of any detailed geographical surveys, although most of their surveying, measuring and time-keeping instruments were already proving vulnerable to the climate.

A few days after this loss they were overtaken by a large Arab merchant caravan, coming in from the coast to Unyamwezi land, and much to their delight the Arabs presented them with the lost load, quite intact. It had been left by the runaway porter in the long grass beside the road. Burton had ordered a search to be made for it, knowing that any porter preferred to desert without carrying thirty-odd pounds on his head. The order was not carried out, because neither Burton nor Speke had made it their business to see that it was; nor had they trained anybody to act in what Burton always called "a subordinate capacity", although the material was there. This sort of situation, therefore, cropped up over and over again. Rarely were any orders carried out at all unless either man took personal charge—something they were bad at doing, and often too unwell to do.

The Arab caravan had caught up with them because Speke had been too ill to be moved for a few days. Now he was better, and the expedition joined up with the Arab merchants. Burton liked this, but Speke is slightly caustic about the manner in which the caravan travelled, although quite what was odd or wrong with this mode of travel he doesn't tell. Yet another opposition of views between the two men was the warmth which Burton felt for the Arab, in contrast to the coldness Speke always showed.

But now they were marching through Ugogo land it was better to join forces and make a show of strength. Not that the Wagogo were known so much for their hostility as for their independence, and their somewhat unpredictable boisterousness. This they gave plenty of evidence of when it came to collecting their dues from the men of "White Land—the mysterious end of the world". This collection, a toll or tax levied against the traveller by headsmen, chief and kings before he was allowed to pass through their territory, was in operation throughout central Africa.

It was a source of considerable annoyance to all the expeditions, and the haggling for more beads or a few different cloths could days. A number of the Wagogo chiefs proved very trying in this respect, but the traveller without his six hundred armed men had to put up with such blackmail. As one Wagogo chief said to Burton ". . . all we had was in his hands". And Burton knew it was true, as did his Arab companions, who moved freely through central Africa by paying their dues, and exploiting the ancient formula of "divide and rule" until each tribe was for ever skirmishing against its neighbour.

The expedition and the Arab caravan went across the high plains of Ugogo at a good rate. It was not pleasant country; one part of it was known as the Fiery Field, a thorny jungle with a tall, hard grass straw, and no water. At the end of this was the limit of Burton's Third Region, the frontier of Ugogo and Unyamwezi, a place called Tura, where they halted for a few days before pressing on to Kazeh.

The most confusing thing about Kazeh is that it never seems to have existed under that name to anybody but Burton and Speke. Stanley the next white man to visit the area, in 1871, found that the main town was called Tabora, as it is today. However, in his book about his expedition with Grant, Speke solves the riddle.

Kazeh was far from being a mythical town; it was in fact the centre, the capital town, of the Arab ivory and slave traders. A substantial place spread over a wide area where the Arab had built himself solid houses and lived in much comfort. Here the expedition remained for over a month, and the second mystery is why they remained so long.

Burton remarks that he was very comfortably housed, and had plenty of time to explore the general area, called Unyanyembe, and cultivate his new-found Arab friends. He certainly wrote up the place and the people of Unyanyembe most fully. Then a little further on in his narrative all has turned sour. He writes: "I was detained at Kazeh from 8th November to the 14th December, 1857, and the delay was one long trial of patience." He writes of illnesses suffered by the guards and porters, he complains now of the attitude of his Arab friends and their sullen resentment to the idea of his expedition going on to Ujiji. He doesn't mention Speke—it is as if his companion were elsewhere—and he doesn't mention his own health.

If Burton doesn't mention Speke, the latter certainly mentions Burton, in his short but pertinent resumé of events at Kazeh. It was here that Speke, in Burton's presence, first heard of a great lake to the north, from one Sheikh Snay. At the same time Snay and his fellow merchants implied that rivers ran into this lake, not from it. It seems that both men discussed the idea of abandoning the journey to Ujiji and going north to the lake called Ukerewe. For the moment to move at all was impossible owing to a lack of porters—most of the expedition's men had dispersed at Kazeh, where they had wives and friends—and then Speke records: ". . . Captain Burton got desperately ill, whilst I picked up all the information I could gather from the Arabs, with Bombay as an interpreter." (Seedy Bombay was the leader of the expedition's men.)

So whilst Burton was ill Speke persisted in his questions about the Ukerewe lake. His persistence was rewarded when he made Snay and his friends confess that what they had said about the rivers running into the lake was totally untrue: the rivers flowed out of it. Furthermore, he gathered that the lake stretched well beyond the equator, and vessels sailed upon it and out of it in that area. From that moment Speke was resolved to march north; from that moment he was sure that Lake Ukerewe would prove to be the source of the Nile.

He had to bide his time, for the northern route was said to be highly dangerous. Burton, it seems, now preferred to head west,

and anyway there wasn't a slave or a porter willing to go anywhere. Speke also decided that the expedition must move, somehow; he writes: "We had now been at Kaze rather more than a
month, and I thought Captain Burton would die if we did not
make a move, so I begged him to allow me to assume the command pro tem, and I would see what I could do to effect a move."
Enough men were found to take the expedition out of Kazeh,
although Burton was still very ill. As Speke writes: "Three days
after he was carried over, and he begged me to take account of his
effects, as he thought he would die." Except to say that they
pushed on to the west, Speke writes no more about the Kazeh
episode. It was obviously a period of importance, both in the
history of the discovery of the Nile sources and in the relationship
between the two men. Burton was not silent about such essential
matters for nothing.

Leaving Kazeh, they had about 150 miles to go through the
Fourth Region, the land of Unyamwezi. This last stage of their
journey appears to have been completed without as much agony
as the previous stages, although Burton fell seriously ill on 18
January. Unlike his mysterious illness at Kazeh, he describes this
affliction and its effect on his spirit most graphically: "At sunset
the attack had reached its height. I saw yawning wide to receive
me '. . . those dark gates across the wild that no man knows'."

He was paralysed and lost all sensation, and his leg muscles
contracted. That he thought he was dying is hardly surprising,
but after ten days he was on the move again. A few days later
Speke suffered an attack of ophthalmia, an affliction he had first
had as a child. It left him almost blind, so that when they came
to their moment of glory, on the top of a steep and stony hill,
with Lake Tanganyika spread out before them, poor Speke could
see nothing but "mist and glare" before his eyes.

A day later, on 14 February 1858, they went by a large canoe
along the shores of the lake to Ujiji. Here just about everything
that could go wrong did. Their supplies were stolen, the local
chief was at first suspicious, and then he began a vicious programme of extortion against them.

This man, called Kannena, was described with derisive relish by Burton: ". . . his aspect was truly ignoble; a short, squat and board-backed figure, with natural 'plumpers', a black skin cut and carved in various patterns, thick straight, stumpy legs, and huge splay feet; his low narrow brow was ever knotted into a peevish frown, his apology for a nose much resembled the pug . . . and a villainous expression lurked about the depressed corners of his thick-lipped, sensual, licquorish mouth." Actually, Burton handled the slow-witted man without much tact, and left himself wide open to Kannena's natural cupidity.

The climate was atrociously humid, their botanical collection was ruined by the damp, books fell away from their bindings, and they were subjected to many of the violent electrical storms which were for ever sweeping the hills around the great lake. It left them without energy, and undoubtedly on edge with others, They still had the lake to explore, to sail to the most northerly point, albeit sail was an elegant description for the primitive method of canoeing they would be forced to take—when they managed to rent a couple of canoes.

As ever, it was Speke who was detached for the job of finding the boats. Burton spent the twenty-seven days that Speke was away in pleasant idleness. ". . . It was chiefly spent in eating and drinking, smoking and dozing." Speke was unsuccessful and arrived back much the worse for wear, to Burton's scorn. (It was during this journey that Speke suffered the famous, and frightening, beetle in the ear episode.) Speke was bitter about Burton's behaviour and lack of understanding, but they did not quarrel, only drew a veil over the business and did not mention it again.

By now it seems that the common ground, little though it was, which they had shared no longer existed. By now they had ceased to speak the same language.

For two canoes Burton paid an exorbitant price; he had to show his companion just how easy it was to obtain the transport required, so he paid and made the sort of arrangement with Kannena that meant the expedition was entirely under this man's command whilst on the water. They had set out on 10 April, north-west to Uvira on that coast; it took them until 26 April to get there.

Uvira was as far north on Lake Tanganyika as they were able to get. Here they discovered that the river "Rusizi" ran into the lake, not out of it, which meant that Tanganyika was not the source of the Nile; but they were not allowed to go further north to see the truth of this for themselves. There was no chance of persuading, or forcing, their escort to venture into an area supposedly crammed full of hostile, hardly human cannibals.

They went back to Ujiji, only to be nearly drowned in a terrific storm. Having just got through that they found themselves involved in a nasty little battle with a tribe on the lake shore which was started by a drunken slave. The wretch attacked the expedition's camp for no other reason than that, being drunk, he required to fight—so Speke mentions, adding, with a rare touch of humour, that the man's behaviour was thoroughly British. They arrived back at Ujiji early in May and lost no time in leaving it: they were now on their way home.

By 19 June 1858, they were back in Kazeh, and the subject of the lake of Ukerewe was again on the agenda. Once more it is difficult to discover the sequence of events and the reasons which led to Speke going off on his own to find the lake. One thing is clear, however; Burton had no intention of leaving Kazeh for any trek to the north—or to any point of the compass, come to that. He wanted to complete his journal of the exploration, up to Kazeh on the way home. He also wanted to write up the northern regions from what he had gathered from the Arab merchants. *The Lake Regions of Central Africa* contains twenty-odd pages under the heading of "The Northern Kingdoms. Karagwah, Uganda, and Unyoro". The subject matter of these pages drifts into some remarks about life in Kazeh, and then deals with Speke's return from his great discovery.

Speke went on this journey because he wanted to go. He had never ceased working over what he had discovered, by word of mouth, during their previous stay in Kazeh. At one point on their way from Ujiji he had tried to persuade Burton to take a north-east route back home. This would have led them to within a couple of marches of the lake; it would also have meant the joint discovery of the lake, but Burton would have none of it—he was anxious to get back to the fleshpots of Kazeh.

It also seems, according to Speke, that he was far from well on the journey from Lake Tanganyika. Speke mentions that his companion was unable to move without the assistance of eight men to carry him in a hammock. And the other thing was that Burton wanted to get rid of Speke for a while.

What Burton writes about Speke's going is both simple and strange. It was a solidly simple reason to send Speke to find out about the lake and the northern territory for geographical purposes, but Burton turns the obvious to the obscure by adding that Speke's "presence at Kazeh was by no means desirable". Why it was undesirable he doesn't make clear: the rest of the passage is in a prose so ambiguous as to be unintelligible. It can be safely assumed at least that the two men were sick of each other's company, and the unexplored lake to the north was a godsend to both.

Speke went off on 9 July 1858, to make one of the greatest discoveries in the history of exploration. His caravan was a scratch one, and it started in an atmosphere of pessimism and general mistrust. It was an uneventful journey, although it could have run into trouble from some bad-tempered tribes whose territory covered the route. If this had happened, Speke would probably have left his bones in Africa: his caravan was both weak in numbers and cowardly in spirit.

In Speke's narrative he names 3 August as being the day . . . "when the vast expanse of the pale blue waters of the N'yanza burst suddenly upon my gaze". In fact, he records seeing a sheet of water about four miles away on 30 July, the most southerly point of the lake. But it was 3 August when he saw properly, felt certain that he had discovered the one source of the great Nile, named it—to himself—Lake Victoria, and knew he must get back to England with all speed to make his claim, and to claim his fame. His audience on that day in August was only interested in what he called his French grey spectacles, peering beneath his wide-awake hat to get a good sight of his "double eyes"—as they chose to call the spectacles.

He spent three days on the edge of the lake, on the shore of a

gulf, in fact, which now bears his name. He took measurements
and readings, and found out from the local tribesmen all he could.
Then he set off for Kazeh and Burton, resolved to do everything
in his power to visit the lake again—not with Burton but with "a
new and extensive expedition".

On 26 August he was with Burton at what he quaintly describes
as the old house in Kazeh. Their meeting was both friendly and
warm; Burton had been worried for Speke's safety in the light
of some rumours of war in the country he had come through.
Speke shrugged these rumours off lightly and just as casually told
Burton that he had found the source of the Nile. The scene must
have been splendidly fraught, the dramatic climax uttered with a
light laugh; the friend's reaction a silence as loud as any thunder-
clap. Within a few days the subject could not be mentioned, and
never was mentioned, face to face, again.

The high-spirited adventure now became a sullen journey back
to the coast, each man convinced that his attitude was a reasonable
one, that his companion was being jaundiced, jealous, and stupidly
self-opinionated. A ludicrous situation, perhaps, but one that had
shadowed the expedition ever since the first visit to Kazeh, and
was inherent in the Royal Geographical Society's directive, with
the vague insistence on an attempt being made to find the Nile
source.

Speke had assumed that the Nile source was found when he set
eyes on the southernmost part of Lake Victoria: thirty-two
thousand square miles of water stretched before him. Some two
hundred miles north there might have been a stream flowing out
of the lake which, if followed, would grow into the Nile. It was
impossible to tell without actually going over the ground. Speke
—like the ancients—could really only make an intelligent guess.

This he did not have the nous to do; for in Burton's book an
intelligent guess was all right, but a passionate conviction springing from the heart and not the head was all wrong, womanish
nonsense. Burton quoted upon the occasion: "I have no other but
a woman's reason. I think him so because I think him so."

Of course Burton had always considered the quest for the "coy
sources", as he called them, to be a rather pointless operation,

more of an idealistic day-dream than a scientific search for the truth. Sympathy must go out to him for his attitude, but, as ever, Burton was the odd man out. Speke knew instinctively better. The public imagination would be caught by the discovery of the source of the Nile; it was just what Middle Victorian England wanted to wave the flag over. Jingoism was settling its malignant roots. Burton's cold, sceptical attitude of mind belonged to the past, and to a time yet to come.

By 3 February 1859 they were back on the coast, at Konduchi, a few miles south of Kaole, from where they started out sixteen months earlier. The next step ought to have been Zanzibar and England, but it wasn't. Burton instead organised an expedition to go south, down the coast some 150 miles, to Kilwa Krsiwan's. This they did, to find that cholera had turned the place into a terrible death trap.

They came away, and eventually arrived on the island of Zanzibar on 4 March 1859. There could only have been one reason for this strange little anti-climax of a journey; that was, to make Speke sweat it out a bit longer before he could announce his discovery to the world. It must also have put him in a foul temper, and have made him more intent than ever to reap his reward, alone.

Speke arrived in England on 8 May 1859. Burton followed thirteen days after. He found that Speke had been furiously—and selfishly—active in those thirteen days. By lectures, letters and social receptions he had spread the word, had celebrated the deed. There was not one influential person or society who did not know that John Hanning Speke had discovered the source of the Nile, and Lake Victoria. Burton was shouldered to one side. The long feud had begun.

Within a year Speke was off on his second expedition, this time in command, and with a companion who suited him perfectly, James Augustus Grant.

RICHARD BURTON

from

The Lake Regions of Central Africa

SEEDY MUBARAK BOMBAY—in the interior the name became Mamba (a crocodile) or Pombe (small beer)—had long before returned to his former attitude, that of a respectful and most ready servant. He had, it is true, sundry uncomfortable peculiarities. A heaven-born "Pagazi", he would load himself on the march with his "T'haka-t'haka", or "chow-chow", although a porter had been especially hired for him. He had no memory: an article once taken by him was always thrown upon the ground and forgotten: in a single trip he broke my elephant gun, killed my riding-ass, and lost its bridle. Like the Eastern Africans generally, he lacked the principle of immediate action; if beckoned to for a gun in the field he would probably first delay to look round, then retire, and lastly advance. He had a curious inverted way of doing all that he did. The water-bottle was ever carried on the march either uncorked or inverted; his waistcoat was generally wound round his neck, and it appeared fated not to be properly buttoned; whilst he walked bareheaded in the sun, his Fez adorned the tufty poll of some comrade; and at the halt he toiled like a charwoman to raise our tents and to prepare them for habitation, whilst his slave, the large lazy Maktubu, a boy-giant from the mountains of Urundi, sat or dozed under the cool shade. Yet with all his faults and failures Bombay, for his un-wearied activity, and especially from his undeviating honesty—there was no man, save our "Negro Rectitude", in the whole camp who had not proved his claim to the title triliteral—was truly valuable.

WE left Mzizi Mdogo on the 9th August, much cheered by the well-omened appearance of a bird with red bill, white breast, and long tail-feathers. The path ran over a succession of short steep hills with a rufous-brown soil, dotted with blocks and stones, thinly veiled with grass, and already displaying signs of aridity in the growth of aloetic and thorny plants, the Cactus and the larger Asclepias, the Euphorbia or Spurge-wort, and the stunted Mimosa. The Calabash, however, still rose a stately tree, and there was a sprinkling of the fine Tamarinds which have lent their name to the district. The Tamarind, called by the Arabs of Zanzibar "Subar", extends from the coast to the Lake Regions: with its lofty stem, its feathery leaflets, and its branches spreading dark cool shade, it is a beautiful feature in African landscape. The acidulated fruit is doubtless a palliative and a corrective to bilious affections. The people of the country merely peel and press it into bark baskets, consequently it soon becomes viscid, and is spoiled by mildew; they ignore the art of extracting from it an intoxicating liquor. The Arabs, who use it extensively in cooking, steam, sun-dry, and knead it, with a little salt and oil to prevent the effects of damp, into balls: thus prepared and preserved from the air, it will keep for years.

On the way we were saddened by the sight of the clean-picked skeletons, and here and there the swollen corpses, of porters who had perished in this place of starvation. A single large body which had lost fifty of its number by small-pox, had passed us but yesterday on the road, and the sight of their deceased comrades recalled to our minds terrible spectacles; men staggering on blinded by disease, and mothers carrying on their backs infants as loathsome objects as themselves. The wretches would not leave the path, every step in their state of failing strength was precious; he who once fell would never rise again; no village would admit death into its precincts, no relation nor friend would return for them, and they would lie till their agony was ended by the raven and vulture, the Fisi and the fox. Near every Khambi or Kraal I remarked detached tents which, according to the guides, were set apart for those seized with the fell disease. Under these circumstances, as might be expected, several of our party caught the infection; they lagged behind and probably threw themselves into some jungle, for the path when revisited showed no signs of them.

We spent 4 hrs. 30 in weary marching, occasionally halting to reload the asses that threw their packs. Near the Mgeta River, which was again forded six times, the vegetation became tall and thick, grasses obstructed the path, and in the dense jungle on the banks of the stream, the Cowhage (*Dolichos pruriens*), and stiff reeds known as the "wild sugar-cane", annoyed the half-naked porters. Thus bounded and approached by muddy and slippery, or by steep and stony inclines, the stream shrank to a mountain torrent, in places hardly fifty feet broad; the flow was swift, the waters were dyed by the soil a ruddy brown, and the bed was sandy and sometimes rocky with boulders of primitive formation, streaked with lines of snow-white quartz. Near the end of the marsh we ascended a short steep staircase of rock and root, with a dwarf precipice overhanging the river on the right, which was dangerous for the laden beasts as they crawled like beetles up the path. At 3 p.m. we arrived at a kraal called Cha K'henge—of the iguana, from the number of these animals found near the stream. It was a delightful spot, equal to Mzizi Mdogo in purity of air, and commanding a fair prospect of the now distant Dut'humi Highlands.

We started on the next day for a long march which concluded the passage of the "Tamarind Hills". Crossing a country broken by dry nullahs, or rather ditches, we traversed a seam of forest with a deep woody ravine on the right, and twice unpacked and reloaded the asses, who lay down instead of breasting the difficulties: a muddy swamp full of water-courses, and the high earth-banks of the Rufuta a Fiumara, here dry during the hot season. Thence, winding along a hill-flank, to avoid a bend in the bed, the path plunged into the sole of the Rufuta. This main-drain of the lower gradients carries off, according to the guides, the waters of the high ground around it into the Mgeta. The bed, which varies from three to sixteen feet in breadth, serpentines abruptly through the hills: its surface is either deep sand or clay, sopped with water, which near the head becomes a thin fillet, ankle-deep, now sweet, then salt: the mud is tinged in places with a solution of iron, showing, when stagnant, prismatic and iridescent tints. The corpses of porters were even more numerous than on the yester: our Muslems passed them with averted faces and with the low "la haul!" of disgust, and a decrepid old Mnyamwezi porter gazed at them and wept for himself. About 2 p.m., turning abruptly from the bed, we crawled up a short stony steep strewed with our asses and their loads; and reaching the summit of a dwarf cone near the foot of the "Goma Pass", we found the usual outlying huts for porters dying of small-pox, and an old kraal, which we made comfortable for the night.

THE women wear a tobe, or long cloth, wrapped tightly round the body, and extending from beneath the arms to the ankles; it is a garb ungraceful as was the European "sacque" of bygone days. It spoils the figure by depressing instead of supporting the bosom, and it conceals none of its deficiencies, especially the narrowness of the hips. The Murungwana, or free-women, is distinguished from the slave-girl, when outside the house, by a cloth thrown over the head. Like the women of the Bedouins and of the Persian Iliyat, even the matrons of the Mrima go abroad unmasked. Their favourite necklace is a string of shark's teeth. They distend the lobes of the ears to a prodigious size, and decorate them with a rolled-up strip of variously-dyed cocoa-leaf, a disk of wood, a plate of chakazi or raw gum-copal, or, those failing, with a betel-nut or with a few straws. The left wing of the nose is also pierced to admit a pin of silver, brass, lead, or even a bit of manioc-root. The hair, like the body, is copiously anointed with cocoa-nut or sesamum oil. Some shave the head wholly or partially across the brow and behind the ears; others grow their locks to half or full-length, which rarely exceeds a few inches. It is elaborately dressed, either in double-rolls rising like bear's ears on both sides of the head, or divided into a number of frizzly curls which expose lines of scalp, and give to the head the appearance of a melon. They have also a propensity for savage "accrochecoeurs", which stand out from the cheek bones, stiffly twisted like young porkers' tails. In early youth, when the short, soft, and crisp hair resembles Astrachan wool, when the muscles of the face are smoothly rounded, and when the skin has that life and texture, and the countenance has that vivacity and amiability which belong only to the young, many of the girls have a pretty piquancy, a little minois chiffonne, a coquettishness, a natural grace, and a caressing look, which might become by habit exceedingly prepossessing. In later life, their charms assume that peculiar solidity which is said to characterise the beauties of Mullingar, and as a rule they are shockingly ugly. The Castilian proverb says that the English woman should be seen at the window, the French woman on the promenade, and the Spanish woman everywhere;—the African woman should be seen nowhere, or in the dark.

*　　*　　*

The discomfort of the halt was not less than that of the boat. At first we pitched tents near the villages, in tall, fetid grass, upon ground never level, where stones were the succedanea for tent-pegs stolen for fuel, and where we slept literally upon mire. The temperature inside was ever in extremes, now a raw rainy cold, then a steam-bath that damped us like an April shower. The villagers, especially in the remoter districts, were even more troublesome, noisy, and inquisitive, than the Wagogo. A "notable passion of wonder" appeared in them. We felt like baited bears: we were mobbed in a moment, and scrutinised from every point of view by them; the inquisitive wretches stood on tiptoe, they squatted on their hams, they bent sideways, they thrust forth their necks like hissing geese to vary the prospect. Their eyes, "glaring lightning-like out of their heads", as old Homer hath it, seemed to devour us; in the ecstasy of curiosity they shifted from one Muzungu to his "brother", till, like the well-known ass between the two bundles of hay, they could not enjoy either. They were pertinacious as flies, to drive them away was only to invite a return; whilst, worst grief of all, the women were plain, and their grotesque salutations resembled the "encounter of two dog-apes". The Goanese were almost equally honoured, and the operation of cooking was looked upon as a miracle. At last my experience in staring enabled me to categorise the infliction as follows. Firstly, is the stare furtive, when the starer would peep and peer under the tent, and its reverse, the stare open. Thirdly, is the stare curious or intelligent, which is generally accompanied with irreverent laughter regarding our appearance. Fourthly, is the stare stupid, which denoted the hebete incurious savage. The stare discreet is that of sultans and great men; the stare indiscreet at unusual seasons is affected by women and children. Sixthly, is the stare flattering—it was exceedingly rare, and equally so was the stare contemptuous. Eighthly, is the stare greedy; it was denoted by the eyes restlessly bounding from one object to another, never tired, never satisfied. Ninthly, is the stare peremptory and pertinacious, peculiar to crabbed age. The dozen concludes with the stare drunken, the stare fierce or pugnacious, and finally the stare cannibal, which apparently considered us as articles of diet. At last, weary of the stare by day, and the tent by night, I preferred inhabiting a bundle of clothes in the wet hold of the canoe; this, at least, saved the trouble of wading through the water, of scrambling over the stern, and of making a way between the two close lines of grumbling and surly blacks that manned the paddle-benches; whenever, after a meaningless halt, some individual thought proper to scream out "Safari!" (journey!)

*   *   *

Twanigana, when safe in the mountains of Usagara, would frequently indulge me in a dialogue like the following, and it may serve as a specimen of the present state of conversation in East Africa:

"The state, Mdula?" (i.e. Abdullah, a word unpronounceable to Negroid organs.)

"The state is very! (well) and thy state?"

"The state is very! (well) and the state of Spikka? (my companion)."

"The state of Spikka is very! (well.)"

"We have escaped the Wagogo (resumes Twanigana), white man O!"

"We have escaped, O my brother!"

"The Wagogo are bad."

"They are bad."

"The Wagogo are very bad."

"They are very bad."

"The Wagogo are not good."

"They are not good."

"The Wagogo are not at all good."

"They are not at all good."

"I greatly feared the Wagogo, who kill the Wanyamwezi."

"Exactly so!"

"But now I don't fear them. I call them ——s and ——s, and I would fight the whole tribe, white man O!"

"Truly so, O my brother!"

And thus for two mortal hours, till my ennui turned into marvel.

Twanigana however was, perhaps, in point of intellect somewhat below the usual standard of African young men. Older and more experienced was Muzungu Mbaya, and I often listened with no small amusement to the attempts made by the Baloch to impress upon this truly African mind a respect for their revelation. Gul Mohammed was the missionary of the party: like Moslems generally, however, his thoughts had been taught to run in one groove, and if disturbed by startling objections, they were all abroad. Similarly I have observed in the European old lady, that on such subjects all the world must think with her, and I have been suspected of drawing the long-bow when describing the worship of gods with four arms, and goddesses with two heads.

Muzungu Mbaya, as the old hunk calls himself, might be sitting deeply meditative, at the end of the march, before the fire, warming his inner legs, smoking his face, and ever and anon casting pleasant glances at a small black earthen pipkin, whence arose the savoury steam of meat and vegetables. A concatenation of ideas induces Gul Mohammed to break into his favourite theme.

"And thou, Muzungu Mbaya, thou also must die!"

"Ugh! ugh!" replies the Muzungu personally offended, "don't speak in that way! Thou must die too."

"It is a sore thing to die," resumes Gul Mohammed.

"Hoo! Hoo!" exclaims the other, "it is bad, very bad, never to wear a nice cloth, no longer to dwell with one's wife and children, not to eat and drink, snuff, and smoke tobacco. Hoo! Hoo! it is bad, very bad!"

"But we shall eat," rejoins the Moslem, "the flesh of birds, mountains of meat, and delicate roasts, and drink sugared water, and whatever we hunger for."

The African's mind is disturbed by this tissue of contradictions. He considers birds somewhat low feeding, roasts he adores, he contrasts mountains of meat with his poor half-pound in pot, he would sell himself for sugar; but again he hears nothing of tobacco; still he takes the trouble to ask

"Where, O my brother?"

"There," exclaims Gul Mohammed, pointing to the skies.

This is a "chokepear" to Muzungu Mbaya. The distance is great, and he can scarcely believe that his interlocutor has visited the firmament to see the provision; he therefore ventures upon the query,

"And hast thou been there, O my brother?"

"Astaghfar ullah (I beg pardon of Allah)!" ejaculates Gul Mohammed, half angry, half amused. "What a mshenzi (pagan) this is! No, my brother, I have not exactly been there, but my Mulungu (Allah) told my Apostle, who told his descendants, who told my father and mother, who told me, that when we die we shall go to a Shamba (a plantation), where . . ."

"Oof!" grunts Muzungu Mbaya, "it is good of you to tell us all this Upumbafu (nonsense) which your mother told you. So there are plantations in the skies?"

"Assuredly," replies Gul Mohammed, who expounds at length the Moslem idea of paradise to the African's running commentary of "Nenda we!" (be off!), Mama-e! (O my mother!) and "Tumbanina", which may not be translated.

Muzungu Mbaya, who for the last minute has been immersed

in thought, now suddenly raises his head; and, with somewhat of a goguenard air, inquires:

"Well then, my brother, thou knowest all things! answer me, is thy Mulungu black like myself, white like this Muzungu, or whity-brown as thou art?"

Gul Mohammed is fairly floored: he ejaculates sundry la haul! to collect his wits for the reply, . . .

"Verily the Mulungu hath no colour."

"To-o-oh! Tuh!" exclaims the Muzungu, contorting his wrinkled countenance, and spitting with disgust upon the ground. He was now justified in believing that he had been made a laughing-stock. The mountain of meat had, to a certain extent, won over his better judgement: the fair vision now fled, and left him to the hard realities of the half-pound. He turns a deaf ear to every other word; and, devoting all his assiduity to the article before him, he unconsciously obeys the advice which many an Eastern philosopher has inculcated to his disciples.

SAID bin Salim, who was ill, who coughed and expectorated, and sincerely pitied himself because he had a cold, became more than usually unsociable: he could enjoy nothing but the society of Brahim, the bawling Baghdadi, and the crowd of ill-flavoured slavery that flocked into the vestibule. My Goanese servant, who connected my aspect with hard labour, avoided it like a pestilence. Already I was preparing to organise a little expedition to K'hokoro and the southern provinces, when unexpectedly,—in these lands a few cries and gun-shots are the only credible precursors of a caravan,—on the morning of the 25th August reappeared my companion [Lieut. Speke].

At length my companion had been successful, his "flying trip" had led him to the northern water, and he had found its dimensions surpassing our most sanguine expectations. We had scarcely, however, breakfasted, before he announced to me the startling fact, that he had discovered the sources of the White Nile. It was an inspiration perhaps: the moment he sighted the Nyanza, he felt at once no doubt but that the "Lake at his feet gave birth to that interesting river which has been the subject of so much speculation, and the object of so many explorers." The fortunate discoverer's conviction was strong; his reasons were weak— were of the category alluded to by the damsel Lucetta, when justifying her penchant in favour of the "lovely gentleman," Sir Proteus:

> "I have no other but a woman's reason.
> I think him so because I think him so."

and probably his sources of the Nile grew in his mind as his Mountains of the Moon had grown under his hand.

What tended at the time to make me the more sceptical was the substantial incorrectness of the geographical and other details brought back by my companion. This was natural enough. Bombay, after misunderstanding his master's ill-expressed Hindostani, probably mistranslated the words into Kisawahili to some travelled African, who in turn passed on the question in a wilder dialect to the barbarian or barbarians under examination. During such a journey to and fro words must be liable to severe accidents. The first thing reported to me was the falsehood of the Arabs at Kazeh, who had culumniated the good Sultan Muhayya, and had praised the bad Sultan Machunda: subsequent inquiries proved their rigid correctness. My companion's principal informant was one Mansur Bin Salim, a half-caste Arab, who had been flogged out of Kazeh by his compatriots; he pronounced Muhayya to be a "very excellent and obliging person", and of course he was believed. I then heard a detailed account of how the caravan of Salim bin Rashid had been attacked, beaten, captured, and detained at Ukerewe, by its sultan Machunda. The Arabs received the intelligence with a smile of ridicule, and in a few days Salim bin Rashid appeared in person to disprove the report. These are but two cases of many. And what knowledge of Asiatic customs can be expected from the writer óf these lines? "The Arabs at Unyanyembe had advised my donning their habit for the trip in order to attract less attention; a vain precaution, which I believe they suggested more to gratify their own vanity in *seeing an Englishman lower himself to their position*, than for any benefit that I might receive by doing so." (*Blackwood, loco cit.*) This galamatias of the Arabs!—the haughtiest and the most clannish of all Oriental peoples.

But difference of opinion was allowed to alter companionship. After a few days it became evident to me that not a word could be uttered upon the subject of the Lake, the Nile, and his *trouvaille* generally without offence. By a tacit agreement it was, therefore, avoided, and I should never have resumed it had my companion not stultified the results of the Expedition by putting forth a claim which no geographer can admit, and which is at the same time so weak and flimsy, that no geographer has yet taken the trouble to contradict it.

*   *   *

After about an hour's march, as we entered a small savannah, I saw the Fundi before alluded to running forward and changing the direction of the caravan. Without supposing that he had taken upon himself this responsibility, I followed him. Presently he breasted a steep and stony hill, sparsely clad with thorny trees: it was the death of my companion's riding-ass. Arrived with toil, —for our fagged beast now refused to proceed,—we halted for a few minutes upon the summit. "What is that streak of light which lies below?" I inquired of Seedy Bombay. "I am of opinion," quoth Bombay, "that that is *the* water." I gazed in dismay; the remains of my blindness, the veil of trees, and a broad ray of sunshine illuminating but one reach of the Lake, had shrunk its fair proportions. Somewhat prematurely I began to lament my folly in having risked life and lost health for so poor a prize, to curse Arab exaggeration, and to propose an immediate return, with the view of exploring the Nyanza, or Northern Lake. Advancing, however, a few yards, the whole scene suddenly burst upon my view, filling me with admiration, wonder, and delight.

Nothing, in sooth, could be more picturesque than this first view of the Tanganyika Lake, as it lay in the lap of the mountains, basking in the gorgeous tropical sunshine. Below and beyond a short foreground of rugged and precipitous hill-fold, down which the foot-path zigzags painfully, a narrow strip of emerald-green, never sere and marvellously fertile, shelves towards a ribbon of glistening yellow sand, here bordered by sedgy rushes, there cleanly and clearly cut by the breaking wavelets. Further in front stretch the waters, an expanse of the lightest and softest blue, in breadth varying from thirty to thirty-five miles, and sprinkled by the crisp east-wind with tiny crescents of snowy foam. The background in front is a high and broken wall of steel-coloured mountain, here flecked and capped with pearly mist, there standing sharply pencilled against the azure air; its yawning chasms, marked by a deeper plum-colour, fall towards dwarf hills of mound-like proportions, which apparently dip their feet in the wave. To the south, and opposite the long low point, behind which the Malagarazi River discharges the red loam suspended in its violent stream, lie the bluff headlands and capes of Uguhha, and, as the eye dilates, it falls upon a cluster of outlying islets, speckling a sea-horizon. Villages, cultivated lands, the frequent canoes of the fishermen on the waters, and on a nearer approach the murmurs of the waves breaking upon the shore, give a something of variety, of movement, of life to the landscape, which, like all the fairest prospects in these regions, wants but a little of the neatness and finish of Art,—mosques and kiosks, palaces and villas, gardens and orchards—contrasting with the profuse lavishness and magnificence of nature, and diversifying the unbroken *coup d'oeil* of excessive vegetation, to rival, if not to excel, the most admired scenery of the classic regions. The riant shores of this vast crevasse appeared doubly beautiful to me after the silent and spectral mangrove-creeks on the East-African seaboard, and the melancholy, monotonous experience of desert and jungle scenery, tawny rock and sun-parched plain or rank herbage and flats of black mire. Truly it was a revel for soul and sight! Forgetting toils, dangers, and the doubtfulness of return, I felt willing to endure double what I had endured; and all the party seemed to join with me in joy. My purblind companion found nothing to grumble at except the "mist and glare before his eyes". Said bin Salim looked exulting,—*he* had procured for me this pleasure,—the monoculous Jemadar grinned his congratulations; and even the surly Baloch made civil salams.

*   *   *

During my twenty-seven days of solitude the time sped quickly; it was chiefly spent in eating and drinking, smoking and dozing. Awaking at 2 or 3 a.m., I lay anxiously expecting the grey light creeping through the door-chinks and making darkness visible; the glad tidings of its approach were announced by the cawing of the crows and the crowing of the village cocks. When the golden rays began to stream over the red earth, the torpid Valentine was called up; he brought with him a mess of Suji, or rice-flour boiled in water, with a little cold milk as a relish. Then entered Muhabanya, the "slavey" of the establishment, armed with a leafy branch to sweep the floor, and to slay the huge wasps that riddled the walls of the tenement. This done he lit the fire— the excessive damp rendered this precaution necessary—and sitting over it he bathed his face and hands—luxurious dog!—in the pungent smoke. Ensued visits of ceremony from Said bin Salim and the Jemadar, who sat, stared, and, somewhat disappointed at seeing no fresh symptoms of approaching dissolution, told me so with their faces, and went away. From 7 a.m. till 9 a.m., the breakfast hour, Valentine was applied to tailoring, gun-cleaning, and similar light work, over which he groaned and grumbled, whilst I settled down to diaries and vocabularies, a process interrupted by sundry pipes. Breakfast was again a mess of Suji and milk,—such civilised articles as tea, coffee, and sugar, had been unknown to me for months. Again the servants resumed their labour, and they worked, with the interval of two hours for sleep at noon, till 4 p.m. During this time the owner lay like a log upon his cot, smoking almost uninterruptedly, dreaming of things past, and visioning things present, and sometimes indulging himself in a few lines of reading and writing.

As evening approached I made an attempt to sit under the broad eaves of the Tembe, and to enjoy the delicious spectacle of this virgin Nature, and the reveries to which it gave birth.

It reminded me of the loveliest glimpses of the Mediterranean, there were the same "laughing tides", pellucid sheets of dark blue water, borrowing their tints from the vinous shores beyond; the same purple light of youth upon the cheek of the earlier evening, the same bright sunsets, with their radiant vistas of crimson and gold opening like the portals of a world beyond the skies; the same short-lived grace and loveliness of the twilight; and, as night closed over the earth, the same cool flood of transparent moonbeam, pouring on the tufty heights and bathing their sides with the whiteness of virgin snow.

On the 29th of March the rattling of matchlocks announced my companion's return. The Masika had done its worst upon him. I never saw a man so thoroughly moist and mildewed; he justified even the French phrase "wet to the bone". His paraphernalia were in a similar state; his guns were grained with rust, and his fire-proof powder-magazine had admitted the monsoon-rain. I was sorely disappointed: he had done literally nothing. About ten days before his return I had been visited by Khamis bin Jumah, an Arab merchant, who, on the part of the proprietor of the dow, gave the gratifying message that we could have it when we pleased. I cannot explain where the mismanagement lay; it appears, however, that the wily "son of Sulayyam" detained the traveller simply for the purpose of obtaining from him gratis a little gunpowder. My companion had rested content with the promise that after three months the dow should be let to us for a sum of 500 dollars! and he had returned without boat or provisions to report ill success. The faces of Said bin Salim and the Jemadar, when they heard the period mentioned, were indeed a study. I consoled him and myself as I best could, and applied myself to supplying certain deficiencies as regards orthography and syntax in a diary which appeared in *Blackwood*, of September 1859, under the title "Journal of a Cruise in the Tanganyika Lake, Central Africa". I must confess, however, my surprise, at, amongst many other things, the vast horseshoe of lofty mountain placed by my companion in the map attached to that paper, near the very heart of Sir R. Murchison's Depression. As this wholly hypothetical, or rather inventive feature,—I had seen the mountains growing upon paper under my companion's hand, from a thin ridge of hill fringing the Tanganyika to the portentous dimensions given in *Blackwood* (Sept. 1859), and Dr Petermann's Mittheilungen, (No. 9, of 1859,)—wore a crescent form, my companion gravely published, with all the pomp of discovery, in the largest capitals, "This mountain range I consider to be THE TRUE MOUNTAINS OF THE MOON". Thus men *do* geography! and thus discovery is stultified.

AT Inenge another female slave was added to the troop, in the person of the lady Sikujui, "Don't know", a "mulier nigris dignissima barris", whose herculean person and virago manner raised her value to six cloths and a large coil of brass wire. The channel of her upper lip had been pierced to admit a disk of bone; her Arab master had attempted to correct the disfigurement by scarification and the use of rock-salt, yet the distended muscles insisted upon projecting sharply from her countenance, like a duck's bill, or the beak of an ornithorhyncus.

"Don't know's" morals were frightful. She was duly espoused —as the forlorn hope of making her an "honest woman"—to Goha, the sturdiest of the Wak'hutu porters; after a week she treated him with a sublime contempt. She gave him first one, then a dozen rivals; she disordered the caravan by her irregularities; she broke every article entrusted to her charge, as the readiest way of lightening her burden, and—"le moindre defaut d'une femme galante est de l'être"—she deserted so shamelessly that at last Said bin Salim disposed of her, at Unyanyembe, for a few measures of rice, to a travelling trader, who came the next morning to complain of a broken head.

THE great labour still remained. Trembling with ague, with swimming heads, ears deafened by weakness, and limbs that would hardly support us, we contemplated with a dogged despair the apparently perpendicular path that ignored a zigzag, and the ladders of root and boulder, hemmed in with tangled vegetation, up which we and our starving drooping asses were about to toil. On the 10th September we hardened our hearts, and began to breast the Pass Terrible. My companion was so weak that he required the aid of two or three supporters; I, much less unnerved, managed with one. After rounding in two places wall-like sheets of rock—at their bases green grass and fresh water were standing close to camp, and yet no one had driven the donkeys to feed— and crossing a bushy jungly step, we faced a long steep of loose white soil and rolling stones, up which we could see the Wan-yamwezi porters swarming, more like baboons scaling a precipice than human beings, and the asses falling after every few yards. As we moved slowly and painfully forwards, compelled to lie down by cough, thirst, and fatigue, the "sayhah" or war-cry rang loud from hill to hill, and Indian files of archers and spear-men streamed like lines of black ants in all directions down the paths. The predatory Wahumba, awaiting the caravan's depar-ture, had seized the opportunity of driving the cattle and plunder-ing the villages of Inenge.

By resting after every few yards, and by clinging to our supporters, we reached, after about six hours, the summit of the Pass Terrible, and there we sat down amongst the aromatic flowers and bright shrubs—the gift of mountain dews—to recover strength and breath. My companion could hardly return an answer; he had advanced mechanically and almost in a state of coma. The view from the summit appeared eminently suggestive, perhaps unusually so, because disclosing a retrospect of severe hardships, now past and gone. Below the foreground of giant fractures, huge rocks, and detached boulders, emerging from a shaggy growth of mountain vegetation, with forest glens and hanging woods, black with shade gathering in the steeper folds, appeared, distant yet near, the tawny basin of Inenge, dotted with large square villages, streaked with lines of tender green, that denoted the water-courses, mottled by the shadows of flying clouds, and patched with black where the grass had been freshly fired. A glowing sun gilded the canopy of dense smoke which curtained the nearer plain, and in the background the hazy atmosphere painted with its azure the broken wall of hill which we had traversed on the previous day.

Somewhat revived by the *tramontana* which rolled like an ice-brook down the Pass, we advanced over an easy step of rolling ground, decked with cactus and the flat-topped mimosa, with green grass and bright shrubs, to a small and dirty khambi, in a hollow flanked by heights, upon which several settlements appeared. At this place, called the "Great Rubeho", in distinction from its western neighbour, I was compelled to halt. My invalid sub. had been seized with a fever-fit that induced a dangerous delirium during two successive nights; he became so violent that it was necessary to remove his weapons, and, to judge from certain symptoms, the attack had a permanent cerebral effect. Death appeared stamped upon his features, yet the Baloch and the sons of Ramji clamoured to advance, declaring that the cold disagreed with them.

On the 12th September the invalid, who, restored by a cool night, at first proposed to advance, and then doubted his ability to do so, was yet hesitating when the drum-signal for departure sounded without my order. The Wanyamwezi porters instantly set out. I sent to recall them, but they replied that it was the custom of their race never to return; a well-sounding principle against which they never offended except to serve their own ends. At length a hammock was rigged up for my companion, and the whole caravan broke ground.

*   *   *

At Henga my companion was taken seriously ill. He had been chilled on the line of march by the cruel easterly wind, and at the end of the second march from Kazeh he appeared trembling as if with ague. Immediately after arrival at the foul village of Hanga —where we lodged in a kind of cow-house, full of vermin, and exposed directly to the fury of the cold gales—he complained, in addition to a deaf ear, an inflamed eye, and a swollen face, of a mysterious pain which often shifted its seat, and which he knew not whether to attribute to liver or to spleen. It began with a burning sensation, as by a branding-iron, above the right breast, and then extended to the heart with sharp twinges. After ranging around the spleen, it attacked the upper part of the right lung, and finally it settled in the region of the liver. On the 10th October, suddenly waking about dawn from a horrible dream, in which a close pack of tigers, leopards, and other beasts, harnessed with a network of iron hooks, were dragging him like the rush of a whirlwind over the ground, he found himself sitting up on the side of his bedding, forcibly clasping both sides with his hands. Half-stupefied by pain, he called Bombay, who having formerly suffered from the "Kichyoma-chyoma"—the "little irons"— raised his master's right arm, placed him in a sitting position, as lying down was impossible, and directed him to hold the left ear behind the head, thus relieving the excruciating and torturing twinges, by lifting the lung from the liver. The next spasm was less severe, but the sufferer's mind had begun to wander, and he again clasped his sides, a proceeding with which Bombay interfered.

Early on the next morning, my companion, supported by Bombay and Gaeotano, staggered towards the tent. Nearing the doorway, he sent in his Goanese, to place a chair for sitting, as usual, during the toils of the day, outside. The support of an arm being thus removed, ensued a second and violent spasm of cramps and twinges, all the muscles being painfully contracted. After resting for a few moments, he called his men to assist him into the house. But neglecting to have a chair previously placed for him, he underwent a third fit of the same epileptic description, which more closely resembled those of hydrophobia than aught I had ever witnessed. He was once more haunted by a crowd of hideous devils, giants, and lion-headed demons, who were wrenching, with superhuman force, and stripping the sinews and tendons of his legs down to the ankles. At length, sitting, or rather lying upon the chair, with limbs racked by cramps, features drawn and ghastly, frame fixed and rigid, eyes glazed and glassy, he began to

c

utter a barking noise, and a peculiar chopping motion of the mouth and tongue, with lips protruding—the effect of difficulty of breathing—which so altered his appearance that he was hardly recognisable, and completed the terror of the beholders. When this, the third and the severest spasm, had passed away, he called for pen and paper, and fearing that increased weakness of mind and body might presently prevent any exertion, he wrote an incoherent letter of farewell to his family. That, however, was the crisis. He was afterwards able to take the proper precautions, never moving without assistance, and always ordering a resting-place to be prepared for him. He spent a better night, with the inconvenience, however, of sitting up, pillow-propped, and some weeks elapsed before he could lie upon his sides. Presently, the pains were mitigated, though they did not entirely cease: this he expressed by saying that "the knives were sheathed". Such, gentle reader, in East Africa, is the kichyoma–chyoma: either one of those eccentric after-effects of fever, which perplex the European at Zanzibar, or some mysterious manifestation of the Protean demon Miasma.

THE fourth division is a hilly table-land, extending from the western skirts of the desert Mgunda Mk'hali, in E. long. 33° 57, to the eastern banks of the Malagarazi River, in E. long. 31° 10: it thus stretches diagonally over 155 rectilinear geographical miles. Bounded on the north by Usui and the Nyanza Lake, to the south-eastwards by Ugala, southwards by Ukimbu, and south-westwards by Uwende, it has a depth of from twenty-five to thirty marches. Native caravans, if lightly laden, can accomplish it in twenty-five days, including four halts. The maximum altitude observed by B. P. therm. was 4050 feet, the minimum 2850. This region contains the two great divisions of Unyamwezi and Uvinza.

The name of Unyamwezi was first heard by the Portuguese, according to Giovanni Botero, towards the end of the sixteenth century, or about 1589. Pigafetta, who, in 1591, systematised the discoveries of the earlier Portuguese, placed the empire of "Monemugi" or Munimigi in a vast triangular area, whose limits were Monomotapa, Congo, and Abyssinia: from his pages it appears that the people of this central kingdom were closely connected by commerce with the towns on the eastern coast of Africa. According to Dapper, the Dutch historian, (1671), whose work has been the great mine of information to subsequent writers upon Africa south of the equator, about sixty days' journey from the Atlantic is the kingdom of Monemugi, which others call "Nimeamaye", a name still retained under the corrupted form "Nimeaye" in our atlases. M. Malte-Brun, senior, mentioning Mounemugi, adds, "ou, selon une autographe plus authentique, *Mou-nimougi*". All the Portuguese authors call the people Monemugi or Mono-emugi; Mr Cooley prefers Monomoezi, which he derives from "Munha Munge", or "lord of the world", the title of a great African king in the interior, commemorated by the historian De Barros. Mr Macqueen ("Geography of Central Africa"), who also gives Manmoise, declares that "Mueno-muge, Mueno-muize, Monomoise, and Uniamese", relate to the same place and people, comprehending a large extent of country in the interior of Africa: he explains the word erroneously to mean the "great Moises or Movisas". The Rev. Mr Erhardt asserts that for facility of pronunciation the coast merchants have turned the name "Wanamesi" into "Waniamesi", which also leads his readers into error. The Rev. Mr Livingstone thus endorses the mistake of Messrs Macqueen and Erhardt: "The names Monomoizes, spelt also Monemuigis and Monomuizes, and Monomotapistas, when applied to the tribes, are exactly the same as if we should call the Scotch the Lord Douglases . . . Monomoizes was formed from Moiza or Muiza, the singular of the word Babisa or Aiza, the proper name of a large tribe to the north." In these sentences there is a confusion between the lands of the Wanyamwezi, lying under the parallel of the Tanganyika Lake, and the Wabisa (in the singular Mbisa, the Wavisa of the Rev. Mr Rebmann), a well-known commercial tribe dwelling about the Maravi or Nyassa Lake, S.W. of Kilwa, whose name

in times of old was corrupted by the Portuguese to Moviazas or
Movisas. Finally M. Guillain, in a work already alluded to, states
correctly the name of the people to be Oua-nyamouezi, but in
designating the country "pays de Nyamouezi", he shows little
knowledge of the Zangian dialects. M. V. A. Malte-Brun, junior
("Bulletin de Geographie", Paris, 1856, Part II, p. 295) correctly
writes Wanyamwezi.

A name so discrepantly corrupted deserves some notice.
Unyamwezi is translated by Dr Krapf and the Rev. Mr Rebmann,
"Possessions of the Moon". The initial U, the causal and locative
prefix, denotes the land, nya, of, and mwezi, articulated m'ezi
with semi-elision of the w, means the moon. The people sometimes pronounce their country name Unyamiezi, which would be
a plural form, miezi signifying moons or months. It is impossible
to investigate the antiquity of the vernacular term; all that can be
discovered is, that nearly 350 years ago the Portuguese explorers
of Western Africa heard the country designated by its present
name.

There is the evidence of barbarous tradition for a belief in the
existence of Unyamwezi as a great empire, united under a single
despot. The elders declare that their patriarchal ancestor became
after death the first tree, and afforded shade to his children and
descendants. According to the Arabs the people still perform
pilgrimage to a holy tree, and believe that the penalty of sacrilege
in cutting off a twig would be visited by sudden and mysterious
death. All agree in relating that during the olden time Unyamwezi was united under a single sovereign, whose tribe was the
Wakalaganza, still inhabiting the western district, Usagozi.
According to the people, whose greatest chronical measure is a
Masika, or rainy season, in the days of the grandfathers of their
grandfathers the last of the Wanyamwezi emperors died. His
children and nobles divided and dismembered his dominions
further partitions ensued, and finally the old empire fell into the
hands of a rabble of petty chiefs. Their wild computation would
point to an epoch of 150 years ago—a date by no means improbable.

These glimmerings of light thrown by African tradition illustrate the accounts given by the early Portuguese concerning the extent and the civilisation of the Unyamwezi empire. Moreover, African travellers in the seventeenth century concur in asserting that, between 250 and 300 years ago, there was an outpouring of the barbarians from the heart of Ethiopia and from the shores of the Central Lake towards the eastern and southern coasts of the peninsula, a general waving and wandering of tribes which caused great ethnological and geographical confusion, public demoralisation, dismemberment of races, and change, confusion, and corruption of tongues.

In these days Unyamwezi has returned to the political status of Eastern Africa in the time of the Periplus. It is broken up into petty divisions, each ruled by its own tyrant; his authority never extends beyond five marches; moreover, the minor chiefs of the different districts are virtually independent of their suzerains. One language is spoken throughout the land of the Moon, but the dialectic differences are such that the tribes in the east with difficulty understand their brethren in the west. The principal provinces are—Utakama to the extreme north, Usukuma on the south,—in Kinyamwezi sukuma means the north, takama the south, kiya the east, and mwere the west,—Unyan-southern declination of the sun, acts like the genial warmth of an English spring. As all sudden changes from siccity to humidity are prejudicial to man, there is invariably severe disease at the end of the summer, when the rains set in.

Travellers from Unyamwezi homeward returned often represent that country to be the healthiest in Eastern and Central Africa: they quote, as a proof, the keenness of their appetites and the quantity of food which they consume. The older residents, however, modify their opinions: they declare that digestion does not wait upon appetite; and that, as in Egypt, Mazanderan, Malabar, and other hot-damp countries, no man long retains rude health. The sequelae of their maladies are always severe; few care to use remedies, deeming them inefficacious against morbific influences to them unknown; convalescence is protracted, painful, and uncertain, and at length they are compelled to lead the lives of confirmed invalids. The gifts of the climate, lassitude and indolence, according to them, predispose to corpulence; and the regular warmth induces baldness, and thins the beard, thus assimilating strangers in body as in mind to the aborigines. They are unanimous in quoting a curious effect of climate, which they attribute to a corruption of the "humours and juices of the body". Men who, after a lengthened sojourn in these regions return to Oman, throw away the surplus provisions brought from the African coast, burn their clothes and bedding, and for the first two or three months eschew society; a peculiar effluvium rendering them, it is said, offensive to the finer olfactories of their compatriots.

The Mukunguru of Unyamwezi is perhaps the severest seasoning fever in this part of Africa. It is a bilious remittent, which normally lasts three days; it wonderfully reduces the patient in that short period, and in severe cases the quotidian is followed by a long attack of a tertian type. The consequences are severe and lasting even in men of the strongest nervous diathesis; burning and painful eyes, hot palms and soles, a recurrence of shivering and flushing fits, with the extremities now icy cold, then painfully hot and swollen, indigestion, insomnolency, cutaneous eruptions and fever sores, languor, dejection, and all the inconveniences resulting from torpidity of liver, or from an inordinate secretion of bile, betray the poison deep-lurking in the system. In some cases this fever works speedily; some even, becoming at once delirious, die on the first or the second day, and there is invariably an exacerbation of symptoms before the bilious remittent passes away.

The fauna of Unyamwezi are similar to those described in Usagara and Ugogo. In the jungles quadrumana are numerous; lions and leopards, cynhyaenas and wild cats haunt the forests; the elephant and the rhinoceros, the giraffe and the Cape buffalo, the zebra, the quagga (?), and the koodoo wander over the plains; and the hippopotamus and crocodile are found in every large pool. The nyanyi or cynocephalus in the jungles of Usukuma attains the size of a greyhound; according to the people, there are three varieties of colour—red, black, and yellow. They are the terror of the neighbouring districts: women never dare to

approach their haunts; they set the leopard at defiance, and, when
in a large body, they do not, it is said, fear the lion. The Colobus
guereza, or tippet monkey, the "polume" of Dr Livingstone
(ch. xvi.), here called mbega, is admired on account of its polished
black skin and snowy-white mane. It is a cleanly animal, ever
occupied in polishing its beautiful garb, which, according to the
Arabs, it tears to pieces when wounded, lest the hunter should
profit by it. The mbega lives in trees, seldom descending, and
feeds upon the fruit and the young leaves. The Arabs speak of
wild dogs in the vicinity of Unyanyembe, describing them as
being about eighteen inches in height, with rufous-black and
shaggy coats, and long thick tails; they are gregarious, running in
packs of from 20 to 200; they attack indiscriminately man and
the largest animals, and their only cry is a howl. About the time of
our autumn the pools are visited by various kinds of aquatic
birds, widgeon, plump little teal, fine snipe, curlew, and crane;
the ardea, or white "paddy-bird" of India, and the "lily-trotter"
(Parra Africana), are scattered over the country; and sometimes,
though rarely, the chenalopex or common Egyptian-goose and
the gorgeous-crowned crane (Balearica pavonina), the latter a
favourite dish with the Arabs, appear. In several parts of Unyamwezi, especially in the north, there is a large and well-flavoured
species of black-backed goose (Sakidornis melanota): the common wild duck of England was not seen. Several specimens of the
Buceros, the secretary-bird (Serpentarius reptilivorus), and large
vultures, probably the condor of the Cape, were observed in
Unyamwezi; the people do not molest them, holding the flesh
to be carrion. The Cuculus indicator, called in Kisawahili "ton-
goe", is common; but, its honey being mostly hived, it does not
attract attention. Grillivori, and a species of thrush, about the
size of common larks, with sulphur-yellow patches under the
eyes, and two naked black striae beneath the throat, are here
migratory birds; they do good service to the agriculturist against
the locust. A variety of the Loxia or grossbill constructs nests
sometimes in bunches hanging from the lower branches of the
trees. The mtiko, a kind of water-wagtail (Motacilla), ventures
into the huts with the audacity of a London sparrow, and the

Africans have a prejudice against killing it. Swallows and martins of various kinds, some peculiarly graceful and slender, may be seen migrating at the approach of winter in regular travelling order: of these, one variety resembles the English bird. The Africans declare that a single species of hirundo, probably the sand-martin, builds in the precipitous earth-banks of the nullahs: their nests were not seen, however, as in Southern Africa, under the eaves of houses. There are a few ostriches, hawks, ravens, plovers, nightjars (Caprimulgidae), red and blue jays of brilliant plume, muscicapae, blackcaps or mock nightingales (Motacilla atrocapilla?), passerines of various kinds, hoopoes, bulbuls, wrens, larks, and bats. We saw but few poisonous animals. The people speak of a yellow and brown-coated snake, eight feet long by five or six inches in diameter; it is probably a boa or rock-snake. Chura or frogs are numerous in the swamps, where the frog-concerts resemble those of the New World; and in the regions about the Tanganyika Lake a large variety makes night hideous with its croakings. Of the ranæ there are many species. The largest is probably the "matmalelo" of S. Africa; it is eaten by the Wagogo and other tribes. A smaller kind is of dark colour, and with long legs, which enable it to hop great distances. A third is of a dirty yellow with brownish speckles. There is also a little green tree-frog, which adheres to the broad and almost perpendicular leaves of the thicker grasses. The leech is found in the lakes and rivers of the interior, as well as in Zanzibar and on both coasts of Africa; according to the Arabs they are of two kinds, large and small. The people neither take precautions against them when drinking at the streams, as the Somal do, nor are they aware of any officinal use for the animals; moreover, it is impossible to persuade a Msawahili to collect them: they are of P'hepo or fiendish nature, and never fail to haunt and harm their captor. Jongo, or huge millepedes, some attaining a length of half a foot, with shiny black bodies and red feet, are found in the fields and forests, especially during the rains: covered with epizoa, these animals present a disgusting appearance, and they seem, to judge from their spoils, to die off during the hot weather. At certain seasons there is a great variety of the papilionaceous family in the vicinity of waters where libellulae or dragon-flies also abound. The country is visited at irregular times by flights of locusts, here called nzige. In spring the plants are covered in parts with the p'hanzi, a large pink and green variety, and the destructive species depicted and described by Salt: they rise from the earth like a glowing rose-coloured cloud, and die off about the beginning of the rains. The black leather-like variety, called by the Arabs "Satan's ass", is not uncommon: it is eaten by the Africans, as are many other edibles upon which strangers look with disgust. The Arabs describe a fly which infests the forest-patches of Unyamwezi: it is about the size of a small wasp, and is so fatal that cattle attacked by it are at once killed and eaten before they become carrion from its venomous effects. In parts the country is dotted with ant-hills, which, when old, become hard as sandstone: they are generally built by the termite under some shady tree, which prevents too rapid drying, and apparently the people have not learned, like their brethren in South Africa, to use them as ovens.

The races requiring notice in this region are two, the Wakimbu and the Wanyamwezi.

The Wakimbu, who are emigrants into Unyamwezi, claim a noble origin, and derive themselves from the broad lands running south of Unyanyembe as far westward as K'hokoro. About masika, wet monsoons, or years ago, according to themselves, in company with their neighbours, the Wakonongo and the Wamia, they left Nguru, Usanga, and Usenga, in consequence of the repeated attacks of the Warori, and migrated to Kipiri, the district lying south of Tura; they have now extended into Mgunda Mk'hali and Unyanyembe, where they hold the land by permission of the Wanyamwezi. In these regions there are few obstacles to immigrants. They visit the Sultan, make a small present, obtain permission to settle, and name the village after their own chief; but the original proprietors still maintain their rights to the soil. The Wakimbu build firmly stockaded villages, tend cattle, and cultivate sorghum and maize, millet and pulse, cucumbers, and water-melons. Apparently they are poor, being generally clad in skins. They barter slaves and ivory in small quantities to the merchants, and some travel to the coast. They are considered treacherous by their neighbours, and Mapokera, the Sultan of Tura, is, according to the Arabs, prone to commit "*avanies*". They are known by a number of small lines formed by raising the skin with a needle, and opening it by points laterally between the hair of the temples and the eyebrows. In appearance they are dark and uncomely; their arms are bows and arrows, spears and knives stuck in the leathern waistbelt; some wear necklaces of curiously plaited straw, others a strip of white cowskin bound around the brow—a truly savage and African decoration. Their language differs from Kinyamwezi.

The Wanyamwezi tribe, the proprietors of the soil, is the typical race in this portion of Central Africa: its comparative industry and commercial activity have secured to it a superiority over the other kindred races.

The aspect of the Wanyamwezi is alone sufficient to disprove the existence of very elevated lands in this part of the African interior. They are usually of a dark sepia-brown, rarely coloured like diluted Indian ink, as are the Wahiao and slave races to the south, with negroid features markedly less Semitic than the people of the eastern coast. The effluvium from their skins, especially after exercise or excitement, marks their connection with the negro. The hair curls crisply, but it grows to the length of four or five inches before it splits; it is usually twisted into many little ringlets or hanks; it hangs down like a fringe to the neck, and is combed off the forehead after the manner of the ancient Egyptians and the modern Hottentots. The beard is thin and short, there are no whiskers, and the moustache—when not plucked out—is scant and straggling. Most of the men and almost all the women remove the eyelashes, and pilar hair rarely appears to grow. The normal figure of the race is tall and stout, and the women are remarkable for the elongation of the mammary organs. Few have small waists, and the only lean men in the land are the youths, the sick, and the famished. This race is said to be long-lived, and it is not deficient in bodily strength and savage courage. The clan-mark is a double line of little cuts, like the marks of cupping, made by a friend with a knife or razor, along the temporal fossae from the external edges of the eyebrows to the middle of the cheeks or to the lower jaws. Sometimes a third line, or a band of three small lines, is drawn down the forehead to the bridge of the nose. The men prefer a black, charcoal being the substance generally used, the women a blue colour, and the latter sometimes ornament their faces with little perpendicular scars below the eyes. They do not file the teeth into a saw-shape as seen amongst the southern races, but they generally form an inner triangular or wedge-shaped aperture by chipping away the internal corners of the two front incisors like the Damaras, and the women extract the lower central teeth. Both sexes enlarge the lobes of the ears. In many parts of the country skins are more commonly worn than cloth, except by the Sultans and the wealthier classes. The women wear the long tobe of the coast, tightly wrapped round either above or more commonly below the breast; the poorer classes veil the bosom with a square of softened skin; the remainder of the dress is a kilt or short petticoat of the same material extending from waist to knee. Maidens never cover the breast, and children are rarely clothed; the infant, as usual in East Africa, is carried in a skin fastened by thongs behind the parent's back. The favourite ornaments are beads, of which the red coral, the pink, and the "pigeon-eggs" made at Nuremberg are preferred. From the neck depend strings of beads with kiwangwa, disks of shell brought from the coast, and crescents of hippopotamus teeth country made, and when the beard is long it is strung with red and particoloured beads. Brass and copper bangles or massive rings are worn upon the wrists, the forearm bears the ponderous kitindi or coil brace-let, and the arm above the elbow is sometimes decorated with circlets of ivory or with a razor in an ivory etui; the middle is girt with a coil of wire twisted round a rope of hair or fibre, and the ankles are covered with small iron bells and the rings of thin brass, copper, or iron wire, called sambo. When travelling, a goat's horn, used as a bugle, is secured over the right shoulder by a lanyard and allowed to hang by the left side: in the house many wear a smaller article of the same kind, hollowed inside and containing various articles intended as charms, and conse-crated by the Mganga or medicine-man. The arms are slender

assegais with the shoulders of the blade rounded off: they are
delivered, as by the Somal, with the thumb and forefinger after a
preliminary of vibratory motion, but the people want the force
and the dexterity of the Kafirs. Some have large spears for
thrusting, and men rarely leave the hut without their bows and
arrows, the latter unpoisoned, but curiously and cruelly barbed.
They make also the long double-edged knives called sime, and
different complications of rungu or knob-kerries, some of them
armed with an iron lance-head upon the wooden bulge. Dwarf
battle-axes are also seen, but not so frequently as amongst the
western races on the Tanganyika Lake. The shield in Unyamwezi
resembles that of Usagara; it is however rarely used.

There are but few ceremonies amongst the Wanyamwezi. A
woman about to become a mother retires from the hut to the
jungle, and after a few hours returns with a child wrapped in
goatskin upon her back, and probably carrying a load of firewood
on her head. The medical treatment of the Arabs with salt and
various astringents for forty days is here unknown. Twins are not
common as amongst the Kafir race, and one of the two is invariably put to death; the universal custom amongst these tribes is for
the mother to wrap a gourd or calabash in skins, to place it to
sleep with, and to feed it like, the survivor. If the wife dies without issue, the widower claims from her parents the sum paid to
them upon marriage; if she leaves a child, the property is preserved for it. When the father can afford it, a birth is celebrated by
copious libations of pombe. Children are suckled till the end of
the second year. Their only education is in the use of the bow and
arrow; after the fourth summer the boy begins to learn archery
with diminutive weapons, which are gradually increased in
strength. Names are given without ceremony; and as in the
countries to the eastward, many of the heathens have been called
after their Arab visitors. Circumcision is not practised by this
people. The children in Unyamwezi generally are the property
not of the uncle but of the father, who can sell or slay them
without blame; in Usukuma or the northern lands, however,
succession and inheritance are claimed by the nephews or sisters'
sons. The Wanyamwezi have adopted the curious practice of

leaving property to their illegitimate children by slave girls or concubines, to the exclusion of their issue by wives; they justify it by the fact of the former requiring their assistance more than the latter, who have friends and relatives to aid them. As soon as the boy can walk he tends the flocks; after the age of ten he drives the cattle to pasture, and, considering himself independent of his father, he plants a tobacco-plot and aspires to build a hut for himself. There is not a boy "which cannot earn his own meat".

Another peculiarity of the Wanyamwezi is the position of the Wahara or unmarried girls. Until puberty they live in the father's house; after that period the spinsters of the village, who usually number from seven to a dozen, assemble together and build for themselves at a distance from their homes a hut where they can receive friends without parental interference. There is but one limit to community in single life: if the Mhara or "maiden" be likely to become a mother, her "young man" must marry her under pain of mulct; and if she die in childbirth, her father demands from her lover a large fine for having taken away his daughter's life. Marriage takes place when the youth can afford to pay the price for a wife: it varies according to circumstances from one to ten cows. The wife is so far the property of the husband that he can claim damages from the adulterer; he may not, however, sell her, except when in difficulties. The marriage is celebrated with the usual carouse, and the bridegroom takes up his quarters in his wife's home, not under her father's roof. Polygamy is the rule with the wealthy. There is little community of interests and apparently a lack of family affection in these tribes. The husband, when returning from the coast laden with cloth, will refuse a single shukkah to his wife, and the wife succeeding to an inheritance will abandon her husband to starvation. The man takes charge of the cattle, goats, sheep, and poultry; the woman has power over the grain and the vegetables; and each must grow tobacco, having little hope of borrowing from the other. Widows left with houses, cattle, and fields, usually spend their substance in supporting lovers, who are expected occasionally to make presents in return. Hence no coast slave in Wanyamwezi is ever known to keep a shukkah of cloth.

The usual way of disposing of a corpse in former times was, to carry it out on the head and to throw it into some jungle strip where the fisi or cynhyaena abounds,—a custom which accounts for the absence of graveyards. The Wanyamwezi at first objected to the Arabs publicly burying their dead in their fields, for fear of pollution; they would assemble in crowds to close the way against a funeral party. The merchants, however, persevered till they succeeded in establishing a right. When a Mnyamwezi dies in a strange country, and his comrades take the trouble to inter him, they turn the face of the corpse towards the mother's village, a proceeding which shows more sentiment than might be expected from them. The body is buried standing, or tightly bound in a heap, or placed in a sitting position with the arms clasping the knees: if the deceased be a great man, a sheep and a bullock are slaughtered for a funeral feast, the skin is placed over his face, and the hide is bound to his back. When a sultan dies in a foreign land his body is buried upon the spot, and his head, or what remains of it, is carried back for sepulture to his own country. The chiefs of Unyamwezi generally are interred by a large assemblage of their subjects with cruel rites. A deep pit is sunk, with a kind of vault or recess projecting from it: in this the corpse, clothed with skin and hide, and holding a bow in the right hand, is placed sitting, with a pot of pombe, upon a dwarf stool, whilst sometimes one, but more generally three female slaves, one on each side and the third in front, are buried alive to preserve their lord from the horrors of solitude. A copious libation of pombe upon the heaped-up earth concludes the ceremony. According to the Arabs, the Wasukuma inter all their sultans in a jungle north of Unyamyembe, and the neighbouring peasants deposit before seed-time small offerings of grain at the Mzimo or Fettiss-house which marks the spot.

The habitations of the eastern Wanyamwezi are the Tembe, which in the west give way to the circular African hut; among the poorer sub-tribes the dwelling is a mere stack of straw. The best Tembe have large projecting eaves supported by uprights: cleanliness, however, can never be expected in them. Having no limestone, the people ornament the inner and outer walls with long lines of ovals formed by pressing the finger tips, after dipping them into ashes and water for whitewash, and into red clay or black mud for variety of colour. With this primitive material they sometimes attempt rude imitations of nature—human beings and serpents. In some parts the cross appears, but the people apparently ignore it as a symbol. Rude carving is also attempted upon the massive posts at the entrances of villages, but the figures, though to appearance idolatrous, are never worshipped. The household furniture of the Tembe differs little from that described in the villages generally. The large sloping Kitanda, or bedstead of peeled tree-branch, supported by forked sticks, and provided with a bedding of mat and cow-hide, occupies the greater part of the outer room. The triangle of clay cones forming the hearth are generally placed for light near the wall-side opposite the front door; and the rest of the supellex consists of large stationary bark cornbins, of gourds and bandboxes slung from the roof, earthen-pots of black clay, huge ladles, pipes, grass-mats, grinding-stones, and arms hung to a trimmed and branchy tree trunk planted upright in a corner. The rooms are divided by party walls, which, except when separating families, seldom reach to the ceiling. The fireplace acts as lamp by night, and the door is the only chimney.

The characteristic of the Mnyamwezi village is the "Iwanza"—a convenience resulting probably from the instinct of the sexes, who prefer not to mingle, and for the greater freedom of life and manners. Of these buildings there are two in every settlement, generally built at opposite sides, fronting the normal Mrimba-tree, which sheds its filmy shade over the public court-yard. That of the women, being a species of harem, was not visited; as travellers and strangers are always admitted into the male Iwanza, it is more readily described. This public-house is a large hut, somewhat more substantial than those adjoining, often smeared with smooth clay, and decorated here and there with broad columns of the ovals before described, and the prints of palms dipped in ashes and placed flat like the hands in ancient Egyptian buildings. The roof is generally a flying thatch raised a foot above the walls—an excellent plan for ventilation in these regions.

Outside, the Iwanza is defended against the incursions of cattle by roughly-barked trunks of trees resting upon stout uprights: in this space men sit, converse, and smoke. The two doorways are protected by rude charms suspended from the lintel, hares' tails, zebras' manes, goats' horns, and other articles of prophylactic virtue. Inside, half the depth is appropriated to the Ubiri, a huge standing bedframe, formed, like the plank-benches of a civilised guard-room, by sleepers lying upon horizontal cross-bars: these are supported by forked trunks about two feet long planted firmly in the ground. The floor is of tamped earth. The furniture of the Iwanza consists of a hearth and grinding-stones; spears, sticks, arrows, and shillelaghs are stuck to smoke in the dingy rafter ceiling, or are laid upon hooks of crooked wood descending from the sooty cross-beams: the corners are occupied by bellows, elephant-spears, and similar articles. In this "public" the villagers spend their days, and often, even though married, their nights, gambling, eating, drinking pombe, smoking bhang and tobacco, chatting, and sleeping like a litter of puppies destitute of clothing, and using one another's backs, breasts, and stomachs as pillows. The Iwanza appears almost peculiar to Unyamwezi.

In Unyamwezi the sexes do not eat together: even the boys would disdain to be seen sitting at meat with their mothers. The men feed either in their cottages or more generally in the Iwanza: they make, when they can, two meals during the day—in the morning, a breakfast, which is often omitted for economy, and a dinner about I p.m. During the interim they chew tobacco, and, that failing, indulge in a quid of clay. It probably contains some animal matter, but the chief reason for using it is apparently the necessity to barbarians of whiling away the time when not sleeping by exercising their jaws. They prefer the "sweet earth", that is to say, the clay of ant-hills: the Arabs have tried it without other effects but nausea. The custom, however, is not uncommon upon both coasts of Africa: it takes, in fact, the place of the mastic of Chios, the kat of Yemen, the betel and toasted grains of India and the farther East, and the ashes of the Somali country. The Wanyamwezi, and indeed the East-African tribes generally, have some curious food prejudices. Before their closer intercourse with the Arabs they used to keep poultry, but, like the Gallas and the Somal, who look upon the fowl as a kind of vulture, they would not eat it: even in the present day they avoid eggs. Some will devour animals that have died of disease, and carrion,—the flesh of lions and leopards, elephants and rhinoceroses, asses, wild cats and rats, beetles and white ants;—others refuse to touch mutton or clean water-fowl, declaring that it is not their custom. The prejudice has not, however, been reduced to a system, as amongst the tribes of southern Africa. They rarely taste meat except upon the march, where the prospect of gain excites them to an unusual indulgence: when a bullock is killed, they either jerk the meat, or dry it upon a dwarf platform of sticks raised above a slow and smoky fire, after which it will keep for some days. The usual food is the ugali or porridge of boiled flour: they find, however, a variety of edible herbs in the jungle, and during the season they luxuriate upon honey and sour milk. No Mnyamwezi, however, will own to repletion unless he has "sat upon pombe"—in other words, has drunk to intoxication; and the chiefs pride themselves upon living entirely upon beef and stimulants.

As has been said, the government of Unyamwezi is conducted by a multitude of petty chiefs. The ruling classes are thus called: Mtemi or Mwame is the chief or sultan, Mgawe (in the plural Wagawe) the principal councillor, and Manacharo, or Mnyapara (plural Wanyapara) the elder. The ryots or subjects on the other hand are collectively styled Wasengi. The most powerful chiefs are Fundikira of Unyamyembe, Masanga of Msene, and Kafrira of Krira. The dignity of Mtemi is hereditary. He has power of life and death over his subjects, and he seldom condescends to any but mortal punishment. His revenue is composed of additions to his private property by presents from travellers, confiscation of effects in cases of felony or magic, by the sale of subjects, and by treasure trove. Even if a man kill his own slave, the slave's effects lapse to the ruler. The villagers must give up all ivory found in the jungles, although the hunters are allowed to retain the tusks of the slaughtered animals.

A few brief remarks concerning Fundikira, the chief of Unyam-wezi in 1858, may serve to illustrate the condition of the ruling class in Unyamwezi. This chief was travelling towards the coast as a porter in a caravan, when he heard of his father's death: he at once stacked his load and prepared to return home and rule. The rest of the gang, before allowing him to depart, taunted him severely, exclaiming, partly in jest, partly in earnest, "Ah! now thou art still our comrade, but presently thou wilt torture and slay, fine and flog us." Fundikira proceeding to his native country inherited, as is the custom, all his father's property and widows; he fixed himself at Ititenya, presently numbered ten wives, who have borne him only three children, built 300 houses for his slaves and dependants, and owned 2000 head of cattle. He lived in some state, declining to call upon strangers, and, though not demanding still obtaining large presents. Becoming obese by age and good living, he fell ill in the autumn of 1858, and, as usual, his relations were suspected of compassing his end by Uchawi, or black magic. In these regions the death of one man causes many. The Mganga was summoned to apply the usual ordeal. After administering a mystic drug, he broke the neck of a fowl, and splitting it into two lengths inspected the interior. If blackness of blemish appear about the wings, it denotes the treachery of children, relations and kinsmen; the backbone convicts the mother and grandmother; the tail shows that the criminal is the wife, the thighs the concubines, and the injured shanks or feet the other slaves. Having fixed upon the class of the criminals, they are collected together by the Mganga, who, after similarly dosing a second hen, throws her up into the air above the heads of the crowd and singles out the person upon whom she alights. Confession is extorted by tying the thumb backwards till it touches the wrist or by some equally barbarous mode of question. The consequence of condemnation is certain and immediate death; the mode is chosen by the Mganga. Some are speared, others are beheaded or "ammazati", —clubbed:—a common way is to bind the cranium between two stiff pieces of wood which are gradually tightened by cords till the brain bursts out from the sutures. For women they practise a peculiarly horrible kind of impalement. These atrocities continue until the chief recovers or dies: at the commencement of his attack, in one household eighteen souls, male and female, had been destroyed; should his illness he protracted, scores will precede him to the grave, for the Mchawi or magician must surely die.

The Wanyamwezi will generally sell their criminals and captives; when want drives, they part with their wives, their children, and even their parents. For economy, they import their serviles from Ujiji and the adjoining regions; from the people lying towards the south-east angle of the Tanganyika Lake, as the Wafipa, the Wapoka, and the Wagara; and from the Nyanza races, and the northern kingdoms of Karagwah, Uganda, and Unyoro.

JOHN HANNING SPEKE

from

What led to the Discovery of the Source of the Nile
(1863)

August 3rd—The caravan, after quitting Isamiro, began winding up a long but gradually inclined hill—which, as it bears no native name, I shall call Somerset—until it reached its summit, when the vast expanse of the pale-blue waters of the N'yanza burst suddenly upon my gaze. It was early morning. The distant sea-line of the north horizon was defined in the calm atmosphere between the north and west points of the compass; but even this did not afford me any idea of the breadth of the lake, as an archipelago of islands (*vide* Map, Bengal Archipelago), each consisting of a single hill, rising to a height of 200 or 300 feet above the water, intersected the line of vision to the left; while on the right the western horn of the Ukerewe Island cut off any farther view of its distant waters to the eastward of north. A sheet of water—an elbow of the sea, however, at the base of the low range on which I stood—extended far away to the eastward, to where, in the dim distance, a hummock-like elevation of the mainland marked what I understood to be the south and east angle of the lake. The important islands of Ukerewe and Mzita, distant about twenty or thirty miles, formed the visible north shore of this firth. The name of the former of these islands was familiar to us as that by which this long-sought lake was usually known. It is reported by the natives to be of no great extent; and though of no considerable elevation, I could discover several spurs stretching down to the water's edge from its central ridge of hills. The other island, Mzita, is of greater elevation, of a hog-backed shape, but being more distant, its physical features were not so distinctly visible.

I no longer felt any doubt that the lake at my feet gave birth to that interesting river, the source of which has been the subject of so much speculation, and the object of so many explorers. The Arabs' tale was proved to the letter. This is a far more extensive lake than the Tanganyika; "so broad you could not see across it, and so long that nobody knew its length." I had now the pleasure of perceiving that a map I had constructed on Arab testimony, and sent home to the Royal Geographical Society before leaving Unyanyembe, was so substantially correct that in its general outlines I had nothing whatever to alter. Further, as I drew that map after proving their first statements about the Tanganyika, which were made before my going there, I have every reason to feel confident of their veracity relative to their travels north through Karague, and to Kibuga in Uganda.

AT night a violent storm of rain and wind beat on my tent with such fury that its nether parts were torn away from the pegs, and the tent itself was only kept upright by sheer force. On the wind's abating, a candle was lighted to rearrange the kit, and in a moment, as though by magic, the whole interior became covered with a host of small black beetles, evidently attracted by the glimmer of the candle. They were so annoyingly determined in their choice of place for peregrinating, that it seemed hopeless my trying to brush them off the clothes or bedding, for as one was knocked aside another came on, and then another; till at last, worn out, I extinguished the candle, and with difficulty—trying to overcome the tickling annoyance occasioned by these intruders crawling up my sleeves and into my hair, or down my back and legs—fell off to sleep. Repose that night was not destined to be my lot. One of these horrid little insects awoke me in his struggles to penetrate my ear, but just too late: for in my endeavour to extract him, I aided his immersion. He went his course, struggling up the narrow channel, until he got arrested by want of passage-room. This impediment evidently enraged him, for he began with exceeding vigour, like a rabbit at a hole, to dig violently away at my tympanum. The queer sensation this amusing

measure excited in me is past description. I felt inclined to act as
our donkeys once did, when beset by a swarm of bees, who buzzed
about their ears and stung their heads and eyes until they were
so irritated and confused that they galloped about in the most
distracted order, trying to knock them off by treading on their
heads, or by rushing under bushes, into houses, or through any
jungle they could find. Indeed, I do not know which was worst
off. The bees killed some of them, and this beetle nearly did for
me. What to do I knew not. Neither tobacco, oil, nor salt could
be found: I therefore tried melted butter; that failing, I applied
the point of a penknife to his back, which did more harm than
good; for though a few thrusts quieted him, the point also
wounded my ear so badly, that inflammation set in, severe
suppuration took place, and all the facial glands extending from
that point down to the point of the shoulder became contorted
and drawn aside, and a string of boils decorated the whole length
of that region. It was the most painful thing I ever remember to
have endured; but, more annoying still, I could not masticate for
several days, and had to feed on broth alone. For many months
the tumour made me almost deaf, and ate a hole between the ear
and the nose, so that when I blew it, my ear whistled so audibly
that those who heard it laughed. Six or seven months after this
accident happened, bits of the beetle—a leg, a wing, or parts of
its body—came away in the wax.

THE SECOND EXPEDITION

From Zanzibar to Lake Victoria; through Karague, Uganda and Unyoro to Gondokoro

September 1860 to February 1863

JOHN HANNING SPEKE
JAMES AUGUSTUS GRANT (1827–92)

ON 9 MAY 1859, the day after his return to England, Speke called at the Royal Geographical Society's offices in London and laid his discovery of Lake Victoria as the probable source of the Nile before Sir Roderick Murchison, the Society's President. By the end of their interview the President was saying: "Speke, we must send you there again." Not "you and Burton", it may be noted. Speke had collared the glory with great speed. More, he had convinced the one person who could set another expedition in motion that he, Speke, was the man to lead that expedition.

It was a twenty-four-hour triumph. And this time the purpose of the expedition was already clear: to find the source of the Nile where it flowed out from the northern end of the lake—assuming that the lake contained the river's source. Speke was sure it did; now he was going back to prove it did.

He set about organising his expedition at once, and with considerable thoroughness. He was also made to lecture, against his own inclination, to the Royal Geographical Society and indeed went on to lecture at a number of other places, presumably still against his own inclination.

It was not long before word got round of Speke's new commission, even to Nairn, in the north of Scotland, where an old friend of his was on half-pay from the Indian Army, having been badly wounded at the relief of Lucknow some eighteen months earlier.

James Augustus Grant had met Speke in India in 1847; they were the same age, got on very well together, and shared a common devotion to the sport of shooting wild animals. Grant was an impressive looking man: handsome, six feet two inches tall, broad shouldered, and of remarkable strength and stamina.

He was also a remarkably nice man, and the catalogue of virtues ascribed to him is a little breath-taking. Kind, gentle, of sweet disposition, even-tempered, loyal—so it goes on.

It is tempting to wonder if he was too good to be true. (He was certainly too true to be good—for Speke.) But the only other side of the coin of Grant's riches was a tendency to be dull, a slight, but not crippling, lack of imagination, and a predisposition to see those he came in contact with in a too rosy light.

Throughout their three years together, often in the most difficult circumstances, frequently under great strain, Grant behaved as Speke's most faithful second-in-command. Never once did he doubt his companion's decisions, never once express surprise or seem perplexed at Speke's more illogical actions. After the proud Lucifer of Burton as a travelling companion, Grant must have seemed like an archangel to Speke. The ideal companion, a self-sufficient oasis of tranquil, rational normality in a desert of irritable, incoherent abnormalities.

They left Portsmouth on 27 April 1860—according to Grant it was 30 April—arriving at the Cape of Good Hope early in July. Here they made a sturdy friend of the Governor of the Cape Colony. He raised an extra £300 for them, and had ten Cape Mounted Riflemen attached to the expedition.

These poor Hottentots are some of the saddest figures in the history of African exploration. Small, homesick creatures, they stand looking out from the record of the journey with reproachful eyes. Volunteers by description, they were obviously nothing else but the first ten men to catch the Sergeant's glance.

They failed to get any further into central Africa than just beyond Kazeh, and were returned to their native land as unadaptable rejects (except for the one who had died earlier).

The expedition sailed from the Cape on 16 July for Zanzibar, making a leisurely voyage up the coast of East Africa. Their ship, the steam corvette *Brisk*, dropped anchor at a couple of ports and then, just after Mozambique, ran down and captured a slave ship sailing in the same direction. There were over five hundred Africans on that ship, which was captained by an Arab with a motley crew of Spanish and Portuguese half-castes. It was not a pleasant thing, as Speke records. "It was no wonder then that every man of the 'Brisk' who first looked upon them did so with a feeling of loathing and abhorrence of such a trade. All over the vessel, but more especially below, old women, stark naked, were dying in the most disgusting 'ferret box' atmosphere . . ." A prize crew was put upon the slaver and she went off to Mauritius, presumably with the wretched slaves still aboard.

Once the *Brisk* made Zanzibar, Speke set about organising his expedition with what he termed "care, expedience and diligence; for I had seen matters go wrong before" (which is the nearest he comes to mentioning Burton in his long record of the exploration). Grant was rather left to his own devices, although, no doubt, he was introduced to the top drawer of the island's society whom Speke had met on his first visit.

Zanzibar struck both men as being a pleasant enough place, and it was certainly more stable politically than when Speke had last left it, a mere sixteen months before. All the old retinue, led by Seedy Bombay, came forward and were promptly engaged; the stores ordered in advance had been delivered; the instruments, equipment and baggage animals were got in order. All in all, things were done as Speke claimed; there was hardly any wandering away from the point to visit a piece of coastland, to study the life of a tribal village, or just to have a look around at a spot that could be interesting. Speke had his destiny to fulfil.

The only diversions were a spot of hippopotamus shooting with the Admiral—presumably the one from the Cape, though his name remains a mystery—and a very strange trip in a Zanzibar "man of war", at the Sultan of Zanzibar's request, to capture a slave ship in port on the African coast opposite the island.

Speke, it appears, was in command, and after a good deal of scouting around and laying-to, they got into the port only to find that the slaver had left three days before. Something went amiss with the navigation after this travesty of an action, and the ship was found to be firmly stuck on a bank of sand. Not wanting to remain in limbo until a friendly tide altered their situation, Speke and Grant took to a small boat with a number of the crew to row them back to Zanzibar.

It took them a couple of days to complete the voyage, and at one time it seemed likely that the current would sweep them up past their destination and on into the Indian Ocean. When they arrived at Zanzibar, they found the ship had got there before them, and the news of their death, or at least of their being swept into the ocean to die, was starting to be spread around the island.

It was a typical piece of negative adventure; a sort of indulgence on the part of the Sultan which started from a false premise, never had any planning behind it or point to it, and could easily have ended in an ignominious distaster. Both men were aware of the risk they had been made to take, and of their own stupidity in accepting it.

It doesn't seem to have occurred to them that the Sultan was perhaps not just being indulgent, that the whole operation had an evil design behind it. It is, of course, unlikely, but just possible. The Sultan was deeply involved in the slave trade, however much he pretended to oppose it when the British put the pressure on. And however friendly the Zanzibar Arabs seemed, it was a surface friendliness. They could well do without Speke and Grant marching through their trading territory, and it is likely that they understood the purpose of the British expedition not as a fanatically obstinate search for the truth, but as the beginning of a vast take-over bid. Perfidious Albion using the source of the Nile search as a cover, as clever as it seemed ridiculous. Be that as it may, Speke hurried things up after this adventure, and his expedition was across from Zanzibar and well into the first stage of its long walk by the middle of October.

By the end of January 1861 they were into Unyanyembe, the Land of the Moon, and near to the place which Speke, Grant and Burton called Kazeh. This time Speke lets us into the secret of the name. They had come, he writes, "within five miles of Kaze, which is the name of a well in the village of Tabora . . ." Nevertheless, both men still continued to call it Kazeh, and as such it remains in the history of the discovery of the sources of the Nile: the point of departure to the unentered equatorial lands and the kingdoms of the three kings—Rumanika of Karague, in the south:

Mtesa of Uganda, in the centre; and Kamrasi of Unyoro, in the north.

As ever, Kazeh proved a difficult place to get away from; Speke and Grant were there for nearly two months. Floods and heavy rain delayed them much of the time; for the rest, it was a matter of waiting for an old friend, Musa, an Indian merchant, to leave with them once the porters were organised.

Musa lived like a king in Kazeh, and quite why he should travel north was never clear, but he was a splendid procrastinator, with all the tricks of that trade. Once Speke found that ". . . to prove to me that he was bent on leaving Kaze the same time as myself, he began eating what he called his training pills—small dried buds of roses with alternate bits of sugar candy. Ten of these buds, he said, eaten dry, were sufficient for ordinary cases, and he gave a very formidable description of the effect likely to follow the use of the same number boiled in rice-water or milk."

In the end they left Musa and his rosebuds behind. The truth was that the local tribes were becoming increasingly hostile to the Arab and Indian traders who lived around the well of Kazeh. Speke's cunning old friend of the earlier expedition, Sheikh Snay, and six other traders were killed in a pitched battle at this time. It was better for Musa to stay at home, only he did not like to admit it. He probably sighed with relief when he found that the two gently deranged white men had slipped off without telling him.

By the end of November 1861 they were in Karague and had met Rumanika, and for the first time in Africa traces of a past civilisation, something of an organised pattern of social behaviour. Rumanika's subjects wore their scanty costume in a particular fashion, with dignity and decorum. They were gentle people, pastoral and homeloving. The royal caste was carefully inter-married with the royal families of surrounding countries; they lived in some style, compared at least with those chiefs whom Speke and Grant had come across earlier; their town had the semblance of a plan about it, and it was set beside a fine lake. Grant was reminded of home; even the climate was reminiscent of a hot day in the English countryside—the Lake District, thought

Grant, and he christened the lake Little Windermere. (Speke claims to have done this too, so perhaps they came to the same conclusion together.)

The explorers were charmed by Rumanika; both saw him as a paragon of virtue divorced from African reality. Undoubtedly, he was a pleasant man of over six foot, with non-African features. Speke considered him to be of the best Abyssinian blood, but surely went too far in tracing his lineage from "Abyssinia and King David". The best that could be said for Rumanika in fact was that he had few bad habits, and his reign was not murderously despotic. He had only killed his mother, and few of his more distant relatives, to achieve undisputed power.

To his kingdom he was everything, King, Prophet and Priest dressing up to play each part. A long white beard as Priest, the oracle's mask as Prophet, a long staff as King, so that he looked like "the picture of the gentle shepherd of his flock".

He had no religion, only a series of rituals based upon a horde of primitive, ancient superstitions, covering every aspect of the individual's life from birth to death, and appeasing every sort of likely disaster to the kingdom's life. Grant thought there were indications of "Jewish worship" in these rituals, but unfortunately he does not give any examples. One significant rite that could be traced back to the beginnings of the kingdom—according to Rumanika—was the burial of the royal dead on an island in the lake, the island being treated as sacred and never visited but for the purposes of a burial.

Another, more grotesque, observance was the manner in which the women of the royal household were kept. In breeding terminology they were artificially fed for fatstock on milk until they literally could not stand up straight, but walked around on all fours. Speke, as we shall see, measured the King's sister-in-law (she had a 52″ bust); and suffered for his action when he told of it upon reaching England.

From the beginning of the journey Grant had gone through the gauntlet of the local illnesses; now at Karague he became completely incapacitated with a poisoned leg. Speke, on the other hand, had remained in extremely good health, as he did for the whole journey, none of the illnesses which he had suffered with Burton reappearing. (It is possible that Speke suffered psychosomatically with Burton, although more likely that he had become immune to African diseases after his first trip.)

There was nothing to be done for Grant, outside the dubious help from native treatment, but to keep him rested and hope that the poison would eventually clear—which meant that Speke would have to either wait patiently with his comrade or press on alone to Uganda.

Within a week or so of their arrival in Karague emissaries had been sent to the King of Uganda to obtain his agreement that the expedition should visit his country. The answer was favourable, and Speke decided to go off alone; he left for Uganda on 10 January 1862.

Grant, as ever, was nice about it. He was also very accurate in his estimation of Speke's compulsive drive to achieve his ends, regardless of the means. "At first sight this appeared to some persons at home as an unkind proceeding, leaving a helpless 'brother' in the heart of Africa; but my companion was not the man to be daunted; he was offered an escort to the north, and all tender feelings must yield to the stern necessities of the case."

But Grant could have been carried on a litter. It would have been a rather painful journey for him, but quite practical. When he eventually left to join Speke, three months later, he began his journey in precisely this way, and only took to walking when his bearers discovered that he could in fact put foot to ground. So why did he remain behind on January 10, wholly at the mercy of Rumanika and a small group of highly unreliable bearers? Speke makes Rumanika responsible for a story that no sick people were ever allowed into Uganda. This was patent nonsense in a continent without frontiers, and where sickness was an accepted part of daily life. As if to prove that such stories were nonsense, Speke records that the King went on to say: "'To show how absurd [the Ugandians] are, your donkey would not be permitted because he has no trousers; and you even will have to put on a gown as your unmentionables will be considered indecorous.'"

This was pure "Alice in Wonderland", as were so many African attitudes and actions displayed for the benefit of the European traveller. They were not meant to be taken seriously. They were part and parcel of the eternal childhood jokes which the African never stopped playing. If taken seriously, they were likely to rebound—from all sorts of queer angles—upon the unfortunate traveller. We may hold the suspicion, perhaps, that on this occasion it suited Speke to take such a farrago of absurdity at face value. He had heard not only that Mtesa of Uganda would welcome his party but that native traders took their ivory up the Nile, from where it flowed out of the Victoria Nyanza to Kidi, a few hundred miles north-west.

Once again his destiny was being dangled, carrot-like, in front of him. Travel with Grant would be slow and faltering, and so once again Speke contrived to make for the Nile source alone. He had not reckoned with Mtesa, of course, and would have to kick his heels for many months before reaching his goal—but reaching it alone even then. As for the gentle Grant, was he being a little ironic—for once—when he wrote that Mtesa was impatient to see the white man but ". . . as a story was got up that no sick person or donkeys were allowed to enter his territory, I had to remain till sufficiently recovered to march"? Needless to add, once in Uganda the subject of sick people on donkeys, with or without "unmentionables", was never brought up in any shape or form.

Grant remained at Karague until April, accepting and suffering like a saint. It was a lonely, mean time for him, unable to move more than a few steps from his bed in his small hut.

Speke arrived on the outskirts of Mtesa's palace on 19 February 1862, and sat conducting a war of nerves with the King for a number of days. Mtesa was anxious to meet the white man; the white man was just as anxious to meet Mtesa; but it was necessary for both to preserve their dignity. Everything, therefore, had to be done with tantalising precision, as if in a delicate slow motion.

Even then their first meeting only resulted in Speke turning on his heel and leaving the court after he considered he had been snubbed. Their long awaited first conversation took most of the day to begin, the King inquiring at regular intervals if Speke had seen him—they were facing each other across a large hut—and moving from one hut to another surrounded by a hundred or so of his wives, who were naked, and his court officials, who spent most of their time grovelling at his feet in excessive salutation.

After the King and the explorer had accepted each other, it was the turn of the Queen Mother. "Fat, fair and forty-five", this lady proved more approachable; she was usually in a state of alcoholic beatitude which helped matters, and soon looked upon Speke as an administer of pills and potions for her wide range of illnesses, real and imaginary. They became firm friends, and through her good offices Speke eventually obtained living quarters within the palace boundaries, something he had set his heart on directly he had arrived in the Ugandian capital.

Here Speke settled down, fitting in with the régime, to await the arrival of Grant, although, before Grant could even start from Karague, Mtesa's co-operation and agreement to receive another white man had to be obtained. It took about a month of persistent application before Mtesa would condescend even to discuss the matter, and it is difficult to discover from Speke's story just how things were resolved. The patient, uncomplaining Grant did not appear at the palace until the end of May, having received messengers on his journey asking him to hurry, as the King had heard he ". . . was beautiful, and he could not eat till he had seen me!" Grant also learned from the messengers that his arrival would be celebrated by a great deal of bloodshed.

The most outstanding manifestation of Mtesa's grotesque reign was the amount of bloodshed. It was not so much a reign of cruelty and terror as one of sheer reckless murder. Mtesa ruled his subjects through the machinery of murder, and nobody raised a voice or a hand to stop him, including Speke and Grant. Even the most factual recital of a day in the administration of the court has a nightmare quality to it.

On two or three mornings a week the King would hold a levee, moving from hut to hut as the whim took him, attended by his sycophantic ministers, a selection of his women, and his

D

younger brothers and half-brothers. These last were a mere handful: when Mtesa came to the throne he had those older than himself and those of about his age murdered. It was an old Uganda custom. These younger brothers were, however, kept handcuffed together and under constant surveillance; Speke found them playful and happy regardless.

The audience attending a levee would sit in total silence, immobile and with heads bowed, for to be seen looking at the royal women, however fleetingly, could mean a nasty death beginning with castration. Whenever the King dealt out his rough justice the appointed "cheer leaders" would give the signal, and an outburst of *n'yanzigging* would take place. *N'yan-zigging* was a cry, rendered onomatopoetically, of approval and admiration. The Waganda were much given to it, and would behave like a demented Greek chorus suiting the action to the word, and performing a series of St Vitus' dances which would go on until the overlooking "detectives" brought order back to the assembly by setting about the chorus with sticks and whips.

Once again there would be silence, and should anybody break that silence by so much as a word or a cough he would be pounced on by a detective, and on the King's unspoken command taken a little way off and maimed. A foot or an ear, a hand or fingers removed—unless Mtesa was feeling particularly ungenerous, when the poor wretch's head would be removed. Should the victim complain of his sentence, the royal musicians would drown the complaint in martial music.

These levees were a primitive court of justice. The ministers acted as a jury if so requested. For most of the time the King, however, was judge and jury. Nothing could be depended upon, Mtesa was either sunshine or storm. Speke records the story of the chief who asked for more. This man had been given a woman by the King as a reward for his part in a raid on Unyoro. Thinking Mtesa in a good humour, he asked for another. This cheerful request turned Mtesa's mood inside out; enraged, he ordered the chief to be seized, taken to the executioner's garden and cut to pieces.

As both white men noticed, the reaction of the assembly to all these blood-curdling happenings was precisely nil. "Fowls in a farmyard could not have been despatched with less emotion," writes Grant. They also noted the bizarre fact that there were no axes or swords in Uganda. Tall, razor-sharp reeds were used by the executioners to cut off whatever part of the human body they had to remove—sawn off would be a more accurate description, although before decapitation the victim was knocked unconscious.

Once again we are back in an obscene "Alice in Wonderland" where the command "Off with her head!" is unremarkable and carried out as a mere routine. For outside the business of the levees, Mtesa would give the order with sickening frequency, and one or other of his three hundred-odd wives would be led away by a royal executioner to the executioner's garden—a square of land on the edge of a river, secluded behind tall grasses—and beheaded. As the harem was for ever being supplied with new, young women, this was presumably one way of disposing of the old ones. And it never took much to arouse the King's wrath. Speke gives an example. ". . . next the whole party took a walk . . . enjoying themselves amazingly, till, by unlucky chance, one of the royal wives, a most charming creature . . . plucked a fruit and offered it to the King, thinking, doubtless, to please him greatly; but he, like a madman, flew into a towering passion, said it was the first time a woman ever had the impudence to offer him anything and ordered the pages to seize, bind, and lead her off to execution." On this occasion Speke demanded the woman's life and the King immediately, and gracefully, granted the request.

It was the only time Speke—or Grant, come to that—interceded between the King and the object of his anger. They preferred, it seems, to divorce Mtesa from his hideous behaviour, to see him as a young king administering his kingdom in the way expected of him. That he was a real king of a kingdom which had certain vestiges of civilisation to it impressed them no end, Speke perhaps more than Grant.

To be fair to both men, it was a rather bewildering situation, for Mtesa always appeared, and obviously was, quite unconcerned with the amount of death he so casually ordained. There was not the slightest murmur ever to be heard against him, and they never got wind of any plot—however sketchy—to dispose of him. He was no conscious-stricken despot, there was nothing fierce or warlike about him, he was not sadistic in that he never witnessed any of his orders being carried out; nor was he plagued by any scruples of emotional involvement with any of his subjects. All that he was was plain for all to see: a carefree, rather spoilt and therefore petulant young king who ruled by divine right. And his subjects were on the whole a contented lot who conformed to the order of things and were quite indifferent to the endless tapestry of murder surrounding them. Like the present-day owner of a smart motor-car, the Waganda must have lived in the illusion that injury and death could only happen to other people.

The point was that life in Uganda was one large illusion, and once Speke and Grant understood this their enforced stay became intolerable. For the Mtesa who broke through the beautiful illusion was a lunatic monster obsessed with his powers of being allowed to kill anything and anybody. A man as stupid as he was vainglorious, greedy, and without a single unselfish thought. Unable to feel pity or compassion for anybody but himself, Mtesa had become the very image of the incarnate anti-god. And behind the contented surface of his kingdom was a world that mirrored his brutal disrespect for human life. Although Speke and Grant only just touch the facts, it is obvious enough that the Waganda took one another's lives on the slightest provocation. The royal executioners set the standard by disposing of their own enemies, along with their routine murdering for the King. After that it was more or less a free for all.

There were other things which made the two travellers long to shake the dust of Uganda off their feet. Around them the Waganda existed without a moral code. If they wanted something, they stole it. If they reckoned they could blackmail the explorers' party for food or drink, they did so without compunction. If they said they would do a thing, it meant no more to them than it would to a forgetful child. All this was corrupting to the expedition's team of servants, porters and guards. At times Speke and Grant seem pretty unsure that they themselves could continue to remain aloof from the depravity. They became aware in the end that Mtesa wanted them to remain in his country—as prize specimens—until he grew tired of them, until he considered there was nothing else in the way of property to be extorted from them.

There was nothing new in this sort of behaviour from chief or tribesmen; the expedition had met with it often enough on their way to Uganda. It was expected and accepted as a hazard of exploration. In Uganda, somehow, these rules in the game seemed infinitely more complicated, the stakes much higher. For here was a country with a civilised façade to it, a place that the traveller felt he could become some part of, where he could live for a few months something that resembled a normal cultivated existence. And, of course, when Speke first arrived he felt just that. Instead of keeping his distance, running his own show, making it quite apparent to Mtesa that he was the representative of a vast and powerful empire—as Baker would surely have done —Speke went out of his way to join in, did everything he could to make himself acceptable to the King. An elementary, instinctive insight into the way Mtesa's mind worked would have warned Speke to keep clear. Unfortunately he was impossibly naïve in his understanding of people. In seeking the King's friendship, in setting out to impress the King, Speke made himself a prisoner of his environment in no time at all, became part and parcel of the bloodiness, the inhumanity of Mtesa's rule.

Grant's arrival in May did nothing to alter the situation, and, taking his cue from Speke, he also settled into a routine of life which centred around Mtesa and the Queen Mother. It was a boring, futile existence, and Grant complains in his mild way about it, as he also complains about the bloodshed and shows some real pity for the sacrificed men and women.

But he did nothing. Perhaps it was understandable. Both men found it impossible to consider the African as a fully paid-up member of the human race, and therefore when they saw him being slaughtered for no good reason with alarming frequency— and as part of the order of things—they had little difficulty in accepting what under any other circumstances they would have totally condemned. So not once did they say in effect to Mtesa, "killing people is wrong". More unforgivably, Speke gave the monstrous child a new toy.

The rifle delighted Mtesa, for it meant he could do the actual killing himself—or get a page to do it—and not have to rely upon his autocratic executioners. (These gentlemen were always coldly polite to Speke and Grant. The travellers sensed the resentment, and put it down to jealousy because the King was so friendly to them. A few more rifles around, and the executioners might have been out of business.)

Mtesa showed his delight upon receiving his first rifle in the way one might imagine. He told a boy page to go outside the palace boundaries, shoot a man, and come back with a full report of the incident. Naturally the page did as required of him, and King and page enjoyed the joke enormously. After a little experience of the weapons, the King got up enough courage to shoot people himself, although he felt it undignified to do so too often. Grant records asking how the King enjoyed a hunting expedition, and was told: "As his highness could not find any game to shoot at, he shot down many people."

Mtesa had plenty of ammunition, having impounded the explorers' stock for the time they were in his country. They let it happen to them, which was not only weak-kneed but stupid, for it left them without the protection necessary to continue their journey. They could not form up the expedition and just march off without placing their lives at the mercy of any rapacious Waganda element—of which there were plenty. So they began the slow process of obtaining Mtesa's agreement that they should leave, and take their arms and ammunition with them.

It took about six weeks of fairly diplomatic bludgeoning before the King quite suddenly gave them their release. He seemed almost pleased to let them go. Probably the jealous executioners and a group of ministers led by one K'yengo, who was actively opposed to the white man, had managed to convince the King that the omens pointing to the future would be bad if the explorers were still about. We learn from Speke that Mtesa turned to consulting the future most anxiously towards the end of their stay, which meant some extra slaughter taking place, and the ceremony of cooking a child and a fowl—both alive—being carried out by K'yengo. This involved steaming them over a cauldron of boiling water for a limited time, when they were examined to see if they were living or dead. Presumably they were still alive, for this meant that the King must take action at once, not remain passive which their death would have indicated.

So on 7 July 1862 the expedition left Mtesa's city of illusions. Speke had lived in it for almost six months, Grant had suffered it for three. For both it was an experience they were unlikely to forget. In terms of the exploration it had been a terrible waste of time. They had still actually to behold the great Nile flowing out from the waters of Lake Victoria.

They headed north, accompanied between Uganda and Unyoro by Mtesa's Minister for Affairs, a plausible and intelligent diplomat called Budja, who travelled with three wives and twenty boy-servants. The journey was painfully slow and they covered only fifty miles in ten days, having to spend long hours at halt whilst Budja negotiated for supplies and sent and received mysterious messages from Mtesa. By 19 July Speke had had enough. By all reports the Nile was to be found two or three marches east; he decided to make for it, leaving Grant to continue the lame progression to Kamrasi.

Grant wrote afterwards: "Speke asked me whether I was able to make a flying march of it along with him. At that time I was positively unable to walk twenty miles a day. . . . I therefore yielded reluctantly to the necessity of our parting; and am anxious to be explicit on this point, as some have hastily inferred that my companion did not wish me to share in the gratification of seeing the river. Nothing could be more contrary to fact. My state of health alone prevented me from accompanying Speke...."

What is not clear is why Speke had to make a "flying march of it". The river was unlikely to vanish suddenly. He did indeed do so, reaching the brink of the Nile by the 21st, but, once there, his progress north, south and west had no urgency to it. In fact it was vacillating and disorganised, and Speke seemed to be quite indifferent to the tricky situation awaiting Grant on his journey into Unyoro. However much the good-natured Grant may protest, the evidence is clear enough: Speke really did not want to share his second moment of discovery with his friend and fellow-traveller. It was a mean way to act, but Speke was driven by his own devil. When it came to the clinch, he was always a compulsive "loner".

So on 21 July 1862 Speke recorded: "Here at last I stood on the brink of the Nile; most beautiful was the scene, nothing could surpass it." And a little later that day he told his men: ". . . they ought to shave their heads and bathe in the holy river, the cradle of Moses—the waters of which . . . men carry all the way from Egypt to Mecca . . ." Seedy Bombay was not impressed, it seems, with these sentiments—or the river—and replied: "We don't look on those things in the same fanciful manner that you do; we are contented with all the commonplaces of life, and look for nothing beyond the present."

Beyond the present, for Speke, was the fact that he had yet actually to see the Nile gushing forth from the lake. Strangely, therefore, he first followed the bank of the river north until he reached the Isamba Rapids. Here he commented on the scenery. "The whole was more fairy-like, wild, and romantic than—I must confess that my thoughts took that shape—anything I ever saw outside of a theatre." After this he turned back, until by 28 July he had reached the "stones", as the falls were called by the Waganda, and saw the Nile flowing out of Lake Victoria. He had done it at last. "The expedition had now performed its functions. I saw that old father Nile without any doubt rises in the Victoria N'yanza, and, as I had foretold, that lake is the great source of the holy river which cradled the first expounder of our religious belief."

He remained at his Nile source for three days and christened the falls the Ripon Falls, after Lord Ripon, a one-time president of the Royal Geographical Society and future Viceroy of India. Always a great one for naming places, he also called the junction of water immediately before the falls the Napoleon Channel, "in token of respect to the French Geographical Society". This

Society had presented Speke with the usual gold medal for his discovery of Lake Victoria. The Napoleon Channel was an odd, somewhat tactless piece of naming; Bonaparte had once boasted that the English Channel would be called Napoleon Bonaparte's Channel after he had crossed it. Speke also made one extremely good sketch of the falls from some high ground before them, took some bearings and measurements, and spent the last days there watching the Waganda fly-fishing and contemplating how happy he could be with wife, family, garden, yacht, rifle and rod settled at the Ripon Falls for life. These few days were an idyll of satisfied ambition and solitary sufficiency.

Meanwhile, Grant on another journey was finding life far from idyllic. There were the usual quarrels and procrastinations, the usual bloody-mindedness of the porters, and this time the additional irritation of Budja and his meticulous attention to a protocol which he appeared to invent as the expedition made its halting way north.

By 26 July they crossed into Unyoro. On the next day they halted nine miles inside the frontier whilst Budja began a series of negotiations with Kamrasi that were veiled in mystery to such an extent that Grant was not sure if anything at all ever actually took place. They did not move. By 8 August a messenger told Grant that Kamrasi did not want him in Unyoro. The King was insulted, Grant was told, because the white men had approached his country by two different routes, and they had also come via Uganda, whose King was an upstart. They must leave Unyoro at once. So much for Budja's diplomacy. On the 10th Grant turned round and went back to a camp just inside Uganda.

Speke was having trouble on the Nile also. After following the river northwards for a few days, some boats were hired and Speke prepared to take the expedition on the Nile into Unyoro. Perhaps it was just as well he did not succeed, in view of Kamrasi's obvious suspicions of the intentions behind the dual approach. No sooner had they crossed the line into Unyoro, than they were set upon by some of Kamrasi's boats. Although Speke tried his best to rally them, his party had no stomach for a fight on the water. They turned back to where they started from, and Speke had to march back, rather red-facedly, to the original camp in Uganda. He had sailed the Nile for twenty-four hours.

By 19 August Speke found Grant kicking his heels on the Unyoro border. They decided that the situation was not good enough. All they now wanted was to get to a civilised town and then back to old England as fast as they could. If Kamrasi went on being stubbornly unfriendly, then they would turn east and try to force their way through to the coast. It was a pretty mad scheme, and thankfully it was never put into operation, for Kamrasi sent an emmissary on the 21st inviting the expedition to enter his territory. Grant wrote: "Hurrah! We march again some miles nearer England. . . ." And march they did, about five miles, and then stopped for a day or two whilst the Waganda–Wunyoro situation brewed up.

Kamrasi had made it clear that he did not want Budja's and the Waganda escort in his territory. To save face, Budja tried every ploy he knew to stop the explorers going forward. By the end of the month he had arranged for Mtesa to send a message to Speke ordering him back to Mtesa's terrible city. This was too much. Budja was told they were going on regardless, which they did. Budja returned to his King, taking with him his people and twenty-eight of the expedition's porters and servants originally from Zanzibar. Speke and Grant had eighteen loyal men left, led by Seedy Bombay; but at last they were really on their way home.

Surrounded by a host of Kamrasi's warriors, the expedition went into Unyoro towards the King's palace. When they reached it, they discovered it to be a "dumpy, large hut" set in low swampy land on the banks of the Kafu (Kuffo, according to Grant). A miserable situation, and they spent some pretty miserable weeks near it—hemmed in by strong-smelling swamps—whilst Kamrasi proved that he was no different from other African kings and princes by refusing to grant them an audience until he felt he had demonstrated his importance.

They were formally introduced to him at a levee on 18 September. Bombay acted as interpreter, stretching the truth a bit in his replies: "Kamrasi: 'Who governs England?' Bombay: 'A

woman.' Kamrasi: 'Has she any children?' Bombay: 'Yes.'
[pointing to Speke and Grant] 'These are two of them.'"

Kamrasi was suitably impressed, although it was hard to
discover quite what impressed him, owing to his complete lack
of expression. According to Grant, Bombay said that Kamrasi
sat there whilst presents were being displayed to him "like a
cow". A tall, rather bovine-faced man, the King of Unyoro
affected a solemn indifference to everything he gazed upon. This
did not stop him from being very greedy, however, and his
constant begging made both explorers grow almost neurotically
short-tempered with him.

The truth—as Baker was to discover—was that poor Kamrasi
lived in fear of losing his kingdom. Surrounded by enemies—
Mtesa and the chiefs of the Madi, Bari and Chopi were among
them—his position was not an enviable one. Neither was his
disposition, since he was rather stupid, very cowardly, at the
mercy of long spells of depression and always anxious and
insecure. An unpleasant man to deal with, but, as Grant was good
enough to admit, Kamrasi did not butcher his subjects like Mtesa;
he was not unkindly. His rule was—by any standards—a very
liberal one. The only people put to death were the worst mur-
derers; for an unpremeditated murder, for instance, a man was
generally flogged and then set free.

Having got so far, the explorers found they were again
prisoners. Their pitifully small party was firmly overlooked by a
few hundred of Kamrasi's warriors. To move on without the
road ahead being opened to them was impossible. Kamrasi's
motives were those of greed and security: he wanted all he could
force out of them, and he hoped they would help him to turn and
attack a number of his enemies.

He was more successful as a beggar than as an aggressor with
Speke and Grant. They flatly refused to help him fight his
endless wars. They suffered somewhat from his raids on their
possessions. Then Speke, for once, put his foot down; having lost
an expensive watch and gold chain to the King's sticky fingers, he
had had more than enough.

He sent Kamrasi a bag of the commonest beads and with it a

message . . . "the beads were for the poor beggar who came to our house yesterday, not to see us but, to beg . . ." The message finished by stating that they did not desire the acquaintance of beggars, so they would not call on the King again. This strong stuff worked, and Kamrasi reduced his requests to reasonable limits.

It would not have helped him very much if he had gone on pleading for things. The expedition's cupboard was almost bare; Speke and Grant were down to their last garments, the medicine chest was all but empty, and as for beads, cloth and sundry presents, their stock was just about exhausted. But there was hope. At some trading station, not so far north, Petherick would have made his base and be actively looking for his fellow-countrymen. He would also have supplies of everything in plenty. That was the theory, anyway, and, to test its truth, Seedy Bombay had been sent off on 22 September with a mixed escort of tribesmen to Faloro, a trading station about a hundred miles up-country on the banks of a Nile tributary.

The Petherick affair was a weary mixture of ill luck, misunderstanding and poor administration. Its only importance is its aftermath, and how that aftermath illuminated one part of Speke's character. The facts are simple, if a little vague. Petherick was the British Vice-Consul at Khartoum, a good-hearted man doing a pretty beastly job. He had travelled quite extensively in the Sudan, and down into Central Africa as far as Kamrasi's old palace, fifty-odd miles north of the present one.

Petherick, like all vice-consuls, had another job. In his case it was trading in ivory. When Speke's expedition was being got up, the R.G.S. arranged for Petherick to meet it with various supplies, once it was in the area of the fateful Gondokoro Station. For this purpose Petherick was given £1,000.

Presumably it was hoped that Petherick would get wind of Speke's progress and whereabouts from the traders who came into Khartoum. There was certainly no time-table available for him, nor was there much in the way of map references. As we have seen, at one time the expedition nearly hived off eastwards, and the general northern approach could hardly be pinpointed to one or another particular route. Time had ceased to mean very much. A quick-moving party could have done the journey from Zanzibar in nine months; now, halted in the middle of Unyoro, they had been travelling for two years. Finally, the sort of gossip about the expedition's progress which Petherick was likely to pick up could be entirely misleading. Speke and Grant were endlessly misinformed about Petherick's movements, this time included, for Petherick was nowhere near Faloro.

They did not know this, however, although Grant's rather cryptic mention of there being at least a chance of Bombay's journey having a purpose can be taken to mean that he was not exactly sure of Petherick's whereabouts. Speke was possibly more hopeful, for he records that he told Kamrasi that Petherick would have been waiting four (African) years in Gani for their arrival. Hopeful or not, there was nothing left for them to do, of course, but sit and wait. Bombay ought to have been able to make the journey and back in a couple of weeks.

At Kamrasi's primitive court, life was slow and boring. Grant wrote: "Our situation was little better than that of a prisoner in a solitary cell. . . . No one was allowed to visit us. . . . Natives from interesting countries all round would visit the King, but *we* could not see them! Dances and parties went on, and we could not attend them. Rain was felt as a relief, as it employed one in reading the gauge every morning."

They did manage to see one group of visitors from the Chopi and Kidi tribes. Savage hunters "without any covering around the loins" who spoke a completely different language from any the expedition had come across. They visited the king's fat wives and sisters, and found them almost as grotesque as those of Rumanika. They heard of the country's superstitions, including one remarkable story of how Kamrasi could divide the waters of the lake (which lake is not made clear) if he so wished. They received odd snippets of news from Mtesa's kingdom, including the sad story of how Budja, their emissary from Uganda to Unyoro, had been killed by a bewitchment perpetrated by one of Kamrasi's officials. But there was no news of Bombay, and the days turned into weeks.

By the middle of October Speke was becoming anxious. Daily he inquired of the King for news of Bombay's journey, and on most days he was told where Bombay was and even what the small expedition was doing. The trouble was that neither explorer could believe what they were being told. Worse, Speke actively feared that Bombay had been made a prisoner by Kamrasi—that was, if he had not been murdered. In that land of "cruelty and deceit" anything was likely. Kamrasi appeared to be involved in some warlike plans, possibly to attack Mtesa, and was often incommunicado; there was an atmosphere of unrest at court, and the reports of Bombay's movements seemed much too glib. So Speke put his ear to the ground, and without much success tried to discover what was going on.

Only one thing was clear. Bombay's disappearing act and the hectic situation at court was bound up with the event of Mtesa's coronation. (He had been on the throne for the statutory three Waganda years before being crowned.) The coronation rites, which included the burning to death of Mtesa's thirty or so brothers, caused the Waganda to be much too involved with their own business to worry about the intentions of their neighbour. It was also obvious that Bombay's mission for his masters had been used by Kamrasi to deliver messages en route calling upon the various tribal leaders to join Kamrasi in operation "Mtesa". (Later, as we shall see, all this was to rebound on Kamrasi. His plan never got off the ground.) Then, just when things were turning rather desperate, Bombay reappeared.

The rest is an anti-climax. Speke makes a simple note in his journal to the effect that Petherick was not there, but some two hundred Turks (meaning the Egyptian Irregulars) were at the outpost waiting for him on Petherick's instructions. Petherick himself ". . . had gone down the river eight days' journey, but was expected to return shortly". Speke also mentions that, as the Turks were unable to read his letter to Petherick, they were doubtful if his party was the one they were to wait for. This should have worried Speke, but it doesn't seem to have done. As for the other message about Petherick's name being cut on a tree as evidence of his having been at Faloro—a typical piece of

African inventiveness—this also should have warned both men that things were not what they seemed. But they took everything at face-value, and on 9 November started off on their march from the Unyoro capital towards the Nile, and what they thought would be a speedy journey back to civilisation with Petherick's help.

There was still over two hundred miles to cover to Gondokoro, heading almost due north and going through country inhabited by five wild and, if reports could be believed, hostile tribes: the Chopi, Kidi, Gani, Madi and Bari. They found, in fact, that these tribes were no more than naturally aggressive to the slave traders, and wild only because the ravages of slave trading had made them into nomads. At the first sign of a trading caravan, they picked up all their worldly possessions and got out of the way. When the caravan was on the march through difficult country, if any soldier could be picked off they had no hesitation in doing so. Speke and Grant did not blame them, and, once they knew the white men were not traders, perfectly good relationships were established, albeit their language was a problem; it reminded Speke of that spoken by the Tibetan Tartars, and most communication took place through a simple sign language.

The expedition's immediate objective was Faloro, of course, with its promise of better things to come. They set out in fine style, getting to the Nile at its junction with the Kuffo river after a couple of days. The Nile trip took four days, and was made in a canoe hollowed out of an immense tree; Grant found it pleasant but "not dignified", a perplexing conclusion which he did not embroider. Here they found that the Nile ran through large swampy lakes and past some magnificent, high, wooded country, and there were plenty of hippopotami and crocodile to shoot at, without much success.

Once back on land, they had the usual trouble in recruiting enough porters from the local tribesmen. Those they did force into the job quite naturally deserted once they found a chance; this slowed up progress, tempers grew short, fresh porters were found by using rather more brutal methods—Grant writes of the seizing of women and cattle as a blackmail—and these press-ganged

men malingered on their way until it was better to dismiss
them and start the whole abysmal process over again. Speke and
Grant curbed their impatience and plodded on. They had learnt
that nothing could be altered in Africa; mistakes and hopeless
incompetence were never resolved, only repeated. They were,
perhaps, almost at the end of their tether, but they were also
coming to the end of their great journey.

On 3 December they got to Faloro. There was no Petherick,
only a large and very black Egyptian called Mahamed, who
commanded the couple of hundred soldiers of mixed Nubian,
African, and Egyptian descent who formed a sort of movable
garrison. Speke's meeting with him is best described in his own
words: "... a very black man, named Mahamed, in full Egyptian
regimentals with a curved sword, ordered his regiment to halt
and threw himself into my arms, endeavouring to hug and kiss
me." Speke would not be kissed, instead he asked about Petherick.
"'And where is Petherick now?' 'Oh, he is coming.'" Speke
wondered why Mahamed was flying three large red flags instead
of English colours. He was told that the colours belonged to one
called Debono, and that Debono was the same as "Petrick", and
that "Petrick" was Mahamed's master.

Speke and Grant were then taken to a large shed which had been
cleared and turned into their living quarters. Here Speke tackled
Mahamed again: "I said 'tell us your orders; there must be some
letters'. He said 'No, I have no letters or written orders, though I
have directions to take you to Gondokoro as soon as you come'."
He went on to express impatience with hanging around at Faloro
waiting for the explorers. Speke then asked for more about
Petherick, phrasing his question rather oddly. "I said 'How is
it Petherick has not come here to meet me? Is he married?' 'Yes,
he is married, and both he and his wife ride fore-and-aft on one
animal at Khartum.'"

They settled down to camp life, thankful for some luxuries,
including soap, and hoping to be away in a few days with or
without the elusive Petherick. Grant mentions that those they
interrogated "... could not or would not tell us anything about
him, excepting that he was twenty marches away to the north,

and that our letter sent him from Unyoro had not been forwarded." The subject of Petherick and his whereabouts was dropped at first and then lost amidst the unpromising situation which quickly developed. For Mahamed had really no intention of quitting Faloro until he had collected as much ivory and as many slaves as he could obtain from the surrounding country. His words to Speke when they met about being anxious to press on were like his messages to Bombay earlier, nothing else but thoughtless lies, although, as Baker discovered later, Mahamed was no fool, and when approached tactfully could be both useful and trustworthy.

Mahommed Wat-el-Mek, to give him his correct name, was the agent or vakeel of a Maltese trader whose name, embroidered on the main flag at Faloro, was, according to Grant, "Andrea de Bono". Whether de Bono was a trader in ivory alone is doubtful. Grant records hearing the cries of a captured girl, and mentions that there were more female than male slaves. But Wat-el-Mek was de Bono's creature, not Petherick's, and there was nothing Speke could do to make him march his regiment to Gondokoro before he wanted to. Yet again the expedition was stuck, and when Speke tried to move off he found that his guards and porters would not go alone across the Bari country, and anyway there was not a guide who would take them.

So for the last time the two explorers had to sit and wait. They wrote about it with admirable understatement, but it must have been a situation worthy of screaming against. Petherick is not mentioned: presumably Speke had already relegated him to the position of a failed friend, a chap who had let the side down, a man who preferred to ride around Khartoum, fore-and-aft with his wife, than plunge into the heart of Africa and rescue his fellow-countrymen.

Life at Faloro was not dull: alarms and excursions were the normal order of things. Wat-el-Mek's soldiery plundered and ransacked every village for some twenty miles around. It was not a question of buying ivory—or slaves—but of stealing them, and at the same time driving off the native cattle and, whenever possible, burning the miserable villages to the ground. Naturally enough, there was the odd reprisal raid for this behaviour, which unfortunately, in both men's view, was never more than a diversion, causing much noise but no damage. This was the really vicious way of exploiting a country that the Egyptian authorities not only condoned but through their corrupt officials actively encouraged. To Speke and Grant it was an eye-opening, distasteful surprise, and no doubt the thought that the British Vice-Consul at Khartoum was mixed up in it—however slightly—strengthened their resolution to place Petherick in a bad light once they got back to England. Although mean of them, this was to some extent understandable after their forced stay at Faloro, for which they held Petherick responsible anyway.

Christmas passed, unrecorded in their journals, and Mahommed began to show signs of organising his "ragamuffin mixture" for the march north. Not that either man could see any trace of urgency in these proceedings, but something positive must have happened for on 11 January 1863 Speke wrote: "Tired beyond all measure with Mahamed's procrastination . . . I now started myself, much to his disgust, and went ahead again, leaving word that I would wait for him at the next place, provided he did not delay more than one day." Within a couple of days Mahommed's vanguard had caught up with the twenty-strong expedition, and together they got to a village called Apuddo, where they settled down to wait for the main party of Egyptians.

There was still no trace of Petherick, but there was some carving on a tree. Grant viewed it and gave his judgment. "I visited the tree on which a European had cut some letters, but they were so indistinct that I walked twice round it before I could distinguish them. . . . I at once concluded that the traveller was not English, because his letters were not deeply cut into the tree as an Englishman would have done it, and also because the letters were curiously formed." When Grant finally reached Khartoum, he discovered the carving had been done by an Italian called Miani, who got as far as Appudo in 1861 but decided to turn back rather than be shut up in Faloro with Mahommed Wat-el-Mek and his troop during the rainy season.

The story of Petherick carving his name on trees must have

sprung from Miani's sad attempt to commemorate his presence in a savage land. Carving one's name on a tree was something expected, perhaps, of all white men. Strangely enough, neither Grant nor Speke did so, but if they had it can be imagined they would have carved deeply for all time. At Apuddo, however, there was plenty of shooting, some of it successful, although Grant complains at not being able to bag a giraffe. By the end of January Mahommed and his main party arrived, and the next day the whole caravan set off for Gondokoro.

They found themselves going through a beautiful, peaceful countryside—it reminded both men of a well-kept English park —and always somewhere near their path was the Nile, running "like a fine highland stream between the gneiss and mica-schist hills" at one point, "placid and broad like a gentle English river running between swelling slopes" at another. They must have felt triumphant, but they hardly expressed it.

Doubtless they felt anxious at times with the Bari setting fire to the grass around their camps, picking off the odd straggler with poisoned arrows, and on the majority of nights threatening to attack; but their sang-froid was by now second nature. Grant records a nice moment of non-panic: "A most anxious night it was. We were all lying encamped upon a grassy slope . . . within a mile of the Nile . . . Frij came to us saying 'Have you heard that the natives are coming to attack us? Mahommed says we must be prepared with our guns for a fight.' 'Do you hear that, Speke?' 'Yes' was the calm reply." Later both men fell asleep waiting for the attack, and awoke next morning to find everything peaceful. The worst that happened was the loss of Grant's umbrella, which was left behind at one halt. Thirty men went back to recover it, but "cold feet were the order of the day, and my old and trusted friend was abandoned".

On the morning of 15 February 1863 they came to the outskirts of Gondokoro, and, after Mahommed's scratch army had fired a ragged and somewhat dangerous salute, Speke and Grant went along the Nile banks and called in at the hut of a merchant friend of Mahommed to inquire of Petherick. It was all beautifully casual, like a stop on a day's stroll through the English countryside.

Petherick was the friend who should have been waiting for them, but their cool inquiry was answered by a "mysterious silence". They were told that it was de Bono whom they should thank for getting them through the immediate hostile country, which was true enough but quite irrelevant as an answer to their question. Then, according to Grant, they were told that a gentleman had just left the merchant's hut. So they made their farewells and set off to walk into the town proper, still in hunt of the legendary Petherick.

Samuel White Baker and his wife Florence had arrived at Gondokoro on 2 February. They were preparing for their journey south to the undiscovered Lake Albert, and they were at the same time proposing to try to locate Speke and Grant. For the moment they were becalmed in Gondokoro waiting for de Bono's caravan to arrive and set off again, when they would join it. On the morning of 15 February Baker heard the salute fired by Mahommed's soldiers, and shortly after that messengers brought him news of two white men with the caravan who had come from the sea. He ran out to see for himself.

"When I first met them they were walking along the bank of the river towards my boats. At a distance of about a hundred yards I recognised my old friend Speke, and with a heart beating with joy I took off my cap and gave a welcome hurrah as I ran towards him."

At first Speke did not recognise Baker, which was not surprising, considering they had not met for ten years, and he had absolutely no idea that Baker was anywhere in Africa. There was a moment of blank incredulity, and then both men began talking at once. Grant was introduced, for they had not met before, and Baker led them to the boat he was living on.

"We were shortly seated on deck under the awning, and such rough fare as could be hastily prepared was set before these two ragged, careworn specimens of African travel, whom I looked upon with feelings of pride as my own countrymen . . . Speke appeared the more worn of the two, he was excessively lean, but in reality he was in good tough condition; he had walked the whole way from Zanzibar, never having once ridden during that wearying march. Grant was in honourable rags; his bare knees projecting through the remnants of trousers that were an exhibition of rough industry in tailor's work. He was looking tired and feverish, but both men had a fire in the eye that showed the spirit that had led them through."

It was a great moment, the first meeting of white man with white man in the unknown and monstrous wilderness of Central Africa. It is rather surprising that it has not found a place in popular legend.

Baker told them the news of the outside world; it was over two years since they had last had letters forwarded on to them from Zanzibar, and they also learnt from him where Petherick really was—at his trading depot some seventy miles due west of Gondokoro. Both men write about this with seething indignation. They felt totally let down by Petherick, and unfortunately they judged his actions before they heard his story. When he did at last arrive, three days later, their meeting was far from cordial, but by then the whole affair had become so divorced from reality that Speke could write seriously: "For I had hurried away from Uganda and separated from Grant at Kari [where Speke went off alone to find the Nile source] solely to keep faith with him."

This was surely a breathtaking fabrication. No meeting place and time was arranged beforehand between either party and such an arrangement anyway would have been quite impossible to keep to. Petherick, in fact, never had any more idea than Baker had about when and where to expect Speke's expedition to surface. He also had had his problems coming down from Khartoum, being grievously sick on the journey; otherwise he would have arrived at Gondokoro many weeks earlier. But if he had done so, it was unlikely that intelligence of Speke and Grant would have reached him. It did not reach Baker, who was most positively concerned with finding his two fellow-explorers.

Speke and Grant stayed on at Gondokoro until 25 February, largely to enable Speke to take his final lunar observation when the moon was in the right position. Neither man spends much time on the miserable place in their books, although they mention the people they met there, including a party of Dutch ladies who

had travelled down from Khartoum with Baker, and they record
the various kindness done to them whilst they rested as guests
of the hospitable Baker. There is one startling omission from their
reports of their stay at Gondokoro, however: not once is Mrs
Baker mentioned. But it is more than this. For some inexplicable
reason Florence Baker not only vanishes from the picture completely, but through both men's neglect is made to seem as if she
was never even in it.

This passage from Speke is typical: "Baker then said he had
come up with three vessels . . . fully equipped with armed men . . .
and everything necessary for a long journey, expressly to look
after us, hoping as he jokingly said, to find us on the equator in
some terrible fix that he might have the pleasure of helping us out
of it. Three Dutch ladies [footnoted as the Baroness Miss A. Van
Capellan, and Mrs and Miss Tinne], also with a view to assist
us in the same way as Baker (God bless them), had come here in a
steamer but were driven back to Khartoum by sickness."

Here Speke makes Baker talk of his plans as if he was alone on
his expedition, something Baker is very careful not to do in his
own book, as we shall see. He also mentions the three Dutch
ladies, warmly and gallantly. One would imagine there wasn't
another European lady within a thousand miles. And Grant, after
praising the same three ladies for coming down from Khartoum
to aid the expedition, goes on about his and Speke's leaving
Gondokoro: "We had heard all the English news from Baker,
we had shared his hospitable table during our stay, seen his
spirited sketches and listened to his animated conversation."

It is difficult to know quite what to make of all this. Perhaps
Mrs Baker was ill, but then the fact might quite properly have
been reported. We know from Baker that she was sick with a
fever about a week before the two men arrived, although not too
sick to get up and deal with a mutiny amongst her husband's
bearers, and save him from a nasty situation. Florence Baker was a
very positive woman, not the sort to vanish into the background,
sharing her Sam's life in the fullest possible manner. Yet she seems
not to be in evidence at all during Speke's and Grant's time in
Gondokoro. Perhaps they did not approve of her, or thought a

Hungarian lady, as the wife of such a decent Englishman as Sam Baker, was not a mentionable subject. None of this seems likely in any reasonable sense, so there is only one explanation left.

Samuel Baker did not let on that he had his second wife with him, and she joined in the deception. It would have been easy enough, since the Bakers had three boats to live on, although quite why Baker should wish to practise such a deceit is not at all clear. Perhaps he didn't trust Speke and Grant to behave as gentlemen should at the sight of a lovely white girl after years away from such delectable creatures. Or did he have cause not to trust Mrs Baker? Or was it all a great joke which Baker forgot to divulge?

Baker only adds to the mystery by failing to make any reference to his wife meeting or being with Speke or Grant during their pause at Gondokoro. There is no knowing any more, and we are left with the final enigma of a journey which had its fair share of such occurrences.

By 30 March 1863 they were in Khartoum, where they stayed for two weeks. The journey to Cairo was not an easy one at that time, entailing a dash of nearly two hundred miles at one stage across the Sahara Desert, but they reached Cairo on 25 May. With them had travelled their eighteen faithful Seedees, led by Bombay, and the four women servants. In Cairo the Seedees and the girls were photographed, and copies of the photographs given to Bombay as proof of their identity during the journey back to Zanzibar via Suez and Aden. They caused quite a sensation in Cairo one way or the other, so it seems, being lodged in the public garden "as the people were afraid to admit them into their houses". Speke paid them off handsomely, and they left for home on 1 June. They arrived in Zanzibar some months later, where they settled down to live happily ever after.

Speke and Grant arrived back in England in July 1863. A little more than a year later Speke was dead.

*   *   *

From the moment Speke landed in England he was—as in 1859 —furiously busy. There were people to meet, receptions to be attended, lectures to be given. He had seen the Nile flowing from Lake Victoria, he had traced its course for many hundreds of miles, he had sailed upon its waters, and the world had to be told of these achievements. He settled down to write his narrative of the exploration. By the end of 1863 the 650-page *Journal of the Discovery of the Source of the Nile* was in the bookshops.

He also found time to bring the Petherick affair to a conclusion, lobbying the people he knew in the right places until Petherick's failure to be on the spot in Africa at the correct time assumed the proportions of a dark betrayal. Petherick and his friends protested in vain that his side of the story remained unheard. By the end of the year the vice-consularship at Khartoum was abolished.

The destruction of Petherick made Speke a host of new enemies. The old enemies, led by Burton, were still baying at the heels of his behaviour after the finding of the Victoria N'yanza. Once the *Journal of the Discovery of the Source of the Nile* was published, a common front against its author was formed, headed by Burton and strongly abetted by the geographer McQueen.

The attack was in depth and developed quickly. Speke's claim to have confirmed that Lake Victoria was the main source of the Nile was questioned sharply. Facts and figures were asked for, the explorer's evidence was turned inside out, the hastily written book was scrutinised for contradictions. A strong case was pretty easily made against Speke's claim.

At the same time Speke's behaviour in general on the expedition was analysed and attacked without mercy. The measuring of Rumanika's fat sister-in-law was made to appear as a sort of twisted sexual indulgence. The praise of Mtesa and the stay at the tyrant's court was held up to ridicule, and suggestions of Speke being involved in some unsavoury sexual immorality were made, snidely but firmly. And the leaving of Grant behind when finding the Nile at the Ripon Falls was castigated as a piece of blackhearted selfishness.

The attack on Speke's finding of the Nile course was stupid and misguided. That on his behaviour in general had some substance in it, but the manner in which it was done was inexcusable, as was the attempt to derive and detract from his really great achievements as an explorer. A difficult, egotistical and exasperating man he undoubtedly was, but then men of his sort are rarely without eccentricity of character. John Hanning Speke would not have achieved what he did in a short lifetime without being a somewhat unfathomable personality, and certainly a very original one.

But he had sooner or later to answer his critics in public, especially Burton; and in September 1864 such a meeting was arranged at the annual conference of the British Association at Bath. Speke went down beforehand and stayed at a cousin's house near by. On the day before their public debate Burton and Speke saw one another, in the conference hall, for the first time in five years. Speke, it seems, was in an agitated, even distressed, state. Something or somebody in the hall was upsetting him, not necessarily Burton. Before that day's session began he rose from his seat and left the hall. As he went he was heard to say: "Oh, I can't stand this any longer."

He went back to his cousin's house and set out almost at once on a shooting trip with his cousin and a gamekeeper. At about four o'clock in the afternoon he was seen to fall from a low wall on to his gun. He lived only a few minutes. At the inquest a verdict was returned of "accidental death".

Grant heard of his friend's death whilst at home in Scotland writing *A Walk Across Africa*. He had got to the finding of the carved tree at Appudo in the narrative. There and then he inserted an obituary in the book in which he reproaches himself for not joining Speke at Bath when invited. ". . . had I gone thither and been with my friend this calamity might have been averted." He goes on to write of the "taunts and doubts" which Speke's discovery had been subjected to, and then sums up Speke's character with typical generosity: "Captain Speke was, in private life, pure-minded, honourable, regardless of self and equally self-denying, with a mind always aiming at great things and above every littleness. He was gentle and pleasing in manner with almost childlike simplicity but at the same time extremely tenacious of purpose."

The obituary finishes with a strikingly bizarre thought. ". . . had the toll of the funeral bells reached the shores of the Nyanza as it touched the hearts of those in the valley of Ilminster, there is one at least—the King of Uganda—who would have shed a tear for the untimely death of the far distant traveller who had sought and found his protection."

A little later Burton published his obituary of Speke, finishing it with a passage well chosen to keep the flames of controversy blazing for some time.

"Lieutenant Speke was uncommonly hard to manage. To a peculiarly quiet and modest aspect and an almost childlike simplicity of manner he united an immense and abnormal fund of self-esteem. He ever held, not only that he had done his best on all occasions but also that no man living could do better. Before we set out on our last journey together, he openly declared that being tired of life he had come to be killed in Africa. I look upon this confession as a kind of whimsical affectation, like that which made him, when he returned to England in 1859 astonish his friends, the Browns, by speaking a sort of broken English as if he had forgotten his vernacular in the presence of strange tongues."

JOHN HANNING SPEKE

from

Journal of the Discovery of the Source of the Nile
(1864)

21st July—Here at last I stood on the brink of the Nile; most beautiful was the scene, nothing could surpass it! It was the very perfection of the kind of effect aimed at in a highly kept park; with a magnificent stream from 600 to 700 yards wide, dotted with islets and rocks, the former occupied by fishermen's huts, the latter by sterns and crocodiles basking in the sun,—flowing between fine high grassy banks, with rich trees and plantains in the background, where herds of the nsunnu and hartebeest could be seen grazing, while the hippopotami were snorting in the water, and florikan and guinea-fowl rising at our feet.

25th—I marched up the left bank of the Nile at a considerable distance from the water, to the Isamba Rapids, passing through rich jungle and plantain-gardens. Nango, an old friend, and district officer of the place, first refreshed us with a dish of plantain-squash and dried fish, with pombe. He told us he is often threatened by elephants, but he sedulously keeps them off with charms; for if they ever tasted a plantain they would never leave the garden until they had cleared it out. He then took us to see the nearest falls of the Nile—extremely beautiful, but very confined. The water ran deep between its banks, which were covered with fine grass, soft cloudy acacias, and festoons of lilac convolvuli; whilst here and there, where the land had slipped above the rapids, bared places of red earth could be seen, like that of Devonshire; there, too, the waters, impeded by a natural dam, looked like a huge mill-pond, sullen and dark, in which two crocodiles, laving about, were looking out for prey. From the high banks we looked down upon a line of sloping wooded islets lying across the stream, which divide its waters, and, by interrupting them, cause at once both dam and rapids. The whole was more fairy-like, wild, and romantic than—I must confess that my thoughts took that shape—anything I ever saw outside of a theatre. It was exactly the sort of place, in fact, where, bridged across from one side-slip to the other, on a moon-light night, brigands would assemble to enact some dreadful tragedy. Even the Wanguana seemed spellbound at the novel beauty of the sight, and no one thought of moving till hunger warned us night was setting in, and we had better look out for lodgings.

28th—At last, with a good push for it, crossing hills and threading huge grasses, as well as extensive village plantations lately devastated by elephants—they had eaten all that was eatable, and what would not serve for food they had destroyed with their trunks, not one plantain or one hut being left entire—we arrived at the extreme end of the journey, the farthest point ever visited by the expedition on the same parallel of latitude as king Mtesa's palace, and just forty miles east of it.

We were well rewarded; for the "stones", as the Waganda call the falls, was by far the most interesting sight I had seen in Africa. Everybody ran to see them at once, though the march had been long and fatiguing, and even my sketch-block was called into play. Though beautiful, the scene was not excatly what I expected; for the broad surface of the lake was shut out from view by a spur of hill, and the falls, about 12 feet deep, and 400 to 500 feet broad, were broken by rocks. Still it was a sight that attracted one to it for hours—the roar of the waters, the thousands of passenger-fish, leaping at the falls with all their might, the Wasoga and Waganda fishermen coming out in boats and taking post on all the rocks with rod and hook, hippopotami and crocodiles lying sleepily on the water, the ferry at work above the falls, and cattle driven down to drink at the margin of the lake,—made, in all, with the pretty nature of the country—small hills, grassy-topped, with trees in the folds, and gardens on the lower slopes—as interesting a picture as one could wish to see.

The expedition had now performed its functions. I saw that old father Nile without any doubt rises in the Victoria N'yanza, and, as I had foretold, that lake is the great source of the holy river which cradled the first expounder of our religious belief. I mourned, however, when I thought how much I had lost by the delays in the journey having deprived me of the pleasure of going to look at the north-east corner of the N'yanza to see what connection there was, by the strait so often spoken of, with it and the other lake where the Waganda went to get their salt, and from which another river flowed to the north, making "Usoga an island". But I felt I ought to be content with what I had been spared to accomplish; for I had seen full half of the lake, and had information given me of the other half, by means of which I knew all about the lake, as far, at least, as the chief objects of geographical importance were concerned.

I now christened the "stones" Ripon Falls, after the nobleman who presided over the Royal Geographical Society when my expedition was got up; and the arm of water from which the Nile issued, Napoleon Channel, in token of respect to the French Geographical Society, for the honour they had done me, just before leaving England, in presenting me with their gold medal for the discovery of the Victoria N'yanza. One thing seemed at first perplexing—the volume of water in the Kitangule looked as large as that of the Nile; but then the one was a slow river and the other swift, and on this account I could form no adequate judgement of their relative values.

Halt, from 19th. Feb. to 7th July. To-day the king sent his pages to announce his intention of holding a levee in my honour. I prepared for my first presentation at court, attired in my best, though in it I cut a poor figure in comparison with the display of the dressy Waganda. They wore neat bark cloaks resembling the best yellow corduroy cloth, crimp and well set, as if stiffened with starch, and over that, as upper-cloaks, a patchwork of small antelope skins, which I observed were sewn together as well as any English glovers could have pieced them; whilst their head-dresses, generally, were abrus turbans, set off with highly-polished boar-tusks, stick-charms, seeds, beads, or shells; and on their necks, arms, and ankles they wore other charms of wood, or small horns stuffed with magic powder, and fastened on by strings generally covered with snake-skin. N'yamgundu and Maula demanded, as their official privilege, a first peep; and this being refused, they tried to persuade me that the articles comprising the present required to be covered with chintz, for it was considered indecorous to offer anything to his majesty in a naked state. This little interruption over, the articles enumerated below* were conveyed to the palace in solemn procession thus:—With N'yamgundu, Maula, the pages, and myself on the flanks, the Union-Jack carried by the kirangozi guide led the way, followed by twelve men as a guard of honour, dressed in red flannel cloaks, and carrying their arms sloped, with fixed bayonets; whilst in their rear were the rest of my men, each carrying some article as a present.

On the march towards the palace, the admiring courtiers, wonder-struck at such an unusual display, exclaimed, in raptures of astonishment, some with both hands at their mouths, and others clasping their heads with their hands, "Irungi! irungi!" which may be translated "Beautiful! beautiful!" I thought myself everything was going on as well as could be wished; but before entering the royal enclosures, I found, to my disagreeable surprise, that the men with Suwarora's hongo or offering, which consisted of more than a hundred coils of wire, were ordered to lead the procession, and take precedence of me. There was something specially aggravating in this precedence; for it will be remembered that these very brass wires which they saw, I had myself intended for Mtesa, that they were taken from me by Suwarora as far back as Usui, and it would never do, without remonstrance, to have them boastfully paraded before my eyes in this fashion. My protests, however, had no effect upon the escorting Wakungu. Resolving to make them catch it, I walked along as if ruminating

* 1 block-tin box, 4 rich silk clothes, 1 rifle (Whitworth's), 1 gold chronometer, 1 revolver pistol, 3 rifled carbines, 3 sword-bayonets, 1 box ammunition, 1 box bullets, 1 box gun-caps, 1 telescope, 1 iron chair, 10 bundles best beads, 1 set of table-knives, spoons, and forks.

in anger up the broad high road into a cleared square, which divides Mtesa's domain on the south from his Kamraviona's, or commander-in-chief, on the north, and then turned into the court. The palace or entrance quite surprised me by its extraordinary dimensions, and the neatness with which it was kept. The whole brow and sides of the hill on which we stood were covered with gigantic grass huts, thatched as neatly as so many heads dressed by a London barber, and fenced all round with the tall yellow reeds of the common Uganda tiger-grass; whilst within the enclosure, the lines of huts were joined together, or partitioned off into courts, with walls of the same grass. It is here most of Mtesa's three or four hundred women are kept, the rest being quartered chiefly with his mother, known by the title of N'yamasore, or queen-dowager. They stood in little groups at the doors, looking at us, and evidently passing their own remarks, and enjoying their own jokes, on the triumphal procession. At each gate as we passed, officers on duty opened and shut it for us, jingling the big bells which are hung upon them, as they sometimes are at shop-doors, to prevent silent, stealthy entrance.

The first court passed, I was even more surprised to find the unusual ceremonies that awaited me. There courtiers of high dignity stepped forward to greet me, dressed in the most scrupulously neat fashions. Men, women, bulls, dogs, and goats, were led about by strings; cocks and hens were carried in men's arms; and little pages, with rope-turbans, rushed about, conveying messages, as if their lives depended on their swiftness, every one holding his skin-cloak tightly round him lest his naked legs might by accident be shown.

This, then, was the ante-reception court; and I might have taken possession of the hut, in which musicians were playing and singing on large nine-stringed harps, like the Nubian tambira, accompanied by harmonicons. By the chief officers in waiting, however, who thought fit to treat us like Arab merchants, I was requested to sit on the ground outside in the sun with my servants. Now, I had made up my mind never to sit upon the ground as the natives and Arabs are obliged to do, nor to make my obeisance in any other manner than is customary in England, though the Arabs had told me that from fear they had always complied with the manners of the court. I felt that if I did not stand up for my social position at once, I should be treated with contempt during the remainder of my visit, and thus lose the vantage-ground I had assumed of appearing rather as a prince than a trader, for the purpose of better gaining the confidence of the king. To avert over-hastiness, however—for my servants began to be alarmed as I demurred against doing as I was bid—I allowed five minutes to the court to give me a proper reception, saying, if it were not conceded I would then walk away.

Nothing, however, was done. My own men, knowing me, feared for me, as they did not know what a "savage" king would do in case I carried out my threat; whilst the Waganda, lost in amazement at what seemed little less than blasphemy, stood still as posts. The affair ended by my walking straight away home, giving Bombay orders to leave the present on the ground, and to follow me.

Although the king is said to be unapproachable, excepting when he chooses to attend court—a ceremony which rarely happens—intelligence of my hot wrath and hasty departure reached him in an instant. He first, it seems, thought of leaving his toilet-room to follow me, but, finding I was walking fast and had gone far, changed his mind, and sent Wakungu running after me. Poor creatures! they caught me up, fell upon their knees, and implored I would return at once, for the king had not tasted food, and would not until he saw me. I felt grieved at their touching appeals; but, as I did not understand all they said, I simply replied by patting my heart and shaking my head, walking if anything all the faster.

On my arrival at my hut, Bombay and others came in, wet through with perspiration, saying the king had heard of all my grievances. Suwarora's hongo was turned out of court, and, if I desired it, I might bring my own chair with me, for he was very anxious to show me great respect—although such a seat was exclusively the attribute of the king, no one else in Uganda daring to sit on an artificial seat.

My point was gained, so I cooled myself with coffee and a

Sir Richard Burton by Lord Leighton (*National Portrait Gallery, London*)

Canoeing on Lake Tanganyika

Ladies' Smoking Party

Speke and Burton (back view) in "The Valley of Death and the Home of Hunger"

Speke in his "exploration outfit" (*Radio Times Hulton Picture Library*)

Grant in his "traveller's uniform" (*Radio Times Hulton Picture Library*)

Grant joins in the dance

Mtesa, with some of his wives, reviews his soldiers. Speke looks on.

Grant being introduced by Speke to the Queen Mother of Uganda

Mtesa, King of Uganda, "Walking like a lion"

Speke's and Grant's "Faithfuls" photographed in Cairo (Seedy Bombay, with hat, in foreground)

Florence Baker

Baker in his travelling costume (*Radio Times Hulton Picture Library*)

Baker the hunter, hunted

The storm on the Albert lake

Baker's first view of the Murchison Falls

The Obbo war dance

pipe, and returned rejoicing in my victory, especially over Suwarora. After returning to the second tier of huts from which I had retired, everybody appeared to be in a hurried, confused state of excitement, not knowing what to make out of so unprecedented an exhibition of temper. In the most polite manner, the officers in waiting begged me to be seated on my iron stool, which I had brought with me, whilst others hurried in to announce my arrival. But for a few minutes only I was kept in suspense, when a band of music, the musicians wearing on their backs long-haired goat-skins, passed me, dancing as they went along, like bears in a fair, and playing on reed instruments worked over with pretty beads in various patterns, from which depended leopard-cat skins—the time being regulated by the beating of long hand-drums.

The mighty king was now reported to be sitting on his throne in the state hut of the third tier. I advanced, hat in hand, with my guard of honour following, formed in "open ranks", who in their turn were followed by the bearers carrying the present. I did not walk straight up to him as if to shake hands, but went outside the ranks of a three-sided square of squatting Wakungu, all habited in skins, mostly cow-skins; some few of whom had, in addition, leopard-cat skins girt round the waist, the sign of royal blood. Here I was desired to halt and sit in the glaring sun; so I donned my hat, mounted my umbrella, a phenomenon which set them all a-wondering and laughing, ordered the guard to close ranks, and sat gazing at the novel spectacle. A more theatrical sight I never saw. The king, a good-looking, well-figured, tall young man of twenty-five, was sitting on a red blanket spread upon a square platform of royal grass, encased in tiger-grass reeds, scrupulously well dressed in a new mbugu. The hair of his head was cut short, excepting on the top, where it was combed up into a high ridge, running from stem to stern like a cockscomb. On his neck was a very neat ornament—a large ring, of beautifully-worked small beads, forming elegant patterns by their various colours. On one arm was another bead ornament, prettily devised; and on the other a wooden charm, tied by a string covered with snake-skin. On every finger and every toe he had

E

alternate brass and copper rings; and above the ankles, half-way up to the calf, a stocking of very pretty beads. Everything was light, neat, and elegant in its way; not a fault could be found with the taste of his "getting up". For a handkerchief he held a well-folded piece of bark, and a piece of gold-embroidered silk, which he constantly employed to hide his large mouth when laughing, or to wipe it after a drink of plantain-wine, of which he took constant and copious draughts from neat little gourd-cups, administered by his ladies-in-waiting, who were at once his sisters and wives. A white dog, spear, shield, and woman—the Uganda cognisance—were by his side, as also a knot of staff officers, with whom he kept up a brisk conversation on one side; and on the other was a band of Wichwezi, or lady-sorcerers, such as I have already described.

I was now asked to draw nearer within the hollow square of squatters, where leopard-skins were strewed upon the ground, and a large copper kettledrum, surmounted with brass bells on arching wires, along with two other smaller drums covered with cowrie-shells, and beads of colour worked into patterns, were placed. I now longed to open conversation, but knew not the language, and no one near me dared speak, or even lift his head from fear of being accused of eyeing the women; so the king and myself sat staring at one another for full an hour—I mute, but he pointing and remarking with those around him on the novelty of my guard and general appearance, and even requiring to see my hat lifted, the umbrella shut and opened, and the guards face about and show off their red cloaks—for such wonders had never been seen in Uganda.

Then, finding the day waning, he sent Maula on an embassy to ask me if I had seen him; and on receiving my reply, "Yes, for full one hour," I was glad to find him rise, spear in hand, lead his dog, and walk unceremoniously away through the enclosure into the fourth tier of huts; for this being a pure levee day, no business was transacted. The king's gait in retiring was intended to be very majestic, but did not succeed in conveying to me that impression. It was the traditional walk of his race, founded on the step of the lion; but the outward sweep of the legs, intended to represent the stride of the noble beast, appeared to me only to realise a very ludicrous kind of waddle, which made me ask Bombay if anything serious was the matter with the royal person.

I had now to wait for some time, almost as an act of humanity; for I was told the state secret, that the king had retired to break his fast and eat for the first time since hearing of my arrival; but the repast was no sooner over than he prepared for the second act, to show off his splendour, and I was invited in, with all my men, to the exclusion of all his own officers save my two guides. Entering as before, I found him standing on a red blanket, leaning against the right portal of the hut, talking and laughing, handkerchief in hand, to a hundred or more of his admiring wives, who, all squatting on the ground outside, in two groups, were dressed in new mbugus. My men dared not advance upright, nor look upon the women, but, stooping, with lowered heads and averted eyes, came cringing after me. Unconscious myself, I gave loud and impatient orders to my guard, rebuking them for moving like frightened geese, and, with hat in hand, stood gazing on the fair sex till directed to sit and cap.

Mtesa then inquired what messages were brought from Rumanika; to which Maula, delighted with the favour of speaking to royalty, replied by saying, Rumanika had gained intelligence of Englishmen coming up the Nile to Gani and Kidi. The king acknowledged the truthfulness of their story, saying he had heard the same himself; and both Wakungu, as is the custom in Uganda, thanked their lord in a very enthusiastic manner, kneeling on the ground—for no one can stand in the presence of his majesty—in an attitude of prayer, and throwing out their hands as they repeated the words N'yanzig N'yanzig ai N'yanzig Mkahma wangi &c. &c. for a considerable time; when thinking they had done enough of this, and heated with the exertion, they threw themselves flat upon their stomachs, and, floundering about like fish on land, repeated the same words over again and again, and rose doing the same, with their faces covered with earth; for majesty in Uganda is never satisfied till subjects have grovelled before it like the most abject worms. This conversation over, after gazing at me, and chatting with his women for a considerable time, the second scene ended. The third scene was more easily arranged, for the day was fast declining. He simply moved with his train of women to another hut, where, after seating himself upon his throne, with his women around him, he invited me to approach the nearest limits of propriety, and to sit as before. Again he asked me if I had seen him—evidently desirous of indulging in his regal pride; so I made the most of the opportunity thus afforded me of opening a conversation by telling him of those grand reports I had formerly heard about him, which induced me to come all this way to see him, and the trouble it had cost me to reach the object of my desire; at the same time taking a gold ring from off my finger, and presenting it to him, I said, "This is a small token of friendship; if you will inspect it, it is made after the fashion of a dog-collar, and, being the king of metals, gold, is in every respect appropriate to your illustrious race."

He said, in return, "If friendship is your desire, what would you say if I showed you a road by which you might reach your home in one month?" Now everything had to be told to Bombay, then to Nasib, my Kiganda interpreter, and then to either Maula or N'yamgundu, before it was delivered to the king, for it was considered indecorous to transmit any message to his majesty excepting through the medium of one of his officers. Hence I could not get an answer put in; for as all Waganda are rapid and impetuous in their conversation, the king, probably forgetting he had put a question, hastily changed the conversation and said, "What guns have you got? Let me see the one you shoot with." I wished still to answer the first question first, as I knew he referred to the direct line to Zanzibar across the Masai, and was anxious, without delay, to open the subject of Petherick and Grant; but no one dared to deliver my statement. Much disappointed, I then said, "I had brought the best shooting-gun in the world—Whitworth's rifle—which I begged he would accept, with a few other trifles; and, with his permission, I would lay them upon a carpet at his feet, as is the custom of my country when visiting sultans." He assented, sent all his women away, and had an mbugu spread for the purpose, on which Bombay, obeying my order, first spread a red blanket, and then opened each article one after the other, when Nasib, according to the usage already mentioned, smoothed them down with his dirty hands, or rubbed them against his sooty face, and handed them to the king to show there was no poison or witchcraft in them. Mtesa appeared quite confused with the various wonders as he handled them, made silly remarks, and pondered over them like a perfect child, until it was quite dark. Torches were then lit, and guns, pistols, powder, boxes, tools, beads—the whole collection, in short—were tossed together topsy-turvy, bundled into mbugus, and carried away by the pages. Mtesa now said, "It is late' and time to break up; what provisions would you wish to have?" I said, "A little of everything, but no one thing constantly." "And would you like to see me to-morrow?" "Yes, every day." "Then you can't to-morrow, for I have business; but the next day come if you like. You can now go away, and here are six pots of plantain-wine for you; my men will search for food to-morrow."

23rd—At noon Mtesa sent his pages to invite me to his palace. I went, with my guard of honour and my stool, but found I had to sit waiting in an ante-hut three hours with his commander-in-chief and other high officers before he was ready to see me. During this time Wasoga minstrels, playing on tambira, and accompanied by boys playing on a harmonicon, kept us amused; and a small page, with a large bundle of grass, came to me and said, "The king hopes you won't be offended if required to sit on it before him; for no person in Uganda, however high in office, is ever allowed to sit upon anything raised above the ground, nor can anybody but himself sit upon such grass as this; it is all that his throne is made of. The first day he only allowed you to sit on your stool to appease your wrath."

I was now requested to shoot the four cows as quickly as possible; but having no bullets for my gun, I borrowed the revolving pistol I had given him, and shot all four in a second of time; but as the last one, only wounded, turned sharply upon me, I gave him the fifth and settled him. Great applause followed this *wonderful* feat, and the cows were given to my men. The king now loaded one of the carbines I had given him with his own hands, and giving it full-cock to a page, told him to go out and shoot a man in the outer court; which was no sooner accomplished than the little urchin returned to announce his success, with a look of glee such as one would see in the face of a boy who had robbed a bird's nest, caught a trout, or done any other boyish trick. The king said to him, "And did you do it well?" "Oh yes, capitally." He spoke the truth, no doubt, for he dared not have trifled with the king; but the affair created hardly any interest. I never heard, and there appeared no curiosity to know, what individual human being the urchin had deprived of life.

*　　　*　　　*

5th—To-day the king went on a visit to his mother, and therefore neither of them could be seen by visitors. I took a stroll towards the N'yanza, passing through the plantain-groves occupied by the king's women, where my man Sangoro had been twice taken up by the Mgemma and put in the stocks. The plantain gardens were beautifully kept by numerous women, who all ran away from fright at seeing me, save one who, taken by surprise, threw herself flat on the ground, rolled herself up in her mbugu, and, kicking with her naked heels, roared murder and help, until I poked her up, and reproached her for her folly. This little incident made my fairies bolder, and, sidling up to me one by one, they sat in a knot with me upon the ground; then clasping their heads with their hands, they woh-wohed in admiration of the white man.

6th—To-day I sent Bombay to the palace for food. Though rain fell in torrents, he found the king holding a levee, giving appointments, plantations, and women, according to merit, to his officers. As one officer, to whom only one woman was given, asked for more, the king called him an ingrate, and ordered him to be cut to pieces on the spot; and the sentence was, as Bombay told me, carried into effect—not with knives, for they are prohibited, but with slips of sharp-edged grass, after the executioners had first dislocated his neck by a blow delivered behind the head, with a sharp, heavy-headed club.

13th—As nothing was done all day, I took the usual promenade in the Seraglio Park, and was accosted by a very pretty little woman, Kariana, wife of Dumba, who, very neatly dressed, was returning from a visit. At first she came trotting after me, then timidly paused, then advanced, and, as I approached her, stood spellbound at my remarkable appearance. At last recovering herself, she woh-wohed with all the coquetry of a Mganda woman, and a flirtation followed; she must see my hair, my watch, the contents of my pockets—everything; but that was not enough. I waved adieu, but still she followed. I offered my arm, showing her how to take it in European fashion, and we walked along, to the surprise of everybody, as if we had been in Hyde Park rather than in Central Africa, flirting and coquetting all the way. I was surprised that no one came to prevent her forwardness; but not till I almost reached home did any one appear, and then, with great scolding, she was ordered to return—not, however, without her begging I would call in and see her on some future occasion, when she would like to give me some pombe.

23rd—To-day occurred a brilliant instance of the capricious restlessness and self-willedness of this despotic king. At noon, pages hurried in to say that he had started for the N'yanza, and wished me to follow him without delay. N'yanza, as I have mentioned, merely means a piece of water, whether a pond, river, or lake; and as no one knew which N'yanza he meant, or what project was on foot, I started off in a hurry, leaving everything behind, and walked rapidly through gardens, over hills, and across rushy swamps, down the west flank of the Murchison Creek, till 3 p.m., when I found the king dressed in red, with his Wakungu in front and women behind, travelling along in the confused manner of a pack of hounds, occasionally firing his rifle that I might know his whereabouts. He had just, it seems, mingled a little business with pleasure; for noticing, as he passed, a woman tied by the hands to be punished for some offence, the nature of which I did not learn, he took the executioner's duty on himself, fired at her, and killed her outright.

24th—The king rose betimes in the morning and called me, unwashed and very uncomfortable, to picnic with him, during the collection of the boats. The breakfast, eaten in the open court, considered of sundry baskets of roast-beef and plantain-squash, folded in plantain-leaves. He sometimes ate with a copper knife and picker, not forked—but more usually like a dog, with both hands. The bits too tough for his mastication he would take from his mouth and give as a treat to the pages, who n'yanzigged, and swallowed them with much seeming relish. Whatever remained over was then divided by the boys, and the baskets taken to the cooks. Pombe served as tea, coffee, and beer for the king; but his guests might think themselves very lucky if they ever got a drop of it.

Now for the lake. Everybody in a hurry falls into his place the best way he can—Wakungu leading, and women behind. They rattle along, through plantains and shrubs, under large trees, seven, eight, and nine feet in diameter, till the beautiful waters are reached—a picture of the Rio scenery, barring that of the higher mountains in the background of that lovely place, which are here represented by the most beautiful little hills. A band of fifteen drums of all sizes, called the Mazaguzo, playing with the regularity of a lot of factory engines at work, announced the king's arrival, and brought all the boats to the shore—but not as in England, where Jack, with all the consequence of a lord at home, invites the ladies to be seated, and enjoys the sight of so many pretty faces. Here every poor fellow, with his apprehensions written in his face, leaps over the gunwale into the water—ducking his head from fear of being accused of gazing on the fair sex, which is death—and bides patiently his time. They were dressed in plantain-leaves, looking like grotesque Neptunes. The king, in his red coat and wideawake, conducted the arrangements, ordering all to their proper places—the women in certain boats, the Wakungu and Wanguana in others, whilst I sat in the same boat with him at his feet, three women holding mbugus of pombe behind. The king's Kisuahili now came into play, and he was prompt in carrying out the directions he got from myself to approach the hippopotami. But the waters were too large and the animals too shy, so we toiled all the day without any effect, going only once ashore to picnic; not for the women to eat—for they, poor things, got nothing—but the king, myself, the pages, and the principal Wakungu. As a wind-up to the day's amusement, the king led the band of drums, changed the men according to their powers, put them into concert pitch, and readily detected every slight irregularity, showing himself a thorough musician.

25th—This day requires no remark, everything done being the counterpart of yesterday, excepting that the king, growing bolder with me in consequence of our talking together, became more playful and familiar—amusing himself, for instance, sometimes by catching hold of my beard as the rolling of the boat unsteadied him.

26th—We started early in the usual manner; but after working up and down the creek, inspecting the inlets for hippopotami, and tiring from want of sport, the king changed his tactics, and, paddling and steering himself with a pair of new white paddles, finally directed the boats to an island occupied by the Mgussa, or Neptune of the N'yanza, not in person—for Mgussa is a spirit— but by his familiar or deputy, the great medium who communicates the secrets of the deep to the king of Uganda. In another sense, he might be said to be the presiding priest of the source of the mighty Nile, and as such was, of course, an interesting person for me to meet. The first operation on shore was picnicking, when many large bugus of pombe were brought for the king; next, the whole party took a walk, winding through the trees, and picking fruit, enjoying themselves amazingly, till, by some unlucky chance, one of the royal wives, a most charming creature, and truly one of the best of the lot, plucked a fruit and offered it to the king, thinking, doubtless, to please him greatly; but he, like a madman, flew into a towering passion, said it was the first time a woman ever had the impudence to offer him anything, and ordered the pages to seize, bind, and lead her off to execution.

These words were no sooner uttered by the king than the whole bevy of pages slipped their cord turbans from their heads, and rushed like a pack of cupid beagles upon the fairy queen, who, indignant at the little urchins daring to touch her majesty, remonstrated with the king, and tried to beat them off like flies, but was soon captured, overcome, and dragged away, crying, in the names of the Kamraviona and Mzungu (myself), for help and protection; whilst Lubuga, the pet sister, and all the other women, clasped the king by his legs, and, kneeling, implored forgiveness for their sister. The more they craved for mercy, the more brutal he became, till at last he took a heavy stick and began to belabour the poor victim on the head.

Hitherto I had been extremely careful not to interfere with any of the king's acts of arbitrary cruelty, knowing that such interference, at an early stage, would produce more harm than good. This last act of barbarism, however, was too much for my English blood to stand; and as I heard my name, Mzungu, imploringly pronounced, I rushed at the king, and, staying his uplifted arm, demanded from him the woman's life. Of course I ran imminent risk of losing my own in thus thwarting the capricious tyrant; but his caprice proved the friend of both. The novelty of interference even made him smile, and the woman was instantly released.

AFTER a long and amusing conversation with Rumanika in the morning, I called on one of his sisters-in-law, married to an elder brother who was born before Dagara ascended the throne. She was another of those wonders of obesity, unable to stand excepting on all fours. I was desirous to obtain a good view of her, and actually to measure her, and induced her to give me facilities for doing so, by offering in return to show her a bit of my naked legs and arms. The bait took as I wished it, and after getting her to sidle and wriggle into the middle of the hut, I did as I promised, and then took her dimensions, as noted below.* All of these are exact except the height, and I believe I could have obtained this more accurately if I could have had her laid on the floor. Not knowing what difficulties I should have to contend with in such a piece of engineering, I tried to get her height by raising her up.

* Round arm, 1 ft. 11 in.; chest, 4 ft. 4 in.; thigh, 2 ft. 7 in.; calf, 1 ft. 8 in. height, 5 ft. 8 in.

This, after infinite exertions on the part of us both, was accomplished, when she sank down again, fainting, for her blood had rushed into her head. Meanwhile, the daughter, a lass of sixteen, sat stark-naked before us, sucking at a milk-pot, on which the father kept her at work by holding a rod in his hand, for as fattening is the first duty of fashionable female life, it must be duly enforced by the rod if necessary. I got up a bit of flirtation with missy, and induced her to rise and shake hands with me. Her features were lovely, but her body was as round as a ball.

*   *   *

24th—Before breakfast I called on poor Usungu, prescribing hot coffee to be drunk with milk every morning, which astonished him not a little, as the negroes only use coffee for chewing. He gave my men pombe and plantains. On my return I met a page sent to invite me to the palace. I found Mtesa sitting with a number of women. He was dressed in European clothes, part of them being a pair of trousers he begged for yesterday, that he might appear like Bana. This was his first appearance in trousers, and his whole attire, contrasting strangely with his native habiliments, was in his opinion very becoming, though to me a little ridiculous; for the legs of the trousers, as well as the sleeves of the waistcoat, were much too short, so that his black feet and hands stuck out at the extremities as an organ-player's monkey's do, whilst the cockscomb on his head prevented a fez cap, which was part of his special costume for the occasion, from sitting properly. This display over, the women were sent away, and I was shown into a court, where a large number of plantains were placed in a line upon the ground for my men to take away, and we were promised the same treat every day. From this we proceeded to another court, where we sat in the shade together, when the women returned again, but were all dumb, because my interpreters dared not for their lives say anything, even on my account, to the king's women. Getting tired, I took out my sketch-book and drew Lubuga, the pet, which amused the king immensely as he recognised her cockscomb.

Then twenty naked virgins, the daughters of Wakungu, all

smeared and shining with grease, each holding a small square of mbugu for a fig-leaf, marched in a line before us, as a fresh addition to the harem, whilst the happy fathers floundered n'yanzigging on the ground, delighted to find their darlings appreciated by the king. Seeing this done in such a quiet mild way before all my men, who dared not lift their heads to see it, made me burst into a roar of laughter, and the king, catching the infection from me, laughed as well: but the laughing did not end there—for the pages, for once giving way to nature, kept bursting—my men chuckled in sudden gusts—while even the women, holding their mouths for fear of detection, responded—and we all laughed together. Then a sedate old dame rose from the squatting mass, ordered the virgins to right-about, and marched them off, showing their still more naked reverses. I now obtained permission for the Wakungu to call upon me, and fancied I only required my interpreters to speak out like men when I had anything to say, to make my residence in Uganda both amusing and instructive; but though the king, carried off by the prevailing good-humour of the scene we had both witnessed, supported me, I found that he had counter-ordered what he had said as soon as I had gone, and, in fact, no Mkungu ever dared come near me.

25th—I have now been for some time within the court precincts, and have consequently had an opportunity of witnessing court customs. Among these, nearly every day since I have changed my residence, incredible as it may appear to be, I have seen one, two, or three of the wretched palace women led away to execution, tied by the hand, and dragged along by one of the body-guard, crying out, as she went to premature death, "Hai Minange!" (O my lord!) "Kbakka!" (My king!) "Hai N'yawo!" (My mother!) at the top of her voice, in the utmost despair and lamentation; and yet there was not a soul who dared lift hand to save any of them.

To call upon the queen-mother respectfully, as it was the opening visit, I took, besides the medicine-chest, a present of eight brass and copper wire, thirty blue-egg beads, one bundle of diminutive beads, and sixteen cubits of chintz, a small guard, and my throne of royal grass. The palace to be visited lay half a mile beyond the king's, but the highroad to it was forbidden me, as it is considered uncourteous to pass the king's gate without going in. So after winding through back-gardens, the slums of Bandowaroga, I struck upon the highroad close to her majesty's, where everything looked like the royal palace on a miniature scale. A large cleared space divided the queen's residence from her Kamraviona's. The outer enclosures and courts were fenced with tiger-grass; and the huts, though neither so numerous nor so large, were constructed after the same fashion as the king's. Guards also kept the doors, on which large bells were hung to give alarm, and officers in waiting watched the throne-rooms. All the huts were full of women, save those kept as waiting-rooms, where drums and harmonicons were placed for amusement. On first entering, I was required to sit in a waiting-hut till my arrival was announced; but that did not take long, as the queen was prepared to receive me; and being of a more affable disposition than her son, she held rather a levee of amusement than a stiff court of show. I entered the throne-hut as the gate of that court was thrown open, with my hat off, but umbrella held over my head, and walked straight towards her till ordered to sit upon my bundle of grass.

Her majesty—fat, fair, and forty-five—was sitting, plainly garbed in mbugu, upon a carpet spread upon the ground within a curtain of mbugu, her elbow resting on a pillow of the same bark material; the only ornaments on her person being an abrus necklace, and a piece of mbugu tied round her head, whilst a folding looking-glass, much the worse for wear, stood open by her side. An iron rod like a spit, with a cup on the top, charged with magic powder, and other magic wands, were placed before the entrance; and within the room, four Mabandwa sorceresses or devil-drivers, fantastically dressed, as before described, and a mass of other women, formed the company. For a short while we sat at a distance, exchanging inquiring glances at one another, when the women were dismissed, and a band of music, with a court full of Wakungu, was ordered in to change the scene. I also got orders to draw near and sit fronting her within the hut. Pombe, the best in Uganda, was then drunk by the queen, and handed to me and to all the high officers about her, when she smoked her pipe, and bade me smoke mine. The musicians, dressed in long-haired Usoga goat-skins, were now ordered to strike up, which they did, with their bodies swaying or dancing like bears in a fair. Different drums were then beat, and I was asked if I could distinguish their different tones.

The queen, full of mirth, now suddenly rose, leaving me sitting, whilst she went to another hut, changed her mbugu for a deole, and came back again for us to admire her, which was no sooner done to her heart's content, than a second time, by her order, the court was clear, and, when only three or four confidential Wakungu were left, she took up a small faggot of well-trimmed sticks, and, selecting three, told me she had three complaints. "This stick," she says, "represents my stomach, which gives me much uneasiness; this second stick my liver, which causes shooting pains all over my body; and this third one my heart, for I get constant dreams at night about Sunna, my late husband, and they are not pleasant." The dreams and sleeplessness I told her was a common widow's complaint, and could only be cured by her majesty making up her mind to marry a second time; but before I could advise for the bodily complaints, it would be necessary for me to see her tongue, feel her pulse, and perhaps, also, her sides. Hearing this, the Wakungu said, "Oh, that can never be allowed without the sanction of the king;" but the queen, rising in her seat, expressed her scorn at the idea of taking advice from a mere stripling, and submitted herself for examination.

I then took out two pills, the powder of which was tasted by the Wakungu to prove that there was no devilry in "the doctor", and gave orders for them to be eaten at night, restricting her pombe and food until I saw her again. My game was now advancing, for I found through her I should get the key to an influence that might bear on the king, and was much pleased to hear her express herself delighted with me for everything I had done except stopping her grog, which, naturally enough in this great pombe-drinking country, she said would be a very trying abstinence.

The doctoring over, her majesty expressed herself ready to inspect the honorarium I had brought for her, and the articles were no sooner presented by Bombay and Nasib, with the usual formalities of stroking to insure their purity, than she, boiling with pleasure, showed them all to her officers, who declared, with a voice of most exquisite triumph, that she was indeed the most favoured of queens. Then, in excellent good taste, after saying that nobody had ever given her such treasures, she gave me, in return, a beautifully-worked pombe sucking-pipe, which was acknowledged by every one to be the greatest honour she could pay me.

28th—My whole thoughts were now occupied in devising some scheme to obtain a hut in the palace, not only the better to maintain my dignity, and so gain superior influence in the court, but also that I might have a better insight into the manners and customs of these strange people. I was not sorry to find the king attempting to draw me to court, daily to sit in attendance on him as his officers are obliged to do all day long, in order that he might always have a full court or escort whenever by chance he might emerge from his palace, for it gave me an opening for asserting a proper position.

3rd—Our cross purposes seemed to increase; for, while I could not get a satisfactory interview, the king sent for N'yamgundu to ascertain why I never went to see him. I had given him good guns and many pretty things which he did not know the use of, and yet I would not visit him to explain their several uses. N'yamgundu told him I lived too far off, and wanted a palace. After this I walked off to see N'yamasore, taking my blankets, a pillow, and some cooking-pots to make a day of it, and try to win the affections of the queen with sixteen cubits bindera, three pints peke, and three pints mtende beads, which, as Waganda are all fond of figurative language, I called a trifle for her servants.

I was shown in at once, and found her majesty sitting on an Indian carpet, dressed in a red linen wrapper with a gold border, and a box, in shape of a lady's work-box, prettily coloured in

divers patterns with minute beads, by her side. Her councillors
were in attendance; and in the yard a band of music, with many
minor Wakungu squatting in a semicircle, completed her levee.
Maula on my behalf opened conversation, in allusion to her
yesterday's question, by saying I had applied to Mtesa for a
palace, that I might be near enough both their majesties to pay
them constant visits. She replied, in a good hearty manner, that
indeed was a very proper request, which showed my good sense,
and ought to have been complied with at once; but Mtesa was
only a Kijana or stripling, and as she influenced all the government of the country, she would have it carried into effect. Compliments were now passed, my presents given and approved of; and
the queen, thinking I must be hungry, for she wanted to eat
herself, requested me to refresh myself in another hut. I complied,
spread my bedding, and ordered in my breakfast; but as the hut
was full of men, I suspended a Scotch plaid, and quite eclipsed
her mbugu curtain.

Reports of this magnificence at once flew to the queen, who
sent to know how many more blankets I had in my possession,
and whether, if she asked for one, she would get it. She also
desired to see my spoons, fork, and pipe—an English meers-
chaum, mounted with silver; so, after breakfast, I returned to see
her, showed her the spoons and forks, and smoked my pipe, but
told her I had no blankets left but what formed my bed. She
appeared very happy and very well, did not say another word
about the blankets, but ordered a pipe for herself, and sat chatting,
laughing, and smoking in concert with me.

The queen and her ministers then plunged into pombe and
became uproarious, laughing with all their might and main. Small
bugu cups were not enough to keep up the excitement of the
time, so a large wooden trough was placed before the queen and
filled with liquor. If any was spilt, the Wakungu instantly fought
over it, dabbing their noses on the ground, or grabbing it with
their hands, that not one atom of the queen's favour might be
lost; for everything must be adored that comes from royalty,
whether by design or accident. The queen put her head to the
trough and drank like a pig from it, and was followed by her

ministers. The band, by order, then struck up a tune called the Milele, playing on a dozen reeds, ornamented with beads and cow-tips, and five drums, of various tones and sizes, keeping time. The musicians dancing with zest, were led by four bandmasters, also dancing, but with their backs turned to the company to show off their long, shaggy, goat-skin jackets, sometimes upright, at other times bending and on their heels, like the hornpipe-dancers of western countries.

It was a merry scene, but soon became tiresome; when Bombay, by way of flattery, and wishing to see what the queen's wardrobe embraced, told her, Any woman, however ugly, would assume a goodly appearance if prettily dressed; upon which her gracious majesty immediately rose, retired to her toilet-hut, and soon returned attired in a common check cloth, an abrus tiara, a bead necklace, and with a folding looking-glass, when she sat, as before, and was handed a blown-glass cup of pombe, with a cork floating on the liquor, and a napkin mbugu covering the top, by a naked virgin. For her kind condescension in assuming plain raiment, everybody, of course, n'yanzigged. Next she ordered her slave girls to bring a large number of sambo (anklets), and begged me to select the best, for she liked me much. In vain I tried to refuse them: she had given more than enough for a keepsake before, and I was not hungry for property; still I had to choose some, or I would give offence. She then gave me a basket of tobacco, and a nest of hen eggs for her "son's" breakfast. When this was over, the Mukonderi, another dancing-tune, with instruments something like clarionets, was ordered; but it had scarcely been struck up, before a drenching rain, with strong wind, set in and spoilt the music, though not the playing—for none dared stop without an order; and the queen, instead of taking pity, laughed most boisterously over the exercise of her savage power as the unfortunate musicians were nearly beaten down by the violence of the weather.

When the rain ceased, her majesty retired a second time to her toilet-hut, and changed her dress for a puce-coloured wrapper, when I, ashamed of having robbed her of so many sambo, asked her if she would allow me to present her with a little English "wool" to hang up instead of her mbugu curtain on cold days like this. Of course she could not decline, and a large double scarlet blanket was placed before her. "Oh, wonder of wonders!" exclaimed all the spectators, holding their mouths in both hands at a time—such a "pattern" had never been seen here before. It stretched across the hut, was higher than the men could reach— indeed it was a perfect marvel; and the man must be a good one who brought such a treasure as this to Uddu. "And why not say Uganda?" I asked. "Because all this country is called Uddu. Uganda is personified by Mtesa; and no one can say he has seen Uganda until he has been presented to the king."

As I had them all in a good humour now, I complained I did not see enough of the Waganda—and as every one dressed so remarkably well, I could not discern the big men from the small; could she not issue some order by which they might call on me, as they did not dare do so without instruction, and then I, in turn, would call on them? Hearing this, she introduced me to he prime minister, chancellor of exchequer, women-keepers, hang- men, and cooks, as the first nobles in the land, that I might recognise them again if I met them on the road. All n'yanzigged for this great condescension, and said they were delighted with their guest; then producing a strip of common joho to compare it with my blanket, they asked if I could recognise it. Of course, said I, it is made in my country, of the same material, only of coarser quality, and everything of the same sort is made in Uzungu. Then, indeed, said the whole company, in one voice, we do like you, and your cloth too—but you most. I modestly bowed my head, and said their friendship was my chief desire.

This speech also created great hilarity; the queen and councillors all became uproarious. The queen began to sing, and the council- lors to join in chorus; then all sang and all drank, and drank and sang, till, in their heated excitement, they turned the palace into a pandemonium; still there was not noise enough, so the band and drums were called again, and tomfool—for Uganda, like the old European monarchies, always keeps a jester—was made to sing in the gruff, hoarse, unnatural voice which he ever affects to maintain his character, and furnished with pombe when his throat was dry.

Now all of a sudden, as if a devil had taken possession of the company, the prime minister with all the courtiers jumped upon their legs, seized their sticks, for nobody can carry a spear when visiting, swore the queen had lost her heart to me, and running into the yard, returned, charging and jabbering at the queen; retreated and returned again, as if they were going to put an end to her for the guilt of loving me, but really to show their devotion and true love to her. The queen professed to take this ceremony with calm indifference, but her face showed that she enjoyed it. I was now getting very tired of sitting on my low stool, and begged for leave to depart, but N'yamasore would not hear of it; she loved me a great deal too much to let me go away at this time of day, and forthwith ordered in more pombe. The same roystering scene was repeated; cups were too small, so the trough was employed; and the queen graced it by drinking, pig-fashion, first, and then handing it round to the company.

Now, hoping to produce gravity and then to slip away, I asked if my medicines had given her any relief, that I might give her more to strengthen her. She said she could not answer that question just yet; for though the medicine had moved her copiously, as yet she had seen no snake depart from her. I told her some strengthening medicine in the morning: for the present, however, I would take my leave, as the day was far gone, and the distance home very great; but though I dragged my body away, my heart would still remain here, for I loved her much.

WE slept the night out, nevertheless, and next morning walked in to Gondokoro, where Mahamed, after firing a salute, took us in to see a Circassian merchant, named Kurshid Agha. Our first inquiry was, of course, for Petherick. A mysterious silence ensued; we were informed that Mr Debono was *the* man we had to thank for the assistance we had received in coming from Madi; and then in hot haste, after warm exchanges of greeting with Mahamed's friend, who was Debono's agent here, we took

leave, to hunt up Petherick. Walking down the bank of the river
—where a line of vessels was moored, and on the right hand a
few sheds, one-half broken down, with a brick-built house
presenting the late Austrian Church Mission establishment—we
saw hurrying on towards us the form of an Englishman, who,
for one moment, we believed was the Simon Pure; but the next
moment my old friend Baker, famed for his sports in Ceylon,
seized me by the hand. A little boy of his establishment had
reported our arrival, and he in an instant came out to welcome us.
What joy this was I can hardly tell. We could not talk fast
enough, so overwhelmed were we both to meet again. Of course
we were his guests in a moment, and learned everything that
could be told. I now first heard of the death of H.R.H. the
Prince-Consort, which made me reflect on the inspiring words he
made use of, in compliment to myself, when I was introduced to
him by Sir Roderick Murchison a short while before leaving
England. Then there was the terrible war in America, and other
events of less startling nature, which came on us all by surprise,
as years had now passed since we had received news from the
civilised world.

Baker then said he had come up with three vessels—one dyabir
and two nuggers—fully equipped with armed men, camels,
horses, donkeys, beads, brass wire, and everything necessary for a
long journey, expressly to look after us, hoping, as he jokingly
said, to find us on the equator in some terrible fix, that he might
have the pleasure of helping us out of it. He had heard of
Mahamed's party, and was actually waiting for him to come in,
that he might have had the use of his return-men to start with
comfortably. Three Dutch ladies, the Baroness Miss A. van
Capellan, and Mrs and Miss Tinne, also, with a view to assist
us in the same way as Baker (God bless them), had come here in a
steamer, but were driven back to Khartum by sickness. Nobody
had even dreamt for a moment it was possible we could come
through. An Italian, named Miani, had gone farther up the Nile
than any one else; and he, it now transpired, was the man who
had cut his name on the tree by Apuddo. But what had become of
Petherick? He was actually trading at N'yambara, seventy miles

due west of this, though he had, since I left him in England, raised a subscription of £1,000, from those of my friends to whom this Journal is most respectfully dedicated as the smallest return a grateful heart can give for their attempt to succour me, when knowing the fate of the expedition was in great jeopardy.

Instead of coming up the Nile at once, as Petherick might have done—so I was assured—he waited, whilst a vessel was building, until the season had too far advanced to enable him to sail up the river. In short, he lost the north winds at 7° north, and went overland to his trading depot at N'yambara. Previously, however, he had sent some boats up to this, under a Vakil, who had his orders to cross to his trading depot at N'yambara, and to work from his trading station due south, ostensibly with a view to look after me, though contrary to my advice before leaving him in England, in opposition to his own proposed views of assisting me when he applied for help to succour me, and against the strongly-expressed opinions of every European in the same trade as himself; for all alike said they knew he would have gone to Faloro, and pushed south from that place, had his trade on the west of the Nile not attracted him there.

JAMES AUGUSTUS GRANT

from

A Walk Across Africa

TWENTY-SIX OUT of sixty who slept inland were attacked with fever; those who had taken quinine recovered, while those who had not died. From this it would appear that risk attaches to certain constitutions from sleeping inland, away from the sea-breeze; although, on the heights of the island, where the soil is a rough red grit or friable clay, I should not anticipate danger. But on these elevated spots there is this disadvantage, that no water is procurable; even in a well forty feet deep I observed there was none.

To one wishing to enjoy good health I would prescribe this recipe: Reside on the shore; be in a boat by sunrise; row to any point on the island, or to the exquisite living formations of coral; walk home between the hedgerows, amongst beautiful clove or mango groves; enjoy the refreshing milk from the cocoa-nut; observe the industry in the fields, the snug country-houses of the Arabs; examine the "diggings" for copal; look at the men washing the elephant-tusks on the sea-shore, or at the immense variety of crazy craft—in short, keep active, and you will find that there are many worse climates than Zanzibar.

*   *   *

Dr Roscher, a German gentleman, while exploring near Lake Nyassa, was murdered in 1859 by natives who coveted his scientific instruments. The sultan of the country, justly indignant, sent four men to Zanzibar to stand their trial for the murder. Two were condemned, and suffered decapitation on the 23d August. I was present, going to the execution with the "surrung" or boatswain of the British Consulate, who cleared the way for me to get near the two men. They squatted outside the fort wall with perfect composure, naked from head to foot, except a waist cloth; neither tied nor handcuffed, and guarded carelessly by a few jesting soldiers. The Sultan's order to proceed with the execution not having arrived, a considerable delay occurred, during which the most intelligent-looking of the two prisoners stated to me that he had committed the act when in a state of unconsciousness! A jail official here announced that the Sultan wished the sahib to give the order, and I informed Colonel Rigby of the circumstance. He at once saw through the timidity of the Sultan, and said, as the sentence had been passed weeks ago, he could give no orders about it. Returning to the place of execution, where both men still sat, we found the mob had increased. An Arab boldly asked me, "Why should two men suffer for one white?" On my remarking that "Sooner or later the men must suffer—the sun was broiling over the poor creatures' heads—would it not be charity to go on with the execution?" the reply was, "They are mere animals, and have no feeling." Still no one would give the order. Again the Sultan was applied to. A rush was now rudely made on the crowd by half-a-dozen handsomely-dressed Arabs, brandishing their shields and swords. I thought it was a rescue, but kept my place; and it appeared they only wanted to get up to the prisioners, around whom every one laughed heartily at the momentary panic. Here one of the guard with whom I had been conversing laid hold of my arm, and, followed by a noisy drummer, the prisoners, and mob, we pushed on for a dozen yards, and stopped in an open space where some cows were lying. A twig of grass pinioned each man, and they were made to sit on the ground, speaking calmly, while the crowd, all crushing around, joked as if at a holiday rout. Another delay occurred; no one had given the order. On being asked, "Might it commence?" I replied, "Yes, certainly; proceed." The executioner at once took his place, drew his sword, weighed it in his hand, threw up his sleeves, and slipped his feet out of his shoes, while the dense mass all seemed breathless. The executioner was a small man, respectably dressed, looking like an Indian "Nubbeebux". The prisoners sat three yards apart, one slightly in advance of the other. The foremost was then ordered to bend his head, when, with one stroke, the back of his neck was cut to the vertebrae; he fell forward, and lay breathing steadily, with his right cheek in his own blood, without a sound or struggle. The executioner, after wiping his sword on the loin-cloth of the dying man, coolly felt its edge. The other victim had seen all, and never moved nor spoke. The same horrible scene was again enacted, but with a different result; the man jerked upwards from his squatting position, and fell back on his left side, with no sound nor after-struggle. Both appeared as if in a sweet sleep; two chickens hopped on the still quivering bodies, and the cows in the open space lay undisturbed. I left the spot, hoping never to witness such another scene.

ON the 2d of October 1860, we started from Bagomoyo on the East African coast for Kazeh, 500 miles in the interior of Africa, latitude 5° south. The part consisted of the following:—

Captain Speke, commanding.
    ,,   Grant, second in command.
Corporal, Cape Mounted Rifles, butcher.
Private "William,", bugler and cook.
    ,,   Middle, Speke's valet.
    ,,   April, Grant's valet, cook, &c.
    ,,   Lemon, useful generally.
    ,,   Reyters, fiddler.
    ,,   Peters.
    ,,   Arries.
    ,,   Jansen.
    ,,   "Jacob" Adams.
Said bin Salem, native commandant.
Bombay, factotum, interpreter.
Baraka, commanding Zanzibar men, interpreter.
Rahan, interpreter ⎫
Frij,   ,,   ⎬ Private servants and
Uledi, valet. "⎭ rifle-carriers.

Mabrook, valet, donkey-man.
Three or four women.
Sixty-four Seedee boys   } Carrying our kit
115 porters of the interior   } and barter.
Eleven mules carrying ammunition.
Five donkeys to carry the sick.

Twenty-five Belooch soldiers escorted us for the first thirteen stages, and we had the undermentioned casualties during the journey:—

Private Peters dead;
Five other privates sent back sick;
About thirty Seedees deserted;
One discharged;
113 porters deserted;
Eleven mules and two donkeys dead;
Fifteen out of twenty goats stolen; and
Our native commandant, the Sheikh, *hors de combat*.

The daily stages have been so well and so fully described by Captain Speke that I shall not dwell upon them, but merely mention a few incidents descriptive of our life in the interior, and the fauna we observed. To accomplish this distance of 500 miles in 71 travelling days, of from 1 to 25 miles per day on foot, took us all the months of October, November, December, and twenty-five days of January, struggling against the caprices of our followers, the difficulties of the countries passed through, and the final desertion of our porters.

Food was not abundant. As it was the dry season, we had to trust to chance and our rifles. One night our entire dinner consisted of two ears of Indian corn, eaten with salt; nothing besides, neither bread nor rice. Bombay very kindly, in the middle of this repast (which was laid out on our "service" of reversed tin lids placed on the tops of wooden boxes as tables), went and brought a cold grilled chicken, very small, and awkwardly flattened out. Though our hunger prompted us to accept the offer, we declined with many thanks. But, while sitting rather silently over our empty tin covers, he again appeared, having foraged five live chickens—thus securing for us not only that night's supper, but food for the next two days. Our supplies of grain frequently ran out in camp, but the sportsman need never starve in the country we passed through; for although we could not always find large game, there were sparrows, doves, or guinea-fowl to be had; while persons who do not sport may take note of the herbs gathered by the natives, and live upon them at a pinch. The spirit of our men sank, and a deep, gloomy silence hung over camp, when we had no grain, and continuous days of bad sport with our rifles. Not a man would obey orders; they refused to march, and discipline had to be upheld in several instances by inflicting corporal punishment for the crime of stealing cloth to buy food. One Seedee, a powerful fellow, roared for mercy during the flogging, and disclosed to us who had been his accomplice in the theft. He was therefore excused the third dozen of lashes, and carried away bound, to be expelled from camp next morning.

We foraged zealously for the camp, and succeeded in giving to every one a little meat. The black rhinoceros would rarely charge, even though he saw us standing close to him; but they always afford considerable excitement by the feints they make, and by their deep hoarse grunt. Their ears were often torn and their tails mutilated, apparently in consequence of their fighting with each other. Our whole camp ate heartily of the rhinoceros; but the flesh, though sweet, requires very sharp teeth. Their young would seem to have great affection. Wounding a large female one night, I next day traced her spoor for four miles, and suddenly came on her squatting like a hare in her form, with her back towards me. There was a great deal of whining or pulling near the spot, which I took to be her dying cries. Advancing cautiously, a different rhinoceros cocked its ears at me, and I felt for an instant at a loss which to fire at: both barrels from "Blanshard" went at my new *young* friend, who rushed off crashing through the underwood, and I only then saw that the poor old lady was cold dead, and she proved so heavy that three of us could not move her. It was the

young one weeping over its mother that caused the plaintive cries
I had heard.

LET me give the reader some idea of our life here. Moossah, an
Indian in whose house we resided, was a fine benevolent old man,
with an establishment of 300 native men and women round him.
His abode had, three years ago, taken two months to build, and it
was surrounded by a circular wall which enclosed his houses,
fruit and vegetable gardens, and his stock of cattle. The lady who
presided over the whole was of most portly dimensions, and her
word was law. Moossah sat from morn till night with his "foon-
dee", or chief manager, and other head servants within sight,
receiving salutes and compliments from the rich and poor at the
front or *gentlemen's* side of the house, while the lady presided over
the domestic arrangements of the interior. We had full access to
both, and no house could be conducted with greater regularity.
At three o'clock in the morning, Moossah, who had led a hard
life in his day, would call out for his little pill of opium, which he
never missed for forty years. This would brighten him up till
noon. He would then transact business, chat, and give you the
gossip at any hour you might sit by him on his carpet. To us it
seemed strange that he never stopped talking when prayers from
the Koran were being read to him by a "Bookeen", or Madagascar
man. Perhaps he had little respect for the officiating priest, as the
same reverend and learned gentleman was accustomed to make
him his shirts! After a mid-day sleep, he would refresh himself
with a second but larger pill, transact business, and so end the day.
The harem department presented a more domestic scene. At
dawn, women in robes of coloured chintz, their hair neatly plaited,
gave fresh milk to the swarm of black cats, or churned butter in
gourds by rocking it to and fro on their laps. By seven o'clock the
whole place was swept clean. Some of the household fed the
game-fowls, or looked after the ducks and pigeons; two women
chained by the neck fetched firewood, or ground corn at a stone;

children would eat together without dispute, because a matron presided over them;—all were quiet, industrious beings, never idle, and as happy as the day was long. When any of Moossah's wives gave birth to a child there was universal rejoicing; the infant was brought to show its sex: and when one died, the shrill laments of the women were heard all night long. When a child misbehaved, we white men were pointed at to frighten it, as nurses at home too often do with ghost stories.

BLACK-ART cases were duly tried, and generally ended in conviction. A cowherd who had sold me some fish died very suddenly; one of his two wives was suspected of having poisoned him; and being tried, she was convicted and condemned. She was taken to the dry bed of the stream, her arms tied behind her, and was killed by having her throat cut from ear to ear. No hyena touched the body, which still more confirmed the belief that she was guilty; for my Seedee cook said, "Has not the hyena the soul of a man? does he not know your thoughts when you determine on shooting him?"

On the 10th of July my servant asked permission to go and see the uchawe. I accompanied him to the outside of the bomah (village fence), where a woman and lad lay on their faces with their arms bound painfully tight, and writhing in torture. Poor creatures! they met with no sympathy from the jeering crowd, but the ropes were slackened at my request. They had been apprehended on suspicion of having bewitched the sultan's brother, who lay sick for fifteen days, and unless they could work off the magic spell they must die. The lad said, "Take me to the forest; I know an herb remedy." On the seventh day from this scene (during which the lad was outside the village, and the woman kept by the sick patient in the stocks) the former was killed and the woman released. I went to see his body the following day, but the hyena (I was told) had taken it away. Nothing remained but blood and the ashes of some hair by a fire. Could they have tortured him by burning? A case of adultery was punished in the most horrible manner, too painful to describe minutely. They had no Divorce Court! The strapping young fellow who had found his way into the harem of the sultan, was tied to railings, stripped, certain parts of his person were smeared and covered with rags, then set fire to by the sultan in person, and he was dragged to the fire outside the village; but before he could reach it, assigais from the hands of the son and daughter-in-law of the sultan pierced his neck and chest, and he was drawn out by one leg like a dog through the gate. The woman who committed this act came in fear to me at night, saying, "Give me protection: it is said I am to be killed for stabbing the adulterer." Though for the moment I detested the woman, I endeavoured to calm her by saying my guns would be her protection, and my men should sleep in her house. On asking her "Why did you soil your hands with such a deed?" she replied, in the most animated way, "Oh, did I not glory in it! did the fellow not come to my bedside one night making propositions to me, and I never could get hold of him since?" The following day she, as usual, wished me good-morning, but I shuddered to think that so handsome a woman and so kind a mother, with four beautiful children who must have seen all, could have committed such an act. The woman who had offended was a middle-aged good-looking person. Nothing whatever was done to her, though she had once before been the cause of a man's death under similar circumstances. Previous to this event she would come often to look at herself in my mirror, but afterwards I did not see so much of her.

SCARCELY a man amongst us escaped fever. We arrived on the 25th of January, and by the 1st February several were laid up. My first attack lasted seven days, the 2d, 4th, 6th, 7th, and 8th terminating in headaches every morning. After twelve days another sharper attack, with delirium at night, but no ague, lasted three days. The third and least severe came on fifteen days afterwards, with drowsiness and profuse perspiration, and terminated in three days. All suffered from after-weakness in the limbs; some from blindness of one eye, the eyelid much inflamed and drooping, accompanied with excessive watering; or no inflammation of the eye, but total blindness of it, and no disease or scale observable. Acute pain rarely accompanied this complaint. Our men ascribed their bad health to not having got accustomed to the water of the country. The natives had no efficient remedies for preventing the recurrence of fever, but took pinches of a pounded plant or wood to cure their headaches, or cupped themselves in the following curious manner: A man put some beeswax into his mouth, applied a small cow's horn to cuts made in the temple of the patient, exhausted the air by suction, and with his tongue shut the hole at the end of the horn with the wax. We had only one fatal case. Quinine and applications of blistering tissue behind the ear and on the temples partially restored health and eyesight.

The following account of my own ailments I give, not with a wish to parade them, but in order to convey information:— Having had fevers twice a-month, in December my usual complaint assumed a new form. The right leg, from above the knee, became deformed with inflammation, and remained for a month in this unaccountable state, giving intense pain, which was relieved temporarily by a deep incision and copious discharge. For three months fresh abscesses formed, and other incisions were made; my strength was prostrated; the knee stiff and alarmingly bent, and walking was impracticable. Many cures were attempted by the natives, who all sympathised with me in my sufferings, which they saw were scarcely endurable; but I had great faith—was all along cheerful and happy, except at the crisis of this helpless state, when I felt that it would have been preferable to be nearer home. The disease ran its course, and daily, to bring out the accumulated discharge, I stripped my leg like a leech. Bombay had heard of a poultice made of cow-dung, salt, and mud from the lake; this was placed on hot, but it merely produced the effect of a tight bandage. Baraka was certain that a serpent had spat upon my leg—"it could not have been a bite". Dr M'nanagee, the sultan's brother, knew the disease perfectly; he could send me a cure for it—and a mild gentle peasant of the Wanyambo race came with his wife, a young pleasing-like person, to attend me. With the soft touch of a woman he examined the limb, made cuts over the skin with a penknife, ordered all lookers-on outside the hut, when his wife produced a scroll of plantain-leaf, in which was a black paste. This was moistened from the mouth and rubbed into the bleeding cuts, making them smart; afterwards a small piece of lava was dangled against my leg and tied as a charm round the ankle. Two days afterwards he found no improvement, and, having repeated some mystic words behind me, another charm of wood and goat's flesh was tied above the knee and round the ankle, much in the same way as a kind lady-friend in Scotland once sent me a string of soda-water corks to be worn at night as a cure for cramp! Paste, very like gun-powder, was rubbed into fresh cuts, and this was repeated without any result, although the charms had been on for two days. M'nanagee, seeing his medical adviser had failed, sent an herb to soak in water and rub over the part; it had a very soothing effect, but did not allay the pain. He had seen me apply the leaves of the castor-oil plant as a hot bandage and forbade their use a second time as being injurious, having given me a delirious fever, and causing a counter-action of profuse discharge of water from the limb. By the fifth month the complaint had exhausted itself; at last I was able to be out of the hut inhaling the sweet air, and once more permitted to behold the works of God's creation in the beautiful lake and hills below me. Never did I experience a happier moment!

WE had daily visits from the women of the country, who came in parties. They were copper-coloured and flat-featured, and wore round their necks a profusion of pendent bead necklaces of the colour of the mountain-ash berry; their ankles were concealed with masses of wire rings. For hours they sat silently before us, smoking, nursing, and shampooing the limbs and necks of their infants; some wore the heavy cloth of the country, others had soiled robes of calico. Young girls, many of them with pleasing faces and plump round figures, wore merely a diminutive cloth about their loins, and infants had a fringe of beads. These women were rarely accompanied by men, but on Speke having taken a women's likeness, the husband requested him to write his (the husband's) name on the picture, so that the people of England might know whose wife she was! We saw some decidedly handsome N'yambo girls on this route: their men attend upon cattle exclusively, while they stay at home doing household work, cooking, coquetting, and showing off their beautiful feet and ankles. Two, in the bloom of youth, sat by us with their arms most affectionately twined round each other's neck, till asked to sit apart that they might be sketched. The arms were at once dropped, exposing their beautiful necks and busts, quite models for a "Greek Slave". Their woolly hair was combed out and raised up from the forehead and over their ears by a broad band from the skin of a milk-white cow; this contrasted strikingly with their transparent light copper skins.

The Waha women are somewhat similar, having tall, erect, graceful figures even without crinoline, and with intelligent features. They are looked upon as an inferior tribe to the Watusi (described at Kazeh), though wearing the hair bound up, and having naked arms, &c., similar to them; but their cow-skin coverings from the waist to the ankle are different, being of a yellow-ochre colour. We put up one day at the settlement of a trader, Sungoro-bin-Tabeeb, of whom we had heard a good deal, as he travelled always in a double-poled tent, and kept sixty wives, who lived like goats inside his tent. We saw five of his women; one was a Hubshee, or Abyssinian, whose appearance disappointed us. Her mouth was large, and, though fair for a negress, and with distinctly bridged nose, she was a poor specimen of her race. Another was of my favourite caste, always distinguishable by their intelligence and easy, polite manner—a Watusi, a beautiful tall girl, with large dark eyes, the smallest mouth and nose, thin lips, small hands, &c. Speke said she much resembled the Somal; her noble race never will become slaves, preferring death to slavery, and they refuse to touch fowls or goats.

One morning, to my surprise, in a wild jungle we came upon cattle, then upon a "bomah", or ring-fence, concealed by beautiful umbrageous large trees, quite the place for a gypsy camp. At the entry two strapping fellows met me and invited my approach. I mingled with the people, got water from them, and was asked, "Would I not prefer some milk?" This sounded to me more civilised than I expected from Africans, so I followed the men, who led me up to a beautiful ladylike creature, a Watusi woman, sitting alone under a tree. She received me, without any expression of surprise, in the most dignified manner; and, after having talked with the men, rose smiling, showing great gentleness in her manner, and led me to her hut. I had time to scrutinise the interesting stranger: she wore the usual Watusi costume of a cow's skin reversed, teased into a frieze with a needle, coloured brown, and wrapped round her body from below the chest to the ankles. Lappets, showing zebra-like stripes of many colours, she wore as a "turnover" round the waist; and, except where ornamented on one arm with a highly polished coil of thick brass wire, two equally bright and massive rings on the right wrist, and a neck pendant of brass wire,—except these and her becoming wrapper, she was *au naturelle*. I was struck with her peculiarly formed head and graceful long neck; the beauty of her fine eyes, mouth, and nose; the smallness of her hands and naked feet—all were faultless; the only bad feature, which is considered one of beauty with them, was her large ears. The arms and elbows were rounded off like an egg, the shoulders were sloping, and her small breasts were those of a crouching Venus—a perfect beauty, although darker than a brunette! Her temporary residence was peculiar—it was formed of grass, was flat-roofed, and so low that I could not stand upright in it. The fireplace consisted of three stones; milk-vessels of wood, shining white from scouring, were ranged on one side of the abode. A good-looking woman sat rocking a gourd between her knees in the process of churning butter. After the fair one had examined my skin and my clothes, I expressed great regret that I had no beads to present to her.

F

"They are not wanted," she said: "sit down, drink this butter-milk, and here is also some butter for you." It was placed on a clean leaf. I shook hands, patted her cheek, and took my leave, but some beads were sent to her, and she paid me a visit, bringing butter and buttermilk, and asking for more presents, which she of course got, and I had the gratification to see her eyes sparkle at the sight of them. This was one of the few women I met during our whole journey that I admired.

MUSICAL instruments were in greater variety in Karague than we had previously met with, and the little plaintive native airs could be picked up and hummed, they were so sweet and pleasing to the ear. There was stringed, wind, and drum music. Their most perfect instrument was the "nanga", of seven or eight strings it may be called national. In one of these, played by an old woman, six of the seven notes were a perfect scale, the seven being the only faulty string. In another, played by a man, three strings were a full harmonious chord. These facts show that the people are capable of cultivation. The "nanga" was formed of heavy dark wood, the shape of a tray, 22 by 9 inches or 30 by 8, with three open crosses in the bottom, and laced with *one* string seven or eight times over bridges at either end; sometimes a gourd, as sounding-board, was tied on to the back. Prince M'nanagee, at my request, sent the best player he knew. The man boldly entered without introduction, dressed in the usual Wanyambo costume, and looked a wild, excited creature. After resting his spear against the roof of the hut, he took a "nanga" from under his arm and commenced. As he sat upon a mat with his head averted from me, never smiling, he sang something of his having been sent to me, and of the favourite dog Keeromba. The wild yet gentle music and words attracted a crowd of admirers, who sang the dog-song for days afterwards, as we had it encored several times. Another player was an old woman, calling herself "Keeleeanyagga". As she played while standing in front of me, all the song she could produce was "sh", "sh", screwing her mouth, rolling her body, and raising her feet from the ground; it was a miserable performance, and not repeated.

Of wind instruments we had the fife and horn. The fife is more common with the Uganda than the Karague people. It is an 18-inch-long hollowed reed, about the thickness of a German flute, is held like a flageolet, has a slit at the top, and six finger-holes. As the Waganda walk smartly along the road, with a light load on their heads, they often while away the time with this rude instrument, out of which some of them bring soft, sweet, flute-like music. The bugle they have is shaped like a telescope, and is made of several pieces of gourd fitting into each other, and covered with cow-skin. It is 12 inches long. An expert performer on this bugle can produce a whole chord, which is varied by the thumb acting as a key.

Drums are of different shapes, according as they are beaten by the hand or by a stick. The drum made for the hand is a 4-feet-long log, hollowed out in the shape of an inverted dice-box, open at the lower end, and covered at the top, which is 1 foot across, with the skin of an ichneumon. It is slung from the left shoulder, and played by tapping and stopping with the fingers. The thirty-three drums seen ranged in line at the ceremony after new-moon were of every possible shape, except round, which they all tried to be. They were trunks of trees hollowed out, and covered over with skin. Two copper kettle-drums had found their way into the collection. The sultan had an excellent band, of its kind, composed of 16 men, who performed several tunes before us. The instruments were 14 bugles and 2 hand-drums. Three ranks, the drummers in the rear, formed in front of us, and played, with great spirit and precision, bugle music in waltz and march time. While "trooping" they advanced, swaying their bodies very gracefully to the music; and as they neared us all halted except the bandmaster, who, as he played, being an active, well-made little man, advanced to our feet, kneeling nimbly on alternate knees in time to the music. The drummers were energetic, smart, mirthful fellows; and their music, sounding so sweetly among the hills, was more pleasant than any performance I had ever expected to witness in Africa. It was called Unyoro music, but at Unyoro we heard none of it in consequence of the moroseness of the king. All the time we were at Karague we saw no dance worth noting; they did not seem much given to dancing, and the war-drum was never sounded. Long may this continue! On such occasions the men take the field and the women beat the drums. An alarm of cattle having been captured was once spread, and the men rushed about in hot haste, armed each with a single spear and their faithful bow and arrows; but it proved false, and the bold Prince Chunderah was disappointed of a raid.

RUMANIKA had a sort of litter made up, on which the Waganda lads were to carry me; my half-dozen Seedees could not have done it, as the country afterwards proved to be precipitous, and full of swamps and marshy drains. On the morning of the 14th April, when a start was made from Karague, Mariboo came into camp with his thirty or forty men, making a noise and saying they had been starved while waiting for the Unyamuezi doctor and myself during the last fortnight, and were determined to move to-day whether I was ready or not. "Bring out the white man. Where is his bedding? Let him get into the conveyance." The property, however, had first to be despatched. I lost sight of it for two days, but none of the loads were plundered. On our journey, the stretcher was changed from the head to the shoulder of the Waganda, who went at the rate of six miles an hour, jostling and paining my limb unmercifully. The coach and four, as I may term it, was put down every mile, or less, that the bearers might rest, laugh, joke, and make a deafening noise with their mumbling language, beating their tongues to the roofs of their mouths. They seldom spoke when in motion, only when one stumbled the others would cry out against him, recommending greater care of their charge. Certainly it was not a safe position to be perched such a height on an open frame of sticks, with rocky precipices, small footing for the men, and very often water below. One great difficulty was to make them carry the conveyance so that the country in front could be seen in travelling; this they, for some reason, refused to do, and persisted in carrying me head first, instead of feet. If a grove of plantain was by the side of the path, it could not be resisted; off all would dash at the fruit, eat, and carry away as much as they were able, sometimes politely offering me a share, or more frequently remaining so long away, as I lay on the stretcher, that it became irritating. The best way was to join as much as possible with them in their frolics; my men did so, and enjoyed the march extremely.

During the march they all carried some small load on their heads, never more than 20 or 30 lb., rolled in the form of a web of cloth, neatly bound round, and having pipes and flutes stuck into it. Each man had a spear and shield over his back; the latter served as an umbrella when rain fell; and thus, with their bark-cloths kilted up, their dress was secure from rain or boggy ground. On arrival in camp, the march costume was changed for a clean suit of bark-cloth as stiff as silk, or for a set of many-coloured goat-skins, with scalloped, pierced edges, in which they made themselves smart, and strutted about like gentlemen. Those who had been able to find dogs led them with strings tied to their waists or wrists as they ran along. Very ridiculous they appeared, for the animals (not accustomed to it) always refused to be led in this way. On coming near habitations, the men shouted and sang, as if carrying some object of triumph. Had I been a dead lion, they could not have made greater noise; and on getting near camp, regardless of cultivated fields, they would plunge into them with malicious delight, trample them down, slash away branches or plantain-trees which came in their way, and deposit the litter inside a grove.

When morning again came, the gay Mariboo, always scrupulously clean and proud of his dress, would appear, followed by his drummer-boy and dog, to announce, by beat of drum, a march or halt. If the former, the shouts of his men coming to join him would be heard in the distance, and Mariboo would answer and receive replies, till one by one all rushed up, spear in hand, as if to attack him, shouting allegiance, and causing their "captain" to spring and bound with delight, while I looked on with admiration at the strange and wild spectacle. After several exhibitions of this sort, it became evident that presents were expected, and if the march was to be a success, a little "tipping" was necessary; consequently, the captain was summoned to receive a gift of beads. His delight, as he handled the beautiful small beads, knew no bounds; his spear was flashed up to my face, while his left hand held his shield, and he finished with a number of nimble antics. His arms laid aside, he repeated, "N'yans, n'yans" (thanks, thanks), perhaps fifty times in succession, with a diagonal motion of both palms at each repetition. This over, another mode of thanks was adopted, and was even more agreeable; he drew his flute from his waist, played some soft music, making his eyes twinkle with delight, and swayed his body as if charmed with his own sweet strains. They certainly are a most joyous race. On our third march from Karague, the ground was so steep, and there was so much danger of my falling off the stretcher, that I was obliged to get out, and be half-carried up the rocky side of the hill, never dreaming that they would run away with my conveyance, which they did on seeing that I was able to put my foot to the ground. For a couple of hours they allowed me to wait there, while they, like a parcel of wicked boys, kept throwing rocks down the precipice, listening in perfect quiet till they heard the last sound of the stones reaching the bottom of the ravine, when all would shout together.

As my caravan daily shortened its distance from the residence of the king, messengers came to inquire for me, where I was to sleep each night, and to hurry on, because the king had heard I was *beautiful*, and he could not eat till he had seen me! These parties were sometimes commanded by boys of thirteen years of age—smart little fellows, who travelled very quickly over the country, never getting fatigued. If they met our caravan on the march, complimentary taps and rolls were sounded by their drummers, and returned by ours. It was not considered etiquette for any of their number to mingle with our baggage-party while moving along; because, if anything should be missed, they might be made answerable for it.

Pokino, the governor of a large territory, was one day announced while I was dressing. His name had been constantly quoted as an authority by Mariboo, and I had a strong desire to see him. On coming out of my hut, he sat surrounded by twenty Waganda in considerable state, and I could not help saying aloud, "Hallo! is this Pokino?" At once all grinned at the mention of the name; no one moved from their seated positions, and my iron chair was placed outside the red cow-skin, on which he alone sat,—a determined, sly-looking functionary, with a bad expression of mouth, and just the man to have an order obeyed. His dress was the ordinary one of the country, robing him in graceful folds of bark-cloth, salmon-coloured, which harmonised well with his dark complexion. Round his bare head he wore a wreath of creepers (*Coccinia Indica*), which made me inquire whether his head ached. A laugh from him, and suppressed titter from his men at my ignorance, immediately followed, and he wished to see my pictures and lucifer-matches; of the former he preferred the buffalo's head, and one representing some slaves in chains; these amused him more than any of the others, and he soon took his departure, walking away slowly with considerable style, as if proud of his tall stout manly figure.

*   *   *

The day of my arrival at the Uganda capital, the 27th of May 1862, was one not only of intense joy, but deep thankfulness. I felt that my prayers for our safety had been heard. Speke and I had been separated for upwards of four months, and on being led by some of his men to the small hut he occupied, we were so happy to be together again, and had so much to say, that when the pages of the king burst in with the royal mandate that his Highness must see me "to-morrow", we were indignant at the intrusion. The morrow, however, came, and with it the same sharp, intelligent boys, to say that my stool might be brought to sit upon in the presence of the king. Accordingly, the present of a gun and some ammunition having been graciously received by him, at three o'clock, dressed in my best suit—i.e., white trousers, blue flannel coat, shepherd's-plaid shirt, a helmet, and a red turban—I sallied forth with Speke and some Seedees to make the call. It may be mentioned, as a curious custom of the court at Uganda, that when I told Speke that I meant to wear knicker-bockers at the levee, he warned me that I should not be considered "dressed" if any portion of my bare leg was left exposed. This costume, because my stockings were not long enough, had therefore to be abandoned for white trousers. In proceeding to the palace we had to make one short descent, cross a bog, with grass thrown over it to keep the feet from being soiled, and rise on a broad road to the top of a hill, on which several hundred houses were built, each surrounded with a screen of tall reeds. The outer gate, having iron bells behind it, was slid aside, and we entered under a cord strung with charms. Here was a wide oblong space, screened all round; one steep-roofed house, beautifully thatched, was the only dwelling visible. Inside its wide threshold sat a single figure; and on the open space in front a mob of bare-headed, well-dressed Africans sat, forming a crescent, and facing "His Majesty M'tessa." Our approach was abruptly stopped, and we were directed to halt. Some minutes elapsed, the court broke up, and the mass of people ran quickly through a wicket that had been opened. We followed, but the doorkeeper closed the gate, and ten minutes elapsed ere we were admitted. We next entered a similar place, but smaller, and stood in the sun, uncomfortable enough, till permitted to be seated on our stools, with our hats off and umbrellas up. M'tessa sat upon a bench of grass, with a dog behind him. His kamaraviona (commander-in-chief) was the only man allowed to sit at his feet; a sister and several women were on his left, also seated on the ground under the shade of the lofty cane-and-grass building. His quick eye detected that part of my hand had been cut off. "How did this happen?" He no doubt fancied that some offence had been committed by me, as it was the custom of his court to maim people by cutting off fingers, feet, or ears for even slight offences. He spoke in whispers to his pages, when Mariboo, the officer who had charge of me from Karague, informed him that I had received the wound in my hand in action; he also told him of the difficulties he had in bring-ing me to his majesty. The people listened with the most perfect decorum, only once interrupted by a sudden arrest. Maulah, the chief "detective", observing some breach of etiquette—probably a man speaking above his breath—suddenly seized the offender, and dragged him away. The look of anguish of the miserable creature thus apprehended was most painful. No one ventured to show sympathy; and Maulah soon returned alone, looking pleased and satisfied.

Conversation is never interrupted by these scenes; music from drums and other instruments drown any noise made by a poor prisoner, or it is continued to please the ears of those attending the levee. The mode of testifying allegiance was curious; the mob suddenly stood up *en masse*, with their long sticks balanced in the air, and charged towards the threshold several times with shouts of praise for their king, who made no acknowledgment. The court broke up, after an hour, by the king walking away on tiptoe, with the most ludicrous swagger, through a screen leading into another enclosure. The doors were opened and shut by men, who watched every movement of the king, for fear they should be discovered off the alert, and punished according to his caprice. A short time afterwards, a third scene was prepared for us. On entering the courtyard, M'tessa leant in a studied, affected attitude against the portico; about two hundred women sat on the ground on one side, and we were told to bring our chairs to within twenty yards of him, facing the women. No men except our Seedee interpreters were present. The remarks of the great potentate, who regarded us with a kindly surprised air, were confined to his favourite women, and seemed to be concerning our appearance. After a time, the thought seemed to strike him that we all ought to remove to some more shaded place. This was the only sensible thing he had done. Making us draw our stools close to the iron chair on which he sat, the conversation turned upon sport, our expedition, &c. A woman ran to fetch the gun he had that day been presented with; two others held spears beautifully polished. He signalled that I was to show my head uncovered to the ladies; a titter followed, and all of us laughed heartily. Another signal, and I was told to place my hat on; this made us all feel less restraint; and the women were not afraid

to return our smiles at the ridiculous formality of the scene. As the
sun was approaching the horizon, this "drawing-room" was
ended by M'tessa walking away, leaving us to reflect on the strange
events of the day. He was a tall, well-built young fellow, sprightly
in manner, very vain, his woolly hair dressed with the greatest
care; small head, remarkably prominent clever-looking clear
eyes, good teeth, and long nails to his hands and feet; the instep
of the latter was, as in most of the Waganda, highly arched,
indicating a well-moulded sinewy leg. His bark-cloth "toga"
had not a speck upon it, and was neatly knotted over the right
shoulder, concealing his whole body. His ornaments of beads
were made with great taste in the choice of colours; the most
minute beads of white, blue, and brown were made into rings and
rosettes, which he wore round his neck and arms. Each finger had
upon it a ring of brass; on the third finger of the left hand he wore
a gold ring, given him by Speke; with these he played while
sitting at his levees, occasionally receiving a golden-coloured
gourd-cup of wine from a maid of honour sitting by his side;
after each sip, a napkin of dark-cloth was used by him to wipe his
mouth. The only unseemly vulgarity he was guilty of while on
his throne was to use his napkin to rub away the perspiration
from his person. On leaving the court, and getting outside the
last gate of the palace, a woman's screams made us look back;
a cord was tied round her wrist, and a man dragged her, almost
naked, down the hill to be executed; she screamed "N'yawoh!
n'yawoh!" (Mother! mother!) in the most bitter anguish. A
second, similar tied, followed slowly, but not uttering a sound. A
shudder of horror crept over me. Had we been the cause of this
calamity? and could the young prince with whom we had
conversed so pleasantly have had the heart to order the poor
women to be put to death?

The road to our hut was crowded by files of men dressed as
"Neptunes", in tattered leaves of plantain, their limbs coloured
with ashes and vermilion, and girdles of long-haired goatskin
(from Usoga) hanging from their backs and waists. Daily these
wild-looking creatures shouted and rushed with all their might
along the roads, spears and shields being held high in the air; they

were M'tessa's men preparing and drilling for a slave-hunting campaign. The day after my first visit to the king, he came to return the call without giving us any warning. We heard a noisy crowd passing outside our enclosure, and immediately, through the fence, came the young king in a tremendous hurry. He was not the puppet of yesterday, but dressed, like a negro sailor, in an open coat of bed-curtain chintz, loose white trousers or "pyjamas", having a broad stripe of scarlet; his feet and head were naked. He was shown into an iron chair, and seeing some books he turned over their pages as a monkey would; asked to see the picture of Rumanika, and said he would like to know when his own portrait was to be done. His brothers, a mob of little ragamuffins, several in handcuffs, sat behind him chattering very familiarly, and tearing all the while at sugar-cane. I was told to show them my hair by taking off my hat. We were asked if we did not admire the leather wideawake made by one of the brothers?—and the vulture, the dove, and the horn-bill his highness had just shot? This scene over, the king rose, ordered Speke to follow him, and, led by the mob of brothers, all rushed madly away. On following them, the chained lads, escorted by two servants, were very much in the rear, and hobbled along, poor little fellows, in perfect good-humour, looking as strong, healthy, and contented as any of the others. It was said that the king, before coming to the throne, always went about in irons, as his small brothers now do. Where could they have got this custom? Wishing to know what had become of Speke, I went in search of him, and found on the way a *flight* of pages—there is no other name for it, as they always go at full speed, their robes flying, when serving the king. They were going with torches to light his highness home; but they knew not what route he had taken. It afterwards appeared that he had entered a house to dine upon boiled beef and wine, a share of which he offered to Speke; then taking a suit of clothes out of the tin box he had got from us, and which was carried to this picnic, he cast aside his torn and dirty suit for another, and went home by torchlight and drums.

My introduction to the king's mother took place on the 1st of June. Captain Speke and myself went with five or six Seedees carrying pads of grass (stools not being permitted), with our gourds of pombe, our sucking-reeds, and umbrellas. The dowager lady had been informed of our intention, but took her time as to seeing us. Walking over one hill to the top of another, in three-quarters of an hour we were at her royal highness's gate. On getting as far as the second courtyard, we were told to wait, with the other visitors, in the drum or ante-house. Here for an hour we were left to smoke, drink, and doze. A musical instrument in the place was new to me—a harmonicon of twelve blocks of wood, which, on being struck, gave out notes as glasses do when played. They rested upon the trunks of plantain, and were isolated from each other by thin reeds. We took our hats off on approaching the old lady, who laughed most heartily, and welcomed us with great cordiality, telling us to sit in front of and near her. She seemed to me like a Tartar woman, being fair-skinned, stout, and short. Her head was shaved, and had a cord tied round it. Conversation was kept up briskly for an hour or so, during which she fondled in her lap a plaything the size and shape of a hedgehog, studded with cowries and beads. She sipped at wine, looked at herself in a small mirror, smoked, and, like any housewife at home, gave orders to her domestics. Quantities of plantain neatly tied up and arranged in line, several basketfuls of boiled beef also tied round with the leaves, were laid out as a present for Mariboo and myself. Each basket of beef was tasted by one of her officers tearing a bit away with his teeth, and we took our leave, very much pleased with her good-humour and homeliness. Many other calls were made upon her by invitation; but although we sat waiting the dowager for hours amongst steaming natives, she did not always give us an interview, saying she was too busy or too tired. Her brother, Katoonzee, an officer of high rank, and with a most *distingue* Uganda air, pointing his toes and showing off his high instep as he walked, was treated with as much ceremony as ourselves, generally being obliged to sit so far distant from her that he had to bawl out to make himself heard. However, the dowager would allow him to whisper jokes into her ear, and be familiar enough when few were present. Any wine intended for us her majesty always tasted before it was presented. This was a condescension on her part not shown to every one.

The people of Uganda require to have the permission of an officer before the barber can use his razor. The women seen about the queen's residence had no hair, neither had she; all were shaved, and only a few in M'tessa's court were allowed to dress their hair in the same aristocratic fashion as the king. One of these women, in the bloom of youth, we one day saw led to execution. She was the fourth female victim that had passed that day. Her back was covered with scars, and blood appeared on her neck. She wept bitterly. Notwithstanding this circumstance, when we went and had an interview with the king, we found him as gay and cheerful as ever. His detective Maulah lived next hut to ours, and the shrieks of poor people, night and day, were quite heart-rending. Not only were their cries heard, but each lash of the stick was distinct; and being in such close proximity to the place of torture was a severe trial. When Maulah captures women, they are asked, "Will you live with so and so?" if they object, the rod is applied, and consent in this way is forced upon them. He and other chief officers were very jealous of Speke's influence with the king, for they knew he could at times obtain an interview, while they had to wait for days. On seeing us return from the palace, Maulah would inquire, "Have you seen the king?" and when we wished for an interview, and asked how it could be brought about, he would coarsely reply, "Are you kings, that you always expected to be received?" Certainly our influence had a most beneficial effect. Not only did Speke save the lives of many, but men about court got him to intercede with the king on several occasions. The executioner Konzah had a favourite son, who was under sentence. The boy, through Speke's inter-cession, was pardoned, and it was thought he would never again be punished; but on Bombay asking this high functionary "how the son was; had anything more been said of it?" the father replied, "My boy was killed yesterday for another offence." A child-page whom we took an interest in, and whom Speke had dressed up very gaily, named Loogohïe (or cloth), got into a dreadful scrape one day for coughing while the king was at dinner. It was thought his little ears would have been cut off, and he laughed very much when he found he had escaped, but he did not expect to live long, as he was always getting into hot water. On my asking what the king had killed when out shooting, Loogohie's reply was that, "As his highness could not get any game to shoot at, he shot down many people."

The king had become so fond of the gun, that, like a young sportsman, he seemed to dream of it. In the early morning his gun or the rattle of the diminutive drums which always accompanied his movements was heard. Interviews were difficult; his whole time was occupied. He had received so many presents from us, he had made so many promises to open the road, and his pages had stolen for him so much of our ammunition, that he at last was ashamed of himself, and suddenly permitted us to leave. For several days neither of us could visit him, being unwell, but Bombay, by showing some pictures to his servants, conveyed such accounts of us that communication was sometimes obtained. In a book he had received from Rumanika, "Kaffir Laws", his highness wished all the birds he had shot to be painted in imitation of our sketch-books. His pages pestered us, and became bold and insolent, walking into our hut, taking up anything they saw to examine it, or coming with the king's orders that our very beds, chairs, guns, shoes, &c., were wanted by the king, and saying there must be no delay about sending them. The union-jack which we had got from Admiral Keppel was also demanded. All these indignities, added to the brutal treatment of the women, made us feel that Uganda was not the "garden of pleasure" we had heard it called, and that the conduct of the king was a worse form of plundering than we had experienced in the Ugogo and southern territories. Here, by robbing us of our ammunition, they had placed us in a defenceless position; and though we did not want their offered hundreds of women and hundreds of cattle, it induced our Seedees to become mutinous, saying, "Although *you* don't take them, we will, for as yet we have received nothing but broken bones for the 2000 dollars' worth of property given to M'tessa." They refused to march with us until they obtained sufficient ball-cartridge. This occurred just previous to our departure, up to which time our men had been gathering a precarious existence from what could be plundered from the gardens.

There were several executioners, men of rank, who were the privy councillors of the king. These men had numbers of followers, distinguished by wearing their mark of office—a short turban of cord—and sometimes carrying a peculiarly-shaped bludgeon. Konzah has been mentioned; another, named Ozzoongoo, was always carried to court in a litter, being an invalid. On meeting him, he would stop to speak, and in expression had nothing repulsive; but when seen with a wreath of black fringe encircling his head, hiding his eyes, and hanging down to near his mouth, his appearance was completely changed, and he reminded one of a black Highland bull looking fiercely through his forelock. Both these executioners were really polite men, always frank when met at the palace—much more so than the kamaraviona (commander-in-chief) who was a proud, haughty young fellow. One day I had the curiosity to follow a poor woman who was led by a boy to be killed. She carried a small hoe, balanced upon her head. No one told me she was under sentence, but the cord on the wrist was sufficient; and after travelling for half a mile, I followed her down to the executioner's gardens. Waiting outside for some time, not a sound was heard, not a person seen. A lazy, yellow-beaked vulture, the cannibal of Uganda, sat perched on the stump of a broken tree; others hovered high overhead, looking on the scene below. This circumstantial evidence was enough for me, and I returned.

At every new moon M'tessa went through an examination of his idol horns; but I should not suppose him to be much of an augur: he was too light-headed and fond of field-sports, of boating, swimming, and music, to give much attention to making rain, &c. He left all these things to the Witchwezee race who were about him, and seldom denied himself to visitors at the time of new moon. On the very day that four of his women were going to execution, at an audience given to ourselves and in our presence, some maidens were offered for his harem. He had detained us in an outer court for a long time, and probably brought us in to enjoy our surprise at the poor naked offerings. Each held by the upper corners an open napkin in front of her, and all were smeared with grease and decorated with girdles and necklaces of beads. After being reviewed without a smile, they were told to face to the right, and march to the "zenana". As was customary, the king then sat on the knees of the matron-like woman who had presented the maidens, and, having ordered all away but ourselves, the interpreters, and some young lads, a conversation began about men and women in general. It is, however, worthy of remark, that M'tessa never behaved indecently by word or deed while women were present.

DE BONO's ivory-traders had selected Faloro, a favourable position, for their camp, situated on the concave side of a hill, with a stream below. Our junction with them at sunset of the 3d December was one of those happy epochs which can never be forgotten. We announced our approach by firing guns when within a few hundred yards of the settlement, and a very lively scene ensued. Turkish banners flew, welcome guns were fired, and an army of well-dressed men, "fezzed" or turbaned, turned out with drums and fifes to greet our arrival and escort us the rest of the way. A procession was formed, with music and colours in the van, the two commanders with drawn sabres went next, and then we followed in our rags of clothes, the soldiers bringing up the rear. As we passed outside the village enclosure others joined, kissing our hands; women shouted shrilly with delight, and we were told to be seated upon a bed covered with leopard-skins placed for us in front of commander "Mahomed's" door. The traders all knew Petherick by name, but they either could not or would not tell us anything about him, excepting that he was twenty marches away to the north, and that our letter sent to him from Unyoro had not been forwarded.

Everything around us looked strange; we had become such "roughs" that the most common object in this semi-civilised life gave us pleasure. Every one seemed so well dressed, they had all

shoes, regular bedsteads, crockery, &c., none of which we had
seen for more than two years. The scenes also in a camp of
Egyptians were new to us. Mahomed, the commander, seated
on a low stool, while being shaved by a barber, excited the wonder
of the Wanyoro. A white napkin being placed on his chest, the
boy strapped the razor with the rapidity of lightning, and, standing with extended arms, passed his instrument over the whole
head and beard at a frightful pace, handing his master a gilt frame
looking-glass when the operation was completed. Donkeys were
ridden at a sharp amble, without saddle or bridle, driven by a long
stick, and the rider seated in the native fashion on the animal's
haunches. Riding-oxen, with halters and ropes through their
noses, were exercised about the village by negro lads, who made
them go at a fast trot. Our bedding and cooking utensils not
having arrived, we requested Mahomed to have some dinner
prepared for us. At once he offered a cow, but it was late, and we
did not wish to wait till it was killed. Coffee in true Arab style
was served, and an attendant stood by offering occasionally tin
mugs full of native-made beer. When dinner was ready, a crowd
squatted beside us, and a woman stood with water to drink. The
repast was minced meat in balls served in a tureen, a roast leg of
goat in another tureen, honey and thin cakes of sorghum; all
looked inviting, and we longed to begin. We found, however,
that there were no spoons, knives, or forks; and we made the
most of it without them, and enjoyed an excellent dinner, which
we had not done for many a day. But the greatest treat was to
come—water was brought us to wash our hands, and luxury of
all luxuries, soap! After the repast was finished, we were gratified
to find that the remains were placed before our Seedees; Mabrook
was so surprised on receiving a cup full of honey, that he inquired
whether it was to be eaten? and after having dined, they all had
soap and water served to them by one of the Nubians. A large
open shed was made over to us, but we could not retire to rest
without a prayer of thankfulness to the Almighty for having
preserved us through so many difficulties, and at length, by His all-
protecting arm, brought us in safety to the boundary of civilisation, after twenty-six months of unceasing toil and anxiety.

At Faloro we found upwards of a hundred men of every Egyptian caste, colour, and costume. They were called by the natives of the country "Toorkee", or Turks; but there was not a true Turk amongst them, and only one or two European coun-tenances. Curly locks were exceptional, and wool predominated. They were adventurers without homes, born in the most northern Egyptian dominions from negro stock. We afterwards ascertained that the bazaar at Khartoum was full of such idlers ready for any employ. The merchants there engage them to go into the interior for the purpose of collecting ivory; guns are put into their hands, an intelligent native is placed over them, and they are sent up the Bahr Abiad (White Nile) as ivory-hunters, not to return perhaps for several years. These were the men we were so glad to meet, but from whom we found it difficult to get away, although they had been at Faloro for nine months previous to our arrival.

The obstacles offered to our departure were many and vexa-tious. The rivers ahead, we were told, would not be fordable for two months, and we could not cross them without using force; besides which, a party was expected to arrive soon from Gondo-koro with ammunition and means of carrying down the tusks in store, and it must be waited for. This we could not assent to. As the streams were getting dry and a march was quite practic-able, our Wanyoro men were ordered to be in readiness, but they had deserted to their homes, and we were helpless. Seeing that delay was inevitable, we proposed a trip to the west, in order that we might have a look at the White Nile, which we had left at Karuma Falls. The reply, however, was, that there was no use looking at the river there, because we should see it two marches ahead on the way to Gondokoro. This information was after-wards confirmed by our standing on a rocky height, from whence the river was seen marked by a long line of mist hanging over its course, which ran from the west in a north-east direction. The next event that startled us was the announcement that a party had to go to a district where a quantity of ivory had been accumu-lated, and that on their return we should all leave together for Gondokoro. There was nothing for it but submission. While we kept their camp eighty started on this razzia or raid, bringing back about a hundred tusks, a herd of cattle, and several slaves. Our importunities to get away were treated as the cravings of children, and we were told, 'Do not fear, you'll get to Gondokoro before next moon.' We surprised them, however, by packing up our luggage and preparing to start with our remaining twenty Seedees.

Our residence amongst the Toorkees reminded me of a military life, for at break of day the *reveille* was sounded regularly with drum and fife; at certain fixed hours we had more music; and at night sentries were placed the same as in a cantonment. But the grand spectacle was their parade every Friday, which was equivalent to our Sunday. We were once requested to attend and see them manœuvre, and anything more ludicrous can hardly be conceived. All were drawn up in line, but no two were dressed alike, neither had they uniform guns. Captain Mahomed stood in front, with drawn "shumshere", in a red jacket and loose Turkish trousers, fez, and silk turban. His second in command had adopted the rifle uniform of green jacket and black braid, loose pyjamas, gaiters, and tasselled fez; he also carried a drawn sword. Speke was the reviewing officer, and I stood on a height in the distance. Bombay, looking very dissipated, thought it his duty to stand alongside of his master; but his appearance, bare-headed, with a dirty shirt worn outside his dress, and holding a spear in his hand, betokened a pretty hard morning's carousing. Our second interpreter, Frij, was also decidedly tipsy, but had not the sense to remain quiet. While the men were marching he would rush wildly at them, flourishing his sword-bayonet, then attempting to show them how to march, blow his boatswain's whistle, repeat the commands, and interfere with the commander, who took it all good-naturedly. The series of manœuvres embraced file-marching, forming square, and open columns of companies—moving in these formations to any flank, over rough ground, to drum and fife music, in slow and quick time. The "general-officer", who had served with Turkish troops in the Crimea, was, of course, obliged to compliment them on their discipline, as their marching and shouldering passed muster; but the commander seemed to be of a different opinion, as any man who lost distance was at once cuffed and shoved out of the ranks, and when one side of the square faced inwards, I thought he would have cut them all down.

After parade, the standards were planted in the open space inside the village, and were there saluted by the men marching round them with drums; or a cow was killed and the colours consecrated by putting some of the streaming blood upon them or on their staffs. This custom was known to our Seedees, who had seen it done by the Sultan of Zanzibar's Mohammedan troops. During the night sentries were posted all over the village, and they performed their duties very regularly, never sleeping, although they sat the whole of their turn of duty upon a stool or stone. This is more than most men could do; but I watched some of them and never saw one fall asleep. Had we asked our Seedees to do this, they would have laughed at us, showing the difference which discipline had made between these two classes of men.

THE THIRD EXPEDITION

*From Gondokoro to Lake Albert and back;
via Latuka, Obbo, Unyoro and Bari*

March 1863 to March 1865

SAMUEL WHITE BAKER (1821–1893)
FLORENCE BAKER (1835–1908)

As we have seen, the Bakers were in Gondokoro preparing for the journey into the interior when Speke and Grant arrived back from their epic walk. The Bakers had been on the African continent for two years, and Samuel Baker knew what he was about. Chapter One of his *The Albert N'Yanza, Great Basin of the Nile* begins with a straightforward statement:

"In March 1861, I commenced an expedition to discover the sources of the Nile, with the hope of meeting the East African expedition of Captains Speke and Grant . . I had not the presumption to publish my intention, as the sources of the Nile had hitherto defied all explorers, but I had inwardly determined to accomplish this difficult task or to die in the attempt. From my youth I had been inured to hardships and endurance in wild sports in tropical climates, and when I gazed upon the map of Africa I had a wild hope, mingled with humility, that, even as the insignificant worm bores through the hardest oak, I might by perseverance reach the heart of Africa."

The only romanticising in that paragraph is the comparison of the author with "the insignificant worm". Those who knew Sam Baker were apt to compare him with the sturdy oak: British and strong. The eldest living son of a family of landed gentry who also had large plantations in the West Indies, Baker had indeed led a tough outdoor life since boyhood. It was also, until the time of the African adventure, a life which had promised much and fulfilled little. Florence was his second wife; his first, Henrietta Martin, was a clergyman's daughter whom he had known since childhood, and whom he married in 1843.

After a short—and probably unhappy—tour of duty in Mauritius on the family estates, Baker and his first wife, with their surviving son (an elder son and daughter had died in Mauritius), went to Ceylon, where they built a home, along with Sam's brother John, who was married to Henrietta's sister. Here they lived for eight energetic and contented years. Besides founding an English settlement in Ceylon, and presumably making things pay, Baker made a little fame for himself as an elephant hunter, publishing a good account of his adventures in two books, *Eight Years in Ceylon* and *Rifle and Hound in Ceylon*. In 1855 both families returned to England, and in the December of that year, whilst holidaying in the Pyrenees, Henrietta died.

There were four children still living of the marriage, all girls (their son had died in Ceylon). These Baker deposited with his dead wife's family, and took himself off to hunt away his despair. For the next four years he wandered around the Balkans and Turkey, mostly shooting some animal or another. These years are very much a blank in his history; they did little else but allow the grief and loneliness to be numbed by action, covered by time. Then in 1859 he drifted into a job with the sort of amateur nonchalance so typical of an Englishman at that time. He became the manager of a British company who were building a railway in Rumania—from the Danube to the Black Sea across a region called the Dobruja—near to the line of the Trojan Wall. By the end of 1860 the railway was constructed, and Baker was on his honeymoon.

No more than that is known of when and where Baker met Florence von Sass and married her. She began her life again as Mrs Baker, and the twenty-four years (if twenty-four years it was) which she had already lived ceased to exist. Legend has it that she had suffered seeing her father and her brothers killed—in what manner and why seems an open question—and she too, therefore, wished to cut adrift from the past, something she succeeded in doing absolutely. She never visited her homeland again, although exactly which country could claim her is again far from clear. Austro–Hungarian of aristocratic connections is probably nearest the truth. None of this mattered. What was important about Florence Baker was her remarkable strength of character, her intelligence and imagination, that she was a perfect match for Sam Baker and that she was very beautiful. They were the right mixture of qualities to start life again with.

*   *   *

Although clear enough in his intentions to find the Nile source, Baker kept his ambition very much to himself when he and Florence left England for Cairo early in 1861. His plans were deliberate and unhurried. Leaving Cairo in April, they arrived in Berber late in May, and proceeded to explore the Nile tributaries which came down from the Abyssinian highlands through the Nubian deserts, flowing mainly, at first, into the Blue Nile. During this time the Bakers were busy learning Arabic, and as much of the Central African languages as they could discover.

Just over a year later they arrived in Khartoum. "A more miserable, filthy, and unhealthy spot can hardly be imagined." Here they were to get their expedition ready, collect men and stores, boats and weapons. They soon discovered the nature of the enemy, led by one Moosa Pasha. "This man was a rather exaggerated specimen of Turkish authorities in general, combining the worst of Oriental failings with the brutality of a wild animal." By "Turk" Baker meant the Egyptian official, the ruling class, the soldiers of the state administered from Cairo. He was under no illusion as to their merit. "The Turk never improves. There is an Arab proverb that—the grass never grows in the footprint of the Turk—and nothing can be more aptly expressive of the character of the nation than this simple adage. Misgovernment, monopoly, extortion, and oppression are the certain accompaniments of Turkish administration."

On top of this there was the fact that more or less the whole of Khartoum was engaged in and dependent upon the slave trade. As with the two previous expeditions from Zanzibar, the presence of a British explorer was not regarded as an advantage. Nobody had the nerve to slit Baker's throat, which would have taken some courage indeed, for the threat of British power was already too considerable in the Middle East for anything too drastic to be done against a subject of the Queen. So every form of non-assistance had to be practised against this fearless Englishman and his equally resolute wife.

At first Baker was frustrated at every turn, and brought almost to despair when his application for assistance to the British Consul in Alexandria, for some trustworthy soldiers and some sailworthy boats, was—after months of delay—turned down flat. Then his spirit reasserted itself or, as he wrote afterwards: "I confess to the enjoyment of a real difficulty—it was perfectly clear that the utmost would be done to prevent my expedition from starting. This opposition gave a piquancy to the undertaking, and I resolved that nothing should thwart my plans. Accordingly, I set to work in earnest."

In a matter of three to four weeks Baker had gathered together his party, and had bought three boats and enough supplies to take the whole expedition to Gondokoro, a journey on the Nile of about six weeks. He also took additional supplies for Speke's party, should they be met up with. The expedition's armed escort, forty-five men, had to be recruited locally. They were made to swear their "fidelity and devotion", shoved into gaudy uniforms Baker had purchased in Cairo, and armed with double-barrelled guns and rifles. Baker looked upon them with awe ". . . a greater set of scoundrels in physiognomy I never encountered." As we shall see, the Bakers turned some of this villainous troop into a reliable—or almost reliable—bodyguard. Here also Baker engaged a German, Johann Schmidt, who had been working in the Sudan for some years as a hunter of animals for European zoos. Schmidt was meant to be the expedition's head man, but his health was failing badly and he died before reaching Gondokoro.

On 18 December 1862 they were all aboard and ready to leave, when the Khartoumese officials tried by two desperate ruses to prevent the inevitable. The first attempt came in the shape of a demand for poll tax on each man of the party. Should Baker refuse to pay—and it was such a ridiculously large sum that he would certainly refuse—then his boats would be detained. Sam Baker shrugged this threat off in true full-blooded adventuring spirit. He hoisted the British flag, declared his expedition under its protection, and added that he would throw overboard any official who might try to board his boats. The miserable poll tax official departed at great speed, and Baker gave the order to cast off.

They made to pull away when a Khartoum government boat bore down swiftly on their vessel, and in the resulting collision the oars of Baker's boat were crushed to pieces. The government boat was commanded by a gigantic native, who proceeded to abuse Baker's crew, and, when asked to supply oars in exchange for those he had smashed, challenged anybody to come aboard his ship and get them. Not one of Baker's crew would take up the challenge. So it was left to Baker himself.

"The insolence of Turkish government officials is beyond description—my oars were smashed and this insult was the reparation; so stepping quickly on board, and brushing a few fellows on one side, I was obliged to come to a physical explanation with the captain which terminated in a delivery of the oars."

Splendid stuff. And so the Bakers began their long journey of exploration.

For once the journey went along without hair-raising incident. It was actually marked by melancholy for much of the way, Johann Schmidt taking to his bed after a few days and dying peacefully on the last day of 1862. Baker was nobly moved by the sight of the German's death.

"I gazed sorrowfully at his attenuated figure, and at the now powerless hand that had laid low many an elephant and lion in its day of strength; and the cold sweat of death lay thick upon his forehead. Although the pulse was not yet still, Johann was gone."

They sailed on down the Nile in line, with the last ship, called the *Clumsy*, living up to its name and always lagging behind through one mishap or another. Some of the "Baker Irregulars" behaved badly, including one Corporal Richarn, who was suffering from post-alcoholic depression after a glorious few weeks in Khartoum. Richarn was, Baker tells us, "an illustration of missionary success", that is, both drunk and useless. Baker had little time for the missionaries: he saw that their teaching of Christianity in Africa would never do more than make a few "surface only" converts. He said that Christianity and civilisation had to go hand in hand. You could not impose the teaching of Christ upon people who were as savage as creatures from the Stone Age; who were to all intents and purposes living as Stone Age primitives. He said this loudly and clearly, and he made himself a few enemies. The enemies were a weak-kneed lot, and Baker ignored them. He showed what could be done by civilised leadership by turning the hopeless Richarn into a first-rate chap by the time the expedition was half-way to the Albert Nyanza. He was not so lucky with his best soldier, Sali Achmet, who was battered to death by a buffalo which Baker had wounded the day before. Sali could have been saved by his comrades, but they preferred to shout their advice to the attacked man from safety, and not try to drive the mad animal away or even take another shot at it. Their behaviour taught Baker a lesson he was not to forget, and he kept them on a tight rein thence until he had instilled some of his own courage into them.

He also learned that he should referee the arguments which his irregulars indulged in over anything there was to argue about; the more trifling the cause, the more heated the argument. (It was all a matter of passing time without effort, Baker concluded quite rightly.) On one occasion a baby hippopotamus was shot and the carcass was found to be scored and pitted with tusk marks. Older hippos had been bullying him, it was decided, but which? One side said the father hippo had done it, the other claimed for the mother. The argument raged all day and could easily have developed into a free fight—these rows often did—so Baker was called in. Was it papa hippo or mama hippo who so badly treated their child? Or was it both perhaps? Baker considered, and then suggested, that "perhaps it was his uncle". "By Allah, it is true!" There was no more argument, and from then on the irregulars began to approach Baker when they needed Solomon's judgement on anything.

Progress was slow and frequently unpleasant. "The luxuries of the country as usual," Baker wrote sardonically, "—malaria, marshes, mosquitoes, misery; far as the eye can reach, vast treeless marshes perfectly lifeless." The misery mentioned was that of the starving Kytch tribe. A people so primitive that they did not know how to plough and sow, and lived upon the land in the manner of apes. "So emaciated that they have no visible posteriors."

Eventually, on 2 February 1863, they floated into Gondokoro, and found they were not welcomed. It was Khartoum, and worse, over again. Baker estimated that there were about six hundred people engaged in the ivory and slave trade residing in the shanty town. Most of them were drunk all day and every day, and spent their time quarrelling and firing their guns in every direction as the spirit moved them. Baker understood the danger he and his wife were in. "Nothing was more probable than a ball through the head by *accident* which might have had the beneficial effect of ridding the traders from a spy."

They kept their eyes skinned and trusted in the Lord, and although possibly they had a few narrow escapes their destiny ran steady for them.

Or almost. Within a few days there were the unmistakable signs amongst the irregulars of discontent and defiance, and it was obvious to Baker that his men had been got at. Things soon came to the boil, and Baker ordered a general parade. One man was so insubordinate that Baker ordered him twenty-five lashes. This sparked off a general mutiny, and although Baker knocked a few men down he was soon surrounded and about to get the worst of it. This was the occasion, already mentioned, when Mrs Baker rushed from her sick bed and by her very presence—coming, too, so unexpectedly—stopped the riot. She was also clever enough to make her Sam forgive the ringleader, whilst at the same time making this man kiss Sam's hand in apology. Such tactics worked like a charm, and, although Baker was left feeling far from happy at the thought of the long journey ahead with such an ill-disciplined crowd, he had for the moment been saved from likely death.

Then on 15 February, as we have seen, Speke and Grant walked into the camp, and Mrs Baker seems to have vanished from the scene for ten days. Before he left, Speke gave Baker some useful information and instructions about the people and places Baker's expedition would encounter as it went south towards Kamrasi's territory. Such was Baker's plan, and once Speke and Grant had departed north he set about putting it into operation. What actually happened was quite different, for the Bakers all but failed to leave Gondokoro and when they did finally they had to go east, not south.

As we know, the two previous explorations from Zanzibar had met with difficulties enough at the start of their journeys. These were nothing to what Samuel and Florence Baker went through, and it was only because of their exceptional courage and determination that they did not find themselves rotting in Gondokoro, unable to move in any direction; a fate which they both realised would result in their deaths, from one cause or another, before many moons passed.

At first it looked as if everything would work out nicely. The man who had brought Speke and Grant into Gondokoro, Mahommed Wat-el-Mek, was setting off again for the interior within a week or so, and readily agreed that the Bakers' expedition should join his large caravan. Baker was pleased but uneasy, for his irregulars were behaving insolently again—which meant they were up to something. Before Baker could put his finger on the trouble, Mrs Baker found it out. The boy Saat—who adored his mistress—and the drunk but loyal Richarn came to her with what they knew of the conspiracy, just about all there was to know. Mahommed was going to leave secretly and suddenly a few days before he had said. With him would go Baker's irregulars, carrying their arms and ammunition.

The effect of this, as the Bakers realised, would have been disaster. To lose the men would be bad enough; to lose their weapons and ammunition also would place them in an impossible situation. Baker acted swiftly and called the irregulars on parade. Only fifteen turned up—the rest had vanished into the seamy background of the slave station. He ordered the fifteen to lay down their arms, and when they seemed reluctant to do so cocked his own rifle and shouted at them: "Down with your guns this moment, sons of dogs!" Baker in his fiercest temper must have been a frightening spectacle, and the irregulars were no match for it. They allowed themselves to be disarmed, and were there and then discharged in writing with the word "mutineer" written above Baker's signature. None of the "mutineers" could read, of course, so no doubt they presented the evidence of their guilt with broad grins to all and sundry. On the other hand, such a discharge from Baker might have been considered as a recommendation by the slave traders.

The Bakers were now left with the boy Saat, one irregular, Richarn, and a quantity of servants and camp-followers. Within a couple of days the deceitful Mahommed led his caravan out of Gondokoro, south back to Faloro. Baker needed help, and there was only one person to turn to in Gondokoro, the rather sinister Koorshid Aga, the Circassian trader. There was never any one thing for which Koorshid Aga could be held responsible. He sat in his small mud palace at Gondokoro, smiling and friendly to everybody. He was a business colleague of Petherick, a friend and an influence with the Egyptian officials at Khartoum, an authoritative figure to the African tribal chiefs, and a friend of King Kamrasi. Presumably he traded in slaves as well as ivory, and for this reason he could not afford to approve the journey which the Bakers were still intent on making. There was no direct evidence that he was behind the Bakers' misfortunes at Gondokoro, but the circumstantial evidence should have been obvious—should have been but was not to Sam Baker, at least so it seems.

Koorshid Aga agreed to help. He would obtain "thirty good blacks at Khartoum" on his next visit there, and bring them back with him. The Bakers would have a six months' wait at Gondokoro, but that was better than "the disgrace of returning to Khartoum beaten, [that] would have been insupportable". Koorshid also agreed to leave ten of his bodyguard with the Bakers whilst they were on their own at Gondokoro, for, once his caravans had left, the trading station would not be a very secure place to live at without an armed bodyguard. All seemed organised and the Bakers slept easily, for one night. The next day Koorshid turned up rather sheepishly and told them that not one of his men would remain behind with them. Baker asked why.

The men's reasons were formidable. He was a spy on the slave trade and a madman to boot, who would lead them into far off countries where everybody would be murdered.

For the moment the Bakers were completely stymied. All they could do, it seemed, was to return to Khartoum—beaten. And this, of course, they would not.

"We were utterly helpless, the whole of the people against us, and openly threatening. For myself personally I had no anxiety, but the fact of Mrs Baker being with me was my greatest care. I dared not think of her position in the event of my death amongst such savages as those around her. These thoughts were shared by her; but she, knowing that I had resolved to succeed, never once hinted an advice for retreat."

This was all very well, but it left them with very little choice but to move on. At first Baker thought to make a dash for it through the hostile Bari country to somewhere called Moir. (Where and what Moir was, except that it was south from Gondo-koro, Baker never makes clear. Why he expected to be able to move on without trouble from Moir he likewise doesn't explain, but he does remark that the people there were friendly—from information received, presumably.) This plan met with strong disapproval from the Bari chief at Gondokoro and from Richarn; Baker therefore dropped it.

He now discovered that a number of his deserters were still in Gondokoro, including his headsman or vakeel, having missed out with Mahommed. What could not be done by reasonable persuasion had to be done by threats. The vakeel was brought to the seat of judgement and told that, if any harm came to the Bakers, he would surely be hanged by the British authorities. A letter arranging this was on its way to Cairo, and at best if he did not co-operate he would be caught and imprisoned sooner or later. It was Baker at his most majestic, and it worked well enough. Some seventeen of the irregulars rejoined the Baker colours, but on condition that Baker would march east and not south; that is, that they would go along with one of Koorshid Aga's caravans, which was due to leave by the eastern route in a few days.

Baker had no option but to accept this condition; all he wanted to do was get away from Gondokoro as soon as he could. Then, almost as if it was the expected thing, Saat discovered a plot amongst the wretched irregulars. They intended to leave Baker at a trading station seven marches from Gondokoro and join a slave trading party. It was hardly a deliberate plot of any cunning, and Baker treated it with the disdain it deserved. He had other problems. Neither of the two trading parties leaving for the eastern province of Latuka wanted him with them. The first of these two caravans, under the command of a Mohammed Her, slipped away before Baker was quite ready. The second caravan, belonging to Koorshid Aga, hastened to follow, at the same time daring Baker to follow them. This did not worry Baker unduly, for he considered that their bark was worse than their bite. What did worry him was the possibility that a warlike tribe in the Ellyria mountains, some forty miles south-east, would be incited to attack him. This tribe had a nasty reputation for massacring the enemies of Koorshid Aga, by ambushing them in a narrow pass.

As Baker put it: "There was no time for deliberation. . . . It was useless to speculate upon chances. . . ." Looked at coldly, the odds against the Bakers ever getting very far were frighteningly high. All they had on their side was courage, determination and what can best be termed a moral superiority. The list against them was a long one. They were being forced to go east instead of south, with a bodyguard of only seventeen irregulars, all of whom were likely to mutiny and desert at any moment. The traders' caravans going in the same direction would have nothing to do with them, and at the same time were quite capable of stirring up the local tribes to attack them, like a swarm of bees. They had neither guide nor interpreter, their animals were badly overloaded, their destination east unknown.

By any reasonable estimate their journey was doomed, and they should never have started. Baker knew it, but he also knew that to be reasonable at that moment was to accept defeat. He faced the odds and began the long journey.

"All had been threatened, and we, perfectly helpless, commenced the desperate journey in darkness about an hour after

G

sunset. 'Where shall we go?' said the men. . . . 'Who can travel without a guide? No one knows the road.' The moon was up and the mountain of Belignan was distinctly visible about nine miles distant. Knowing that the route lay on the east side of that mountain, I led the way, Mrs Baker riding by my side, and the British flag following close behind us as a guide for the caravan of heavily laden camels and donkeys . . . and thus we started on our march in Central Africa on the 26th of March, 1863."

By the end of the first day's march the Bakers' little party had overtaken Koorshid's caravan and at the base of the Belignan mountains found a village, and from this village found a guide to take them to the Ellyria mountains. Baker had also conceived the idea of getting through these mountains, with their hostile tribe, before Koorshid's men. There was some thirty miles to go of rough country, much of it little better than a jungle. By a dint of what Baker calls persuasion, setting an example himself and knocking a few heads together, the expedition was made to move on and to keep on moving. They were helped by two Latukas who deserted Koorshid's caravan after a fracas and joined Baker as additional guides. Things went pretty smoothly, and even the village that tried to stop them—and were convinced that Florence Baker was Baker's son—were diverted from being too much of a nuisance by the antics of Mrs Baker's pet red Abyssinian monkey.

This monkey seems to have had racialist tendencies of a positively human sort. With the Bakers he was tame and affectionate, with the black men he was the opposite, biting their legs and making insulting grimaces at them should they come nearer to him than he felt they should. On this occasion, and on others, his primate apartheid inclinations were of considerable value. The expedition managed to move on without difficulty; for as the village said in its wisdom, nobody who was hostile to them would travel about with a pet monkey anyway, and one as amusing as Wallady was a guarantee of peaceful intentions.

Then on the borders of the Ellyria country, when the Bakers and one guide had gone on ahead of their main party, they were suddenly and unexpectedly overtaken by Koorshid Aga's party.

It was a terrible moment, and it could have proved disastrous but for Florence Baker's presence of mind and strength of personality. As the trading party filed past the Bakers, threatening their Latuka guides with shooting, they noticed that the caravan's leader, Ibrahim, was the last of the line and therefore easily approachable. Mrs Baker implored her Sam to make contact, but he would not, could not, so Florence called to the man, and then with Baker joining in he stopped and the first friendly contact was made. Between them the Bakers set about the task of getting Ibrahim on their side.

Ibrahim himself, so it seems, did not take much convincing that the Bakers would be kind friends and true. His men were another matter and he readily admitted it, but, as we shall see, fate was for once in the Bakers' court and the men were won over almost accidentally. For the moment they were safe to march through the Ellyria tribe without the danger of ambush, and both caravans halted side by side in the beautiful valley of Ellyria. The tribal chief was not so beautiful. Baker drew a sketch of him and recorded: "Of all the villainous countenances that I have ever seen that of Legge excelled. Ferocity, avarice, and sensuality were stamped upon his face. . . ." He appears to have been a greedy, unhelpful drunkard who was in fact no better and no worse than many other chiefs and kings Baker was to encounter over the next two years.

They set off out of the beautiful valley into the country of the Latuka with Ibrahim's party, much to the amazement and sulky hostility of the Baker irregulars. On the way Ibrahim warned Baker that his men meant to desert him at the first trading station in Latuka. This was a threat Baker was already aware of, and he was determined to deal with it firmly and finally this time; for once he would be able to act from a position of strength, for Ibrahim was by now eating from his hand.

Within a few days they came to the station, just outside the town of Latome, and were greeted with a display of excessive friendliness by the caravan of Mahommed Her, which had left Gondokoro a few days earlier than the two arriving parties. Both Baker and Ibrahim were suspicious of this greeting, and within hours their suspicions were confirmed, trouble beginning with Her declaring that Ibrahim had no right of way through the Latuka country and that such right of way belonged to his party only. Naturally Ibrahim was having none of this, and Her was literally brushed aside when he became too insulting. Ibrahim had nothing to fear, for his party outnumbered Her's by a third, and once he had dealt with the trouble he gave orders for his caravan to move on. Baker therefore gave his orders, and as he expected only Richarn, and a reformed villain called Sali, took any notice.

So Baker waited for the storm to break. It was his headsman, Bellaal, who came forward and announced the intentions of the irregulars. "Not a man shall go with you—go where you like with Ibrahim, but we won't follow you." Baker told him to put down his gun. The man answered that he would not, thereupon Baker delivered his favourite right hook to the man's jaw, Bellaal collapsed in a heap, and Baker rushed into the group of, by now wavering mutineers, seized them, and physically made them begin loading. They moved off and soon caught up Ibrahim. The crisis was over; he had acted decisively at the right moment and he had won.

As so often with Baker, or at least with the narrative of the journey, the dramatic action was fast and furious for some days. Approaching a village, one of Ibrahim's porters dropped his load and ran off. He would normally have been shot down by the armed men of the trader's party, but Baker gave pursuit first, and getting between the escaping man and the fire power caught the creature. The man clung to Baker's horse and Baker protected him, asking Ibrahim to spare his life and making the man promise to carry his load to the end of the journey. The incident impressed Ibrahim's men a lot. The speed of Baker's horse, and Baker's courage at going after a man armed with a spear, were both praised. And the Latuka porters praised him also for protecting one of their own kind. In all Baker had made allies, and he had also taken the first step in assuming the powers of leadership over Ibrahim's polyglot irregulars.

Soon after this episode Baker discovered that the miserable

Bellaal and four others had sneaked away, carrying their weapons and ammunition, and joined Mahommed Her's caravan. An impressive scene followed, with Baker cursing the deserters in front of his own and Ibrahim's irregulars. "Inshallah, the vultures shall pick their bones!" Baker meant it to be theatrical and writes that he expressed himself with intense hatred; he knew that such a curse would not be forgotten easily, and it was not.

The two parties wound their way through some fine country to Tarrangolle, the capital of Latuka, a town of about three thousand houses, each with its own stockaded courtyard. Baker was impressed by the Latuka people. Both sexes were physically imposing, a fact rendered obvious by their near nudity; they were also frank, pleasant people with lively intelligences. He decided they were not pure negro, but were probably of Galla origin—a province bordering on Abyssinia—and thus were able to take care of themselves against the slave traders far better than the Bari and Madi tribes in the same region. They were also rich in cattle, something that acted like a magnet to the greedy Egyptian traders, and, as we shall see, could cause a great downfall.

The Bakers made themselves comfortable at Tarrangolle; they would have to stay there whilst Ibrahim went to Gondokoro to collect ammunition and supplies, and returned with them. They made friends with the chief and with one Bokke, his head wife. Florence Baker was the object of much attention by Bokke and other Latuka women, and the fact that Baker claimed her as his only wife was the cause of great amusement. Baker sadly acknowledged that they would never believe him. Polygamy was the only state of matrimony they could conceive of, and Baker, unlike Burton, found polygamy a depressing condition of life in Africa. He wrote:

"Polygamy is, of course, the general custom; the number of a man's wives depending entirely upon his wealth, precisely as would the number of his horses in England. There is no such thing as *love* in these countries, the feeling is not understood, nor does it exist in the shape in which we understand it. Everything is practical, without a particle of romance. Women are so far appreciated as they are valuable animals."

Here at Tarrangolle Baker saw how the Egyptian (Turks) irregulars acted against their own interests by their brutal cupidity towards people as friendly as the Latuka. Once Ibrahim had left on his flying visit to Gondokoro, Baker was for ever having to curb the men Ibrahim had left behind. Fundamentally he understood that their stupidity would explode in their—and his men's—faces. It was a truth that the Egyptians could not grasp, even though they were outnumbered and no match for the efficient Latuka fighting man. Not even the cautionary tale of Mahommed Her's party could stop their thoughtless rampaging for more than a few days—and the story was a horrifying one.

The main body of Her's party had carried out a slave raid on a near-by Latuka town. It had been successful, and on their way back they had been told of a place where a great herd of cattle was kraaled. They got there, and began to drive away the seemingly unprotected animals. But this time the Latuka were prepared to fight, and had chosen their battlefield well. It was mountainous country with plenty of shelter from the traders' bullets and one path that appeared to be an escape route. Slowly at first the Latuka drove Her's men towards this path. Behind the protection of the rock-strewn land, a spear was as useful a weapon as a gun. The traders' ordered retreat became a rout, and they fled down the path not to freedom but to the edge of the precipice. Over two hundred of them were forced to their destruction on the rocks some five hundred feet below.

The news was brought to Tarrangolle and to Baker with much rejoicing. Baker took his chance. "Where," he asked solemnly, "are the men who deserted from me?" In answer two of his expedition's guns were laid at his feet. They were covered in blood and sand. Baker read out the numerals on the stocks and then the names of the men who had owned them. That was an awe-inspiring moment.

"'Are they all dead?' I asked. 'All dead,' the men replied. 'Food for the vultures?' I asked. 'None of the bodies can be recovered,' faltered my vakeel. 'Only two guns have been found, the men are all killed.' 'Better for them had they remained with me and done their duty. The hand of God is heavy,' I replied."

From this time on there was "an extraordinary change in the manner of both my people and those of Ibrahim. . . ." This was hardly surprising: when Baker went about the two camps, the men would say to him, quietly, "My God. Master," to which Baker modestly replied, "There is a God." The high adventure was beginning to take shape.

For the moment, however, life at Tarrangolle was more tedious than adventurous, although the Bakers were far better at settling in—but remaining apart—and keeping themselves busy and amused than their fellow explorers of the Nile source. Long discussions on every subject between, and including, life and death were had with the intelligent chief of the Latuka, Commoro. This man had a severely rational, materialistic outlook on all things, including the goal of Baker's exploration.

"He said, 'Suppose you get to the great lake, what will you do with it? If you find the large river does flow from it, what then? What's the good of it?'"

There was no answer Baker could give which satisfied him. Their dialogues were illuminating to the Bakers, for they made them realise properly, for the first time, how narrowly circumscribed was the African's abstract thinking; how rigid his attitude towards new ideas and new knowledge.

Conservation may have had its frustration limitations; the hunting field around the town, on the other hand, was just about limitless and Baker, the Hunter, got to work. His hunting was in fact very necessary for the general health and comfort of the expedition, for although the Latuka had thousands of cattle the Bakers could hardly ever procure one for eating. Sam kept the larder full, therefore, with everything from wild fowl to elephant. His armoury was sufficient for a regiment of hunters, with rifles of every shape, size and weight.

From a small boy he had been a passionate collector of guns, and he writes about his favourite rifles with great affection: the little double-barrelled No. 24 made by Thomas Fletcher, gunmaker of Gloucester, to whom he gives quite a testimonial ". . . in many years' hard work it has never been out of order, nor has it ever been in a gunmaker's hands." Then there were the pair of No. 10 polygroove rifles made by one Reilly of Oxford Street. They weighed fifteen pounds and carried seven drachms (about an ounce) of powder without, for Baker at least, a "disagreeable recoil". They were extremely accurate, and once again worked perfectly although often mistreated by his irregulars. But the real wonder weapon was an elephant gun which fired a half-pound percussion shell and was christened "Baby". (Ibrahim's men rechristened it, rightly, "Child of a cannon".) It was even something of a trial to Baker. He refers to it as an instrument of torture to the hunter, for it ". . . was not sufficiently heavy for the weight of the projectile . . . the recoil was so terrific that I spun round like a weathercock in a hurricane." Not surprisingly he rarely used it, but whenever he did he got a "bagging". And when it was fired, for cleaning purposes, by his men one always propped up the other; which meant that they both fell on their backs whilst Baby flew up and over to land yards behind them. Baker's testimonial to the firm that made it, Holland of Bond Street, is short and to the point. ". . . I could highly recommend it for Goliath of Gath, but not for men of A.D. 1866."

An elephant hunt on 17 April is recorded in some detail by Baker, as is the previous day's shoot, which was not successful, owing to a thunder-storm. Baker enjoyed every moment of this storm, his men did not.

"How delightful to be really cool in the centre of Africa! I was charmingly wet—the water was running out of the heels of my shoes which were overflowing . . . the whole scene had changed. It was no longer the tropics; the climate was that of old England [and it] restored me; the chilled air refreshed me and I felt at home again . . . I turned round to see how my followers were enjoying it. Dear me! I hardly knew my own people. Of all the miserable individuals I ever saw, they were superlative. . . . 'Charming day!' I exclaimed to my soaked and shivering followers, who looked like kittens in a pond . . . where was my naked guide? He was the most pitiable object I ever saw with teeth chattering and knees knocking together with cold, he crouched under the imaginary shelter of a large tamarind tree;

he was no longer the clean black who had started as my guide, but the cold and wet had turned him grey, and being thin, he looked like an exaggerated slate-pencil."

The elephant hunt was a fifteen-hour-day affair in which Baker fought a series of duels with a large bull elephant he had wounded a number of times. Baker and his elephant were well matched for courage: every time Baker lodged a ball in the elephant, risking his life to get near enough, the bull turned and chased him. His horse was unfit—it died a few days later—and at the best rather a slow animal. The last charge became a chase of half a mile, at the end of which the elephant was within ten yards of the horse's tail. Baker was saved only by the screams of the elephant making the horse find a little extra speed. It was a narrow squeak of the sort Baker was used to taking in his stride. Lesser men would have suffered from shock afterwards. Baker positively flourished on the danger. He was, of course, used to it after the years of hunting in Ceylon, in the Balkans, and more recently in the Sudan and Abyssina. But it was a sport which often led him to take risks that he should not have taken as the leader of an expedition of exploration. This elephant hunt was one such risk and, as we shall see, there were others.

A week or so later Ibrahim arrived back from Gondokoro. This settled his caravan down a little, but beneath the surface politeness and the formal behaviour of Ibrahim and the Lakuta chiefs there was always a tension. Not a day went by without a quarrel which developed into a fight between the Latuka and the Egyptian irregulars; over and over again the war drums were beaten and both sides made preparations for a battle. The battle noises always petered out, but it was nerve-racking to be in the midst of such behaviour all the time, particularly as Baker found himself acting as a mediator between the two camps. He did the job splendidly, like an efficient present-day United Nations Keeper of the Peace, using a mixture of reason and toughness, and now and again subduing everybody with a display of lèse majesté.

Then quite suddenly the chance of escaping from the situation arose with the arrival of some messengers from the Obbo tribe.

They brought with them presents for both Baker and Ibrahim, a gesture that could be read as an invitation to visit and trade, although at the same time Baker discovered that the Obbo knew he was a white man who did not want slaves or ivory. There was plenty of ivory in Obbo, however—slaves were not mentioned—and Ibrahim decided to take a small party to the district at once. It was a journey in the right direction, south-west, and so Baker decided to go with Ibrahim. He left most of his baggage in his camp, with a few men as guards, in the care of Commoro. He knew that as he had put Commoro on his honour all would be well—this was one of the redeeming features of the African which Baker saw as a ray of light in much darkness. It suggested the possibility that better things could arise in the not too distant future.

They left Tarrangolle on 2 May and spent their first night without cover (they had left their tents behind), soaked to the skin under their untanned ox-hides, which were just as wet and gave off ". . . an exceedingly disagreeable raw smell, very attractive to hyenas". After that miserable experience things got better rapidly, and within a couple of days they were making their way through some of the most lovely country they had ever seen in Africa. This led them into the main Obbo village—Baker doesn't give it a name—where they were greeted by the old chief, Katchiba.

The Bakers found the Obbo a pleasant, easygoing race, good-looking and clean. They were also the only people they were to come across on their journey who did not ask for presents of any sort. Katchiba was an unorthodox chief who ruled his tribe by a mixture of cunning and sorcery. The sorcery was based upon the traditional gullibility of the tribe: Katchiba was supposed to be able to control the weather and the productivity of both cattle and women. These imaginary powers he manipulated with such cunning that all believed in him emphatically—all, that is, except Katchiba, who openly acknowledged to Baker that his powers consisted only of doing, or saying, the right thing at the right time. Thus he ruled supreme, with wives in every village, and loyal subjects who carried him pick-a-back between the villages whilst his devoted wives accompanied him with pots of beer. Rumour had it, Baker records, that frequently Katchiba finished a journey with the beer-pots empty and himself being carried by two men.

Besides being a buffoon magician, the chief knew all there was to know about his little kingdom, and he warned Baker that it would not be possible to cross the Asua river until the rainy season was over, and that would not be until December. The Asua was in the direct path of Baker's route to the "great basin of the Nile", some thirty miles to the south, and since Ibrahim was busy collecting ivory, and anything else he could lay his hands on, Baker decided to make a quick reconnaissance down to the river, leaving Florence Baker in the good hands of old Katchiba, who promptly placed her under the protection of a powerful spell.

Baker took three men, a change of clothes, a cooking pot, and four good horses. They rode hard for the first couple of hours, and then came across a herd of magnificent bull elephants. The temptation was too much for Baker, and although his men turned their backs on the whole activity he galloped off, determined to get in a quick pot-shot. After a mile or so of stalking he singled out an immense fellow, rode up to it fast, took a shot and missed, whereupon the bull turned and charged. Baker's horse, Filfil, was no hunter, and an angry bull elephant was more than it could face. It panicked, reared, and threw Baker before turning tail and going off at full pelt, with the elephant—luckily for Baker—in hot pursuit.

Baker was left "in a most inglorious position", his rifle and compass somewhere amongst the high grass. After a bit of searching he found both, but Filfil was nowhere to be seen. He limped back to his three despondent men, shamefaced, resolving to improve his ways. "As a rule hunting during the march should be avoided, and I had now paid dearly for the indiscretion." It was a pious hope if nothing else.

They camped in the open that night, finding a dry plateau of rock where there was wood for a fire and clear rainwater to drink in the rock's hollows. It was the sort of picturesque lair that Baker found most satisfying, and he slept like a romantic hero, beneath the velvet African sky, ready for action.

". . . my couch was quickly and simply made upon the hard rock, softened by the addition of an armful of green boughs, upon which I laid an untanned ox-hide and spread my Scotch plaid. My cap formed my pillow, I packed my cartouche pouch and belt within it, and my handy little Fletcher rifle lay by my side beneath the plaid, together with my hunting knife. This was an exceedingly practical arrangement, as in case of an alarm I rose from my couch armed, capped and belted at a moment's notice."

There were no alarms, only the cries of the nocturnal hunting beasts and their victims sounding within the uninhabited open plains of the Obbo.

On the next day they arrived at a miserably dirty town called Farajoke, and here again Baker was told by all and sundry that it was quite impossible to cross the Asua whilst it was in full flood. So he decided to leave at once and not bother with any further reconnoitering. The truth was that he was far from happy at the thought of his wife at the tender mercies of both Ibrahim's and his own armed ruffians. The thirty miles back were covered in one day, and Baker discovered that his fears were groundless.

"I found my wife looking remarkably well, and regularly installed *at home*. Several fat sheep were tied by the legs to pegs in front of the hut; a number of fowls were pecking around the entrance, and my wife awaited me on the threshold with a large pumpkin shell containing a gallon of native beer. *Dulce domum* although but a mud hut the loving welcome made it happier than a palace."

Whilst this was all very cosy it was not actually getting the Bakers anywhere, as Sam realised, even though he tried to disguise the inevitability of being committed to Ibrahim's schedule as a stalemate caused by the rainy season. The rain would have made movement difficult, but it would not have made it impossible. Thus when Ibrahim decided to return to Tarrangolle Baker found it convenient to do likewise. They were blessed by Katchiba for the journey with a great deal of spitting and the blowing of whistles, and supplied with a guide to whom the old chief had granted powers of control over the elements, and set off on 21 May with the whole town turning out to wish them a good journey. This they were granted, the only delay being caused by Baker getting lost for a few hours one evening after he had unsuccessfully tried hunting some giraffe. He seems to have forgotten his stern words to himself about the inadvisability of hunting when on the march, and only comments on the skill needed to get the better of a giraffe. In a few days they were back at Tarrangolle, and began a term in which exasperation and patience were evenly, and intolerably, mixed.

Ibrahim was not going back to Gondokoro until he had scoured the countryside for ivory, cattle and—although Baker doesn't say so—human beings. The terminology, trading party, was a misnomer: Ibrahim's party, like all the Egyptian traders' groups, was an armed force of marauders who whenever they saw the chance pillaged, sacked and captured the helpless African. It made Baker's blood boil to see this going on around him and to be able to do next to nothing about it. He also observed how the basically friendly Latuka were being transformed into a surly, sullen enemy, and knew the outcome could only be the expulsion of Ibrahim's cut-throats from Tarrangolle, and with them his own little expedition.

They tried to make themselves comfortable, uneasy though they were, in Tarrangolle. There was not much to do except hunt a bit and make as much contact as possible with Ibrahim and his personal bodyguard. One character, whom Baker christens Sinbad the Sailor, had travelled widely, and spent most of his idle time telling endless tall stories of his adventures. Sinbad had visited England as a steward on an Egyptian boat, berthing at the London Docks. His experiences were strictly amorous, and on this occasion printable.

"He had been to a ball at an 'English Pasha's in Blackwall' and had succeeded wonderfully with some charming English ladies excessively 'décolletée', upon whom he felt sure he had left a lasting impression as several had fallen in love with him on the spot supposing him to be a Pasha."

By the middle of June, as Baker had foreseen, Ibrahim announced his intention of leaving Tarrangolle and going back to Obbo. The Latuka were making preparations for an attack in no uncertain manner. Baker was bitter about the situation, and wrote sardonically in his journal: "It is remarkably pleasant travelling in the vicinity of the traders, they convert every country into a wasp's nest, they have neither plan of action nor determination, and I, being unfortunately dependent upon their movements, am more like a donkey than an explorer, that is saddled and ridden away at a moment's notice." They left on 23 June, by which time Florence Baker was ill with a bilious fever and had to be carried in a sort of home-made covered wagon.

On most days it rained in torrents. Florence Baker was safe and dry in her shelter, although far from well; Sam was no longer "charmingly wet" but just soaked through, and he cursed the downpours and felt as miserable about them as his men. And there were snakes, driven out of their nests in the rocks, causing panic among both the Africans and the Egyptians. Baker records killing an enormous puff adder, almost six feet long and fifteen inches in girth; and when he set about dissecting it, all hell broke loose.

"Hardly had I secured the fangs when a tremendous clap of thunder shook the earth. . . . Again the lightening flashed and almost simultaneously a deafening peal roared from the black cloud above us just as I was kneeling over the arch enemy to skin him. He looked so Satanic with his flat head and minute cold grey eye, and scaly hide, with the lightening flashing and the thunder roaring around him. I felt like St Dunstan with the devil, and skinned him."

By the beginning of July they were installed in their old hut in Katchiba's Obbo town. Both were ill of the fever and out of action. Smallpox was ravaging the region and "the natives were dying like flies in winter". The weather was atrociously unhealthy with low dense cloud, a good deal of rain, and a depressing overall dampness in the atmosphere when it wasn't actually raining. The Bakers dosed themselves with herbal medicines and patent medicines, both of which seemed to have had little effect. They also treated their men whenever they were allowed, although most of the irregulars preferred to suffer loudly and take no other medicine but the strong Obbo beer. The boy Saat, however, was always prepared to try a cure from his beloved mistress's hands, although it had to be explained to him that it was not necessary to swallow the wrapping paper also.

It was an unhappy time. The Obbo were harmless enough, but some of their habits were rather distasteful.

"I have had great difficulty in breaking my cow-keeper of his disgusting custom of washing the milk-bowl with cow's urine, and even mixing some with the milk. . . . The Obbo natives wash out their mouths with their own urine."

As Baker noted, the reason for these customs was probably the almost total absence of salt in the country. Knowing why did not help, though, and the Bakers did their own milking, or if this was impossible gave up drinking the beverage.

The waiting, the fevers, the behaviour of Ibrahim's irregulars gave Baker good cause for despair. He reviewed the position, therefore, clarified the dangers and worked out a plan. One danger that could lie ahead worried him most: the present could be coped with, but should Ibrahim move south into Kamrasi's Unyoro in his usual fashion—sacking and pillaging—then Baker knew his expedition would stand very little chance of getting through Unyoro; and to find his great lake Baker had to travel through Kamrasi's kingdom. So he decided he must plan against this all too likely possibility, and his strategy was a simple one. "My plan is to prevail on Ibrahim to commence an ivory trade in Kamrasi's country that might be legitimately conducted, instead of the present atrocious system of robbery and murder." He worked out a route for the trading caravans which presumed the Nyanza would be found, and that from it the Nile would be found to be navigable up to Gondokoro. It was a shot in the dark which was later proved quite practicable. He also reckoned that contact and understanding must be made with Kamrasi personally, and that the barter for ivory would have to be more sophisticated than beads and bracelets; printed cottons and English made clothing, he considered, would be the thing.

Meanwhile there was nothing to do but ride the violent fevers, work on Ibrahim and wait. The journal Baker kept (which he produced in his *The Albert Nyanza*) is very sparse at this time. On 23 August he records the death of his last camel. All his horses were already dead, and only eight donkeys out of twenty-one were still alive. This was not surprising, for the animals came from the dry heat of the Sudan, and it was like planting a desert cactus in a Scottish glen. Almost the next entry, dated 6 October, records: "I have examined my only remaining donkey, he is a picture of misery . . . and is about to start to join his departing comrades. . . . With his loose skin hanging to his withered frame he looked like the British lion on the shield over the door of the Khartoum Consulate. In that artistic effort the lion was equally lean and ragged . . . a pictorial illusion to the smallness of the Consul's pay; the illustration over the shabby gateway utters 'Behold my leanness! £150 per annum!'"

The Consul was, of course, the much misunderstood Petherick. Speke did not deprive him of much of an income at least.

By December Baker was in a more cheerful mood and congratulating himself, and his wife, on having "an extraordinary influence" over Ibrahim and his thugs. The rain had ceased, and Baker's plan to get Ibrahim to go south into Unyoro looked as if it would work. The lack of even a shower was worrying old Katchiba, and for once he seemed stumped for ideas to satisfy his people that things would soon be all right. So he came to Baker and explained his troubles.

"'You don't know my people; if I am fool enough to give them rain before they give me the goats they would let me starve! . . . Do you know, they have positively threatened to kill me unless I bring rain? . . . Have you any rain in your country? How do you bring it? Are you a rainmaker?'"

Baker saw the drift; his advice was being sought on the possibility of rain falling soon.

"'Well, I don't think we shall have any steady rain, but I think we may have a heavy shower in about four days.' 'Just my opinion,' said Katchiba, delighted. 'I will give them in four or five days just one shower.' To give effect to his declaration he gave several toots upon his magic whistle. 'Do you use whistles in your country?' I only replied by giving so shrill and deafening a whistle on my fingers that Katchiba stopped his ears. . . . 'Whistle again,' he said, and once more I performed like the whistle of a locomotive. 'That will do, we shall have it,' said the cunning old rainmaker. . . . In a few days a sudden storm of rain and violent thunder added to Katchiba's renown . . . my whistle was considered infallible."

They set out for Unyoro with Ibrahim's party on 5 January 1864. Both were recovering from fevers; Florence Baker rode an ox, but Baker's animal bolted as they started off and was not seen again. The first day's march of eighteen miles left Baker exhausted, but on the second day he managed to exchange a gun for an ox, and from then on recovered his health and strength rapidly. Another three days of fast travel and they reached the Asua river. Now almost dry it was, Baker saw, an impossible river to ford in full spate, but he wished he had at least visited it during the rainy season; it must have been a glorious spectacle rushing down towards the Nile, "the great drain of the country".

Camp was pitched in the dry bed of the river; there was only a thin shallow stream flowing through the deepest point of the bed. Baker shot an antelope for supper, they built a fire of immense proportions and settled down for a peaceful night's rest. When Baker woke in the morning he was alone with his party. After the first moment of anger and near-panic he discovered that the wretched "Turks" had gone off to raid a village, and quite naturally had thought it wise not to inform Baker of their intentions. The next day they arrived back, having lost their standard bearer but having gained about three hundred head of cattle and a number of slaves.

This must have infuriated Baker, although he doesn't give more than a hint of his feelings. It was precisely the type of behaviour he was trying to stamp out. Luckily the raid was on a Madi village: if it had been on an Unyoro one it could have stopped the whole journey in its tracks. He did not remonstrate with Ibrahim this time, for nothing must be allowed to slow up the journey south. Within a couple of days they were thirty miles beyond the Asua and at Shooa, a mountainous and healthy region. On their way they had seen many burnt-out villages, the work of Speke's and Grant's friend Mahommed Wat-el-Mek, de Bono's agent. Ibrahim told Baker that Shooa was considered by de Bono to be his territory, but Ibrahim had ambitions to exploit the territory and if necessary expel Wat-el-Mek, for Shooa was a land flowing with milk and honey! The people of Shooa were easy to get along with, which meant, so far as Ibrahim was concerned, that they were easy to use. If there had been ivory to be had, then the chances of getting Ibrahim to move on to Unyoro would have been very feeble indeed; as it was, ivory was in short supply, and although Ibrahim's men were anxious—and a little afraid—about that country, greed overcame their fear without much effort. So with Baker in charge they set out from Shooa on 18 January.

This change of situation is mentioned quite casually by Baker. "The Turks knew nothing of the route south, and I accordingly took the lead of the entire party. I had come to a distinct understanding with Ibrahim that Kamrasi's country should belong to *me*; not an act of felony would be permitted; all were to be under my government and I would insure him at least 100 cantars of tusks." As a hundred cantars was ten thousand pounds in weight, it was rather a rash promise, but it probably did the trick of bringing Ibrahim under Baker's command. Baker knew how to mix authority with a little straightforward bribery in the nicest proportions.

The journey into Unyoro was a far from simple matter. Kamrasi's kingdom was bounded by the Nile flowing from Lake Victoria, at the Ripon Falls, into Lake Albert. As we have seen, Speke called this river the Somerset. It could be crossed at only a few places; one of these, the Karuma Falls, was Baker's first objective. They had to cross some pretty terrible country, including a number of swamps, in one of which poor Florence Baker found herself first left on the bank as being too heavy to carry—she was only a small woman—and then carried by her Sam, rather clumsily, it seems.

". . . when in the middle of the swamp the tenacious bottom

gave way, and I sank, and remained immovably fixed, whilst she floundered frog-like in the muddy water. I was extricated by the united efforts of several men and she was landed by being dragged through the swamp."

This was not the first, or the last, somewhat unladylike situation Florence Baker was to experience on this expedition. She took this, and all the others, in her stride, however, dried herself out and got on with the march.

They reached the Somerset River at a point twenty miles to the west of the Karuma Falls. Baker blamed this error in navigation on his guide, who, along with a slave woman called Bacheeta, was in league with Kamrasi's enemy, one Rionga. The whys and wherefores of this Machiavellian plot are hard to come by; Baker seems sure it was a plot, and they were now in Rionga's territory, which might not help them to cross into Kamrasi's. It might have been just bad navigation, for Rionga's people were of no help or hindrance, remaining on their islands in the middle of the two-hundred-yard-wide river and refusing the expedition food or assistance. They pushed on to the Falls, where the first Unyoro Chiefs were met and the strange pantomime of introduction and acceptance began.

This is where Baker had to identify himself with Speke by wearing the sort of suit which he assumed Speke wore (a wrong assumption surely?). At the same time some fine presents for the King were displayed, thus putting the chiefs in a somewhat delicate position. There was no doubt that Kamrasi had been given a nasty fright shortly after Speke and Grant left him two years earlier, accepting into his kingdom those who claimed to be friends of the explorers and finding that they had only come to spy out the land before attacking. When they did, along with Rionga's men, they were beaten off, but at a cost; and Kamrasi had closed his frontiers to trading parties ever since. The false friends were obviously Arabs operating for De Bono; Kamrasi, like most Africans, had difficulty in distinguishing the European from the Arab, much to the former's chagrin.

The chiefs had met Speke and Grant; they were impressed by Baker's resemblance to the former; they were even more impressed by the gorgeous presents so titillatingly placed on show. So they sent a messenger down-country to their king—a three-day journey—telling him about Baker. A wait of six days was something Baker did not intend to put up with. He could not, in fact, for the whole of his expedition was almost without food, and there was nothing behind them but the wilderness they had just traversed. So he threatened to leave, and take his presents with him. Then he said he was quite prepared to come across with his wife and a couple of servants only, and of course the presents. This worked, and in the first darkness the Bakers were ferried to the far bank accompanied by the boy Saat, the old faithful Richarn, and the new faithful Ibrahim.

Once actually amidst the Unyoro, Baker brought into play the full powers of his personality and authority. He upheld the character of the Englishman in general, and, standing facing the chiefs and headmen, declared:

"You MUST trust me, as I trust entirely in you, and have placed myself in your hands; but if you have ever had cause to mistrust a white man, kill me at once!—either kill me, or trust in me, but let there be no suspicions."

Baker reports that the Unyoro seemed pleased with the conversation, as well they might. There was much discussion of Speke and Grant, and Baker discovered that Speke had been nicknamed Mollegge—the bearded one—and Grant rather delightfully Masanga—the elephant's tusk—because of his great height. He also spoke about the finger that Grant had missing (a wound at Lucknow), and this was something they all remembered and nobody else had ever mentioned. Baker writes, "this crowned my success'. Florence and he bedded down for the night on bundles of straw beneath the open sky, watched over in turn by Richarn, Saat and Ibrahim. Things were not going to be very simple, or very pleasant, and they were certainly going to be very slow; but a start had been made.

The next day the Bakers found themselves the centre of attraction for some six hundred Unyoro. It was a fine opportunity to ask questions about the Nyanza, and Baker took it. He ought not to have bothered: not a man, woman or child would

utter a word in reply to his questions. Kamrasi had forbidden
them to speak, or so it appeared by the fact that upon questioning
many would draw a forefinger across the throat and say "Kamrasi". Some of the old men replied with a neat sense of comedy.
"We are children, ask the old people who know the country."
De Bono's gangsters had obviously asked a lot of geographical
questions, and had been given truthful and unsuspecting answers.
From now on the geography of Unyoro was a state secret. Even
Baker decided it was useless to persevere. He turned to the
immediate problems of getting the rest of the expedition across
the river and then marching to Kamrasi's capital.

Baker was beginning to learn how to turn the extreme slowness
of action to advantage. He organised a market and got supplies
ferried across to his starving expedition. Each boat returned with a
few presents for the headsmen, and bearing the gifts one or two
of the expedition's best men. The right sort of interchange was
taking place; Mrs Baker was using the charms of her long blonde
hair to fascinate, Baker was striving manfully to seem patient
and mild. On 29 January the messengers from Kamrasi returned,
and with them were three men of Speke's expedition. Baker was
inspected again and said to be "Speke's own brother", and this
time, when the Unyoro tried to delay, Baker threw an effective
fit of temper, with the result that the rest of the expedition was
allowed across the water. What is more, within two days they
began the march to Kamrasi's palace.

The first days of the march are recorded by Baker with the
prefixes "F. dreadfully ill. F. very ill. F. seriously ill." It was the
beginning of a whole series of fevers for the next six months
which almost killed Florence Baker. Her husband was also ill at
this time, but not so badly, although it put him in a snarling
temper. Kamrasi is called a tyrant, without provocation, and the
Unyoro, who were described upon first meeting as civilised, polite
and clean savages, are now termed filthy, unintelligent brutes.
Baker was a difficult man to share a camp with at times. Eventually they were led to the miserable collection of huts in the middle
of a swamp where Speke and Grant had lived whilst they negotiated their way with Kamrasi. Florence was now better, Baker

was intermittently running fevers. Kamrasi was in his rudimentary palace the other side of the river Kafur, which wandered through the swamp to join the Somerset. He seemed, Baker considered, a most abject coward, terrified of meeting even Baker's relatively weak expedition, delaying the evil moment hour by hour with perfunctory excuses.

There was a good, if bizarre, reason for the King's delaying tactics that later on becomes understandable, as we shall see. Neither Baker nor Ibrahim had any idea of the deception being played on them, which was not surprising. Their main concern was to obtain Kamrasi's blessing to press on to the great lake. Or so it seemed to Baker at the time, albeit his record of events over this period is sketchy, and, for him, not at all clear. When he was ready Kamrasi met the impatient Englishman and received his presents with dignity. The first thing Baker did was to question him about the distance to the lake. Kamrasi's reply was rather staggering: it would take six months, and a man in Baker's condition would never reach it—he would die on the road. The matter was dropped.

Once again the fever gripped both the Bakers. The daily interviews with Kamrasi were purgatorial. The rest of their time was spent prone in their miserable mud hut. They had no quinine left and were therefore entirely at the mercy of the fever running its normal course: a week or so of high temperature for five hours a day. They were also at the mercy of the usual African and Arab stratagems, so that, once Ibrahim had exchanged blood with Kamrasi, Baker was left in the cold. Or, as he put it in somewhat subdued terms: "It was arranged that Ibrahim now belonged to Kamrasi, and that henceforth our parties should be entirely separate."

On 16 February, the Englishman and his young wife were "pictures of despair". On this day also their porters deserted, and it rained until the mud floor of their hut became a quagmire into which Baker sank to the ankles and had hardly enough strength to release himself. They were visited by one of the headsmen, who came to see what he could obtain for himself, told them that the lake was only ten days away, and was suitably rewarded.

The next meeting with Kamrasi was a bad-tempered event. Baker taxed the King with deceiving him about the distance to the lake. Kamrasi became cross and admitted it was only twenty days away, then asked for Baker's little double-barrelled Fletcher rifle. Baker turned on his heel and left the man. As ever, this blunt behaviour produced some kingly favours, and the Bakers were allowed to move out of the swamp into the higher ground of Kamrasi's palace.

Within a few days they were feeling better. They were also just about alone. On 21 February Baker records bleakly: "Ibrahim and his men marched this morning on their return to Karuma, leaving me here with my little party of thirteen men." It was the sort of circumstance that Baker really rather delighted in, as we have seen. Now his only thought was procuring porters and marching to the basin of the Nile. Kamrasi was bribed to help with a gun and some beads, and much to Baker's disgust produced the watch and the beautiful Blissett rifle which he had filched from Speke. The watch "was dead" and the rifle was without ammunition. Baker could not, so he said, do anything about either unless Kamrasi left them with him. This the King was not prepared to do, reckoning quite correctly that Baker would hold on to them and see they were returned to their rightful owner. This, although Baker was not to know it, could never have happened. In six months Speke would be dead.

When they set off a few days later the signs of something being got up against them were in the air. Kamrasi came to see them on their way and immediately began demanding everything he set eyes on, including the Turkish handkerchief Florence Baker wore upon her head. Baker did not like the atmosphere one little bit and tried to take his leave, but Kamrasi had one further request. He would let Baker off the hook on one condition. ". . . you must leave your wife with me!"

Baker's own description of this "infamous proposal" cannot be bettered, as we shall see. His wrath was terrible, and made more so by the revolver that he was pointing at the king. Mrs Baker joined in, followed by her servant woman, Bacheeta. Kamrasi was both amazed and overawed. He had really meant no harm.

It was his custom to give wives to his visitors, he thought Baker might have had no objection to giving Mrs Baker away, exchange was no robbery, but he did not mean to offend, so please no more fuss, it will never be mentioned again. With this apology, Baker was allowed to start, being joined by about three hundred Unyoro warriors as an escort. "A Satanic escort", in fact, as they wore animal skins with the tails of cows strapped on behind, antelope horns fitted upon their foreheads, and false beards.

The march was a harrowing one through flat marshland beneath a broiling sun, surrounded by the half-crazed satanic escort—they were drinking large amounts of strong beer—with Baker totally unsure if he was being taken by the correct route and Mrs Baker full of fears that the mad escort might suddenly snatch her and take her to their King. Then whilst crossing a swamp, which meant running across a carpet of water grass and weeds, Florence Baker was seen to stop, turn purple in the face, and begin literally to sink into the watery ground. Just in time she was pulled clear but lay as if dead, her body as taut as a wire rope, her eyes wide open. It was a severe sunstroke.

Thus she remained for five days, being carried on a litter during the march and watched over nightly by a sleepless Baker. On the dawn of the sixth day she startled Baker by saying "Thank God", woke up, and then lapsed into the jabberwock of madness. That evening it seemed she was all but dead. "My men put a new handle to the pickaxe that evening, and sought for a dry spot to dig her grave." Baker slept for the first time that night for seven nights, and woke in the morning to see Florence calm and still, lying in what seemed the final peace of death. He bent over her in sorrow, only to see that she was sleeping naturally, her breathing normal. She opened her eyes and they were clear. As Baker remarks, "God alone knows what helped us."

They rested for two days and then continued, carrying Florence on a litter. Their first stop was a rather pleasant village, and although Baker's guides had been telling him for some days that he was near to the lake, he had hardly taken notice of them. It was not surprising, of course, for his wife's illness had driven the purpose of his exploration from his mind; anyway, to take what his guides said as truth would have been rash. So the long range of mountains just discernible to the west he took to be the near boundary of his goal. No, the chief guide told him, what you see is the range to the west of the lake; the far side. The lake itself was but a short march from the village. Baker hardly dared believe when he and Florence started out the next morning, 14 March 1864. They came to the top of a granite cliff; there some fifteen hundred feet below them was the great sheet of water. Baker was humble in his triumph, his wife exhausted and grateful to be alive. He meant to give three cheers, but instead could only reflect on the vanity of man in searching for the Nile sources for so many hundreds of years.

His Unyoro guides stood looking down with him at a sight they knew well. They had never sought the sources of the Nile, they were indifferent to the ambitions of the curiously minded, vain European. To them the only mysteries were at the other end of the Nile, the sea into which the river flowed, the strange white man who had arrived among them coming down the river after crossing the mythical sea. They led Baker down to the shore, he rushed into the lake and drank deeply, if perhaps not wisely. A little later Baker's irregulars drifted down, led by Richarn and Saat. They were "perfectly astounded at the appearance of the lake . . . two of them had already seen the sea at Alexandria and they unhesitatingly declared that this was the sea, but that it was not salt". Then Baker called the lake the Albert N'yanza and rested in the satisfaction of a job completed.

That night the little expedition had a feast in honour of the discovery, during which Baker made a slightly tactless speech, reminding the irregulars of their dilatory behaviour in the past twelve months and pointing out that if they had done what they were told always the Albert N'yanza would have been reached a lot sooner. However, all was forgiven, Mrs Baker was restored to health, there was plenty to eat and drink, and come to that the irregulars were willing to forgive Baker his omissions. They told him "Thank Allah" and started on the meal.

"At sunrise on the following morning I took the compass and . . . went to the borders of the lake to survey the country."

Viewed through his powerful telescope the scene took Baker's breath away. Like Speke seeing Lake Victoria for the first time, the knowledge that he was the first European to see the Albert N'yanza, to set foot on its shore, threw Baker into a romantic rapture. Pride at his achievement was mixed with a poetic latitude for the facts. "Here was the great basin of the Nile that received EVERY DROP OF WATER [Baker's capitals], even from the passing shower to the roaring mountain torrent that drained from Central Africa towards the North. This was the great reservoir of the Nile." Baker goes on for some pages in this fashion. Mostly it was intelligent guesswork; it was also a hymn to the practical function of exploration. Only Florence Baker, standing by his side whilst the conquered territory was being observed, is, unfortunately and unintentionally, reduced to a slightly less than splendid dignity by the rhetorical flourish of Baker's vision. "My wife, who had followed me so devotedly, stood by my side pale and exhausted—a wreck upon the shores of the great Albert Lake that we had so long striven to reach."

Having made his sketches, taken readings, made measurements, Baker was anxious to press for Gondokoro. If he could get there before the very end of April the traders' boats would be available to take them up the Nile to Cairo. Otherwise it would mean a six months' wait. To get back to Gondokoro was not all that simple, particularly as Baker was intent on boating up the lake to the point where the Somerset river (the Victoria Nile) ran into the Albert N'yanza. To organise two canoes of the right size with boatmen to paddle them took eight days, and a pretty miserable time was had by all during this wait, the whole expedition, from the boy Saat to the toughest woman cook, being laid low with a local fever.

With typical ingenuity Baker built a cabin of reeds and ox-hide on the larger canoe so that the convalescing Mrs Baker would not have to suffer rain or sun, then they set off in fine style. The first day on the lake went like a dream; they beached in darkness near a village, and the boatmen strolled inland to collect food for the morrow. It was too much to expect that things would go smoothly for long, and by the morning Baker discovered that the boatmen had deserted, the village was nothing but three fishing huts, there was not a soul to be seen anywhere, and his own men claimed they had no idea how to paddle a canoe. Baker congratulated himself that the paddles had been well guarded—otherwise they certainly would have vanished with the boatmen—and set about teaching his irregulars to propel the canoes. It took time, and was at first a matter for tears and laughter. "Pull they certainly did, but—ye gods who watch over boats!—round and round we pirouetted, the canoes waltzing and polkaing together in their great ballroom, the Albert N'yanza."

Then it rained; they managed to go forward a few miles before beaching. Baker set about making rudders out of two of the paddles. With a rudder he would have some say in the direction of his own canoe, and he hoped that Richarn would learn to steer the other. His men took shelter from the rain. They were a sorry sight:

"They were perfectly apathetic with despair, as their ridiculous efforts at paddling had completely extinguished all hope within them. They were quite resigned to their destiny, and considered themselves as sacrificed to geography."

Baker chivvied them along on the next morning, and by the end of the day they were managing to steer straight and paddle with reasonable efficiency. Soon after this they ran into a storm. They were really lucky to escape with their lives here, although Baker treats the occasion as just another dramatic adventure.

After the storm the journey was literally plain sailing. Baker calls it monotonous, although the presence of herds of hippopotomi and elephants bathing on the shores enlivened the scene on some days. Strangely enough, Baker resisted the temptation to have "a pot shot", or possibly his chaps had grown wise to his weakness and kept the canoes at a long range. On the thirteenth day of the voyage they floated through a vast mass of vegetation into the township of Magungo, where the river Somerset sluggishly discharged into the Albert Lake. Some eighteen miles north the White Nile could be clearly seen flowing out from the lake, and Baker knew that if he could reach it with his boats he would be back at Gondokoro in a matter of days. It was a

tantalising objective, but he put it on one side. He had promised
Speke that he would thoroughly explore the Somerset from the
lake to the Karuma Falls, and Baker was not a man to go back
on his word. He knew what it was likely to mean. ". . . although
by this circuitous route I might lose the boats from Gondokoro
and become a prisoner in Central Africa, ill and without quinine,
for another year." He put the choice and its risk to his wife, and
without hesitation she agreed that the promise to Speke must be
kept.

They were in the most deplorably unhealthy country. A
marsh of tall grass enclosed the river on both sides. It was always
raining, and the Somerset itself was foul smelling from the dense
islands of decaying vegetation floating on its almost still waters.
Both the Bakers were too ill to do anything but totter into their
canoe and lie down as still as logs whilst they were paddled
extremely slowly up the river. The men also were a sorry sight.
". . . looking back to the canoe that followed in our wake, I
observed all my men sitting crouched together sick and dis-
spirited, looking like departed spirits being ferried across the
melancholy Styx."

Two days of this, and they heard the thunder of a great
waterfall. By a dint of persuasion, and the promise of some beads,
Baker got their canoe to within three hundred yards of the
majestic fall. He called it the Murchison Falls, and thought it
quite rightly to be the greatest waterfall of the Nile. He was
also impressed by the huge numbers of crocodile lying on a near-
by sandbank, and when they made for the water could not resist
the chance to use the little double-barrelled Fletcher rifle on one
immense brute. His aim was true and the crocodile dropped dead,
but at the same time the sudden noise of the rifleshot caused the
hired boatmen to take cover in the bottom of the canoe. They
had never heard a gun fired before, and were naturally terrified.
Baker hardly helped matters by firing off the other barrel. The
canoe was out of control and thrown into a bank of reeds. Here it
disturbed the slumbers of a very large bull hippo who promptly
charged the offending object, lifting it half out of the water.
There were, even Baker admits, a few moments of panic before

they righted themselves and the angry hippo submerged and disappeared. Then Baker stopped to look at and consider the number of crocodile heads rising out of the water in anticipation. It was a sobering moment. "Fine fun it would have been for these monsters . . . the fat black woman, Karka, would have been a dainty morsel."

What he does not admit is the fact that once again his propensity to blaze away at the nearest animal target all but led to disaster. Florence Baker was probably used to this somewhat disconcerting habit of her husband's, but even so one can only hope that she scolded him about this occasion and nagged him not to do it again.

At the Murchison Falls they said goodbye to their canoes and, led by a deputation from the island town of Patooan, followed the course of the river by land until they came to the island in the centre of the river, one hundred and fifty yards wide and about half a mile long. They were ferried to this long high street, shown a dilapidated hut and left. Both were still far from well, with the fever still on them. That night it rained as usual, and the roof gave no protection; ill and tired, they just lay while the rain poured down on them. Baker was stoical about the situation. "Our servants and people had, like all natives, made themselves much more comfortable than their employers, nor did they attempt to interfere with our misery in any way until summoned to appear at sunrise."

They lay in their stinking hut on Patooan for days, virtually prisoners of the frightened Unyoro. Kamrasi was in the middle of one of the many wars between himself and a couple of neighbouring tribes: there was little food to be had, and not a chance of obtaining porters to go in any direction. "There was no end to the difficulties and trouble in this horrible country." It was a cry from the heart. However, weak and ill as he was, Baker had no intention of being trapped on a poverty-stricken island. By now dreams of making Gondokoro in time for the boats had faded, and it was impossible to go north through Kamrasi's enemies anyway. Or rather, if he had been fit and well he would have risked it, without porters, as a forced march. But both

Florence and he were too weak to walk more than a quarter of a mile without fainting from exhaustion. So he thought to get his expedition taken to Kamrasi's capital. There at least they might be more comfortable.

The headman of Patooan was in fact only too happy to get rid of his prisoners, and escorted them across to the mainland, dumped them without ceremony in a deserted village, and left them after promising to send messages to the King. Here they remained for two months, living on "a mess of black porridge ... that no English pig would condescend to notice ..." and a spinach-like plant that grew among the wilderness of rank grass. The whole area was lifeless and deserted, for Kamrasi's war had put paid to the normal way of life. For most of the time the Bakers were too ill to do anything but lie and dream of the good things of England ... "an English beef-steak and a bottle of pale ale". They were obviously suffering from malnutrition which, coupled with the fever, left them convinced they would be dead within a short time.

Although Baker writes that this was their mood, inactive, fatalistic, without hope, it was not entirely the truth. He never gave up scheming to get the expedition led, and indeed carried, to Kamrasi; messengers went back and forth all the time. In the end the usual show of "white man's temper" worked. If, stated Baker, the King requires me to be a friend and an ally against his enemies, then why ever leave me in these terrible surroundings to live like a wretched beggar? This is no way to treat a man who is quite as powerful as your king, and who comes from a country that is the greatest in the world. I have had enough of this and demand to be taken to this bad-mannered coward you call your King. As ever, this worked; the King sent an escort and gave Baker a token of his friendship. This was, rather neatly, two pages of the English Church service translated into a local tongue by a German missionary, with some notes in the margin in Speke's handwriting.

When they arrived at Kamrasi's movable capital, they found ten of Ibrahim's party waiting to greet them. These "Turks" had been left behind as hostages; they were delighted to meet up with

Baker's men, and amazed to find the Bakers alive. Rumour had reached them of Mrs Baker's death weeks back, and of Baker's soon after. They came to pay their respects, kissing Florence Baker's hand and exclaiming quite rightly, "By Allah, no woman in the world had a heart so tough as to dare to face what she had gone through. Thank Allah, be grateful to Allah." It was a warming welcome and it lifted the Bakers' spirits no end. They felt that after all they might live to see England again.

No sooner were they settled in the hut given them, than much to their surprise a clownish, undignified Kamrasi appeared. Baker was perplexed at the change in the King's behaviour, the lack of formality. He reproached the King for his recent unfriendliness and received the reply that *he* was not the real king but only his younger brother. It had been a complete deception, but one that Baker had been told about by the servant woman, Bacheeta, as he recalled. Understandably he had paid little attention to Bacheeta's words, as she was always grumbling about something or somebody. However, from this time on Bacheeta was paid attention to—much to her delight.

After this little pantomime in falsehood the expedition was looked after quite reasonably, and after the usual African formal haggling—rather like the game of consequences—Baker was introduced to the real Kamrasi. He was only mildly impressed by the King, although the King and his subjects were completely bowled over by Baker, who had attired himself in a full-dress Highland costume of the Athole tartan—an outfit he was rather surprisingly carrying around central Africa with him. (The effect must have been surrealistic. There are times when Baker's behaviour is wistfully reminiscent of Beachcomber's Big White Carstairs.)

Taking his clue from Speke—who believed that Kamrasi's family must have originally come from the Semitic tribes of the north—Baker questioned the King about his ancestry, but discovered only that Kamrasi's grandfather had the unlikely name of Cherrybambi. All the King wished to speak of were his fears and anxieties for the security of his kingdom. He was certainly in an unenviable position, as Speke had discovered, with wars of long standing between himself and Mtesa, Rionga and Fowooka flaring up along his borders. His main attitude was one of panic. Beneath his large, dignified exterior a small, frightened man was trying to get out. Naturally he tried to inveigle Baker in his schemes to rout his enemies and naturally he had no success. Then by chance Baker took over the situation.

It all began one evening with the news of an impending attack by Fowooka, plus the armed irregulars of the trader De Bono led by Mahommed Wat-el-Mek. Kamrasi had no appetite for a fight against the traders' guns, and, dressed like a rather exotic long distance runner, he was prepared for headlong flight. Baker found the business laughable and took control, hoisting the Union Jack—on the flagpole already erected in his little court-yard—and telling Kamrasi that he was now under its protection and that he, Baker, would defend him from attack. Then he got together a party of his own and Kamrasi's men and sent them as emissaries to the enemy camp. The men came back with a group of De Bono's irregulars, who made the journey primarily to see if Baker was really alive. They quickly found out that he was, and very active into the bargain. Beneath the old flag in his courtyard he gave them a lecture to the effect that Unyoro was now under British protection, and Baker as the British representa-tive had given the trading rights in Unyoro to Ibrahim. De Bono's men were suitably impressed, for Baker was already a legendary figure, and seemingly indestructible. They took the message back to Mahommed, who promptly dropped all his aggressive intentions against Kamrasi and instead turned his coat and attacked his ally, Fowooka.

It was all highly satisfactory for Kamrusi in particular, who waited until Mahommed's party left and then moved against the demoralised Fowooka. Complete victory was achieved, and Kamrasi's army returned with a herd of goats and a large number of women and children. (It was always a case of women and children first when the spoils of battle were divided. There were no men taken prisoner. The old men were left to starve, the others were quickly killed.) Some of the women were the royal wives, one of whom was recognised by the complaining Bacheeta as being her former mistress. The Bakers did their best to see that these captives were treated with reasonable humanity, although they were not able to stop the murder of a number of useless older women. Compared to Burton, Speke or Grant, Baker was a model of how to make friends and influence African leaders. His methods were instinctive, based on sound common sense and carried out in the absolute belief that he was superior in courage and intellect to the African. Most significantly, and unlike the other three explorers, he never allowed his wife or himself to get involved in the affairs of the African on their terms: his involvement was strictly on his terms only. (And he never allowed his arms to be impounded as did Speke and Grant. Kamrasi suggested such a thing once only. He received a short, rude reply. Baker does not give his actual words.)

Kamrasi was now in a seventh heaven of security; he begged Baker never to leave him. Baker made it quite clear that he would only stay for the next six months; it was a better spot than Gondokoro, which wasn't saying much, but Gondokoro had nothing to recommend it until the boats arrived next February. Kamrasi's capital, called Kisoona, was a wretched place, in fact. Surrounded by high grass and swamp, a collection of wood and reed huts that were always being accidentally set on fire, a noisy dirty town where the men only too often spent the nights singing and drinking. (The women, who did all the work in the fields, were naturally tired at night and slept.) The Bakers had made themselves a comparatively fine town residence in Kisoona, extending their hut by a couple of extra rooms and placing a stockade around their courtyard and garden. To minimise the risk of fire—Baker was literally sitting on his supply of gunpowder—the huts within a thirty yard circumference of his stockade were pulled down, which made life a lot quieter also.

Here Baker became the power behind Kamrasi's throne, the great white father of the Unyoro. He also had Ibrahim's ten irregulars to control, for whilst his own chaps had learnt, more or less, how to behave themselves, the Turks were still pretty hopelessly the victims of their own uncontrollable tempers. Always

H

ready to take offence, for ever bursting with misconceived pride, quite unable to resist an opportunity to bully and steal, Baker was endlessly rescuing them from fraught situations of their own making. He was also steadily bringing them under control, a process which was helped by his discovery that the Turks were down to their last five rounds of ammunition per man, and at the rate they banged away on any old excuse they would soon be carrying their guns as an empty threat. He told the leading Turk that if they continued to behave so stupidly he would withdraw his protection, and Master Turk had better think of the consequences. They did, so far as they could, and mended their ways considerably. Of course, Baker also made quite sure that Kamrasi knew how well armed and supplied were the Turks and his own men. When the King showed signs of getting beyond himself, he was quickly brought to heel. "I advised Kamrasi not to talk too big, as he had lately seen what only ten guns had effected in the fight with Fowooka, and he might imagine the results that would occur should he even hint at hostility (with the Turks). . . . The gallant Kamrasi turned almost green at the bare suggestion of this possibility."

Kamrasi was a memorable coward, as Baker was to discover yet again. On 6 September intelligence was brought to Kisoona that Mtesa was marching towards them intent on devouring Kamrasi's kingdom. Bacheeta had an explanation for Mtesa's attack, gleaned by her own one-woman intelligence service. This was simply that Mtesa considered Kamrasi was stopping Baker's expedition from visiting Uganda with many valuable presents. Baker thought Bacheeta probably right, for she ". . . picked up information in the camps almost as correctly as a Times Correspondent". Whatsoever the real explanation, it put poor Kamrasi into a state of panic, although Baker saw things rather differently. "This was very enjoyable," he wrote at the thought of a fight. However, he could not get Kamrasi to march to the Karuma Falls region and there do battle against the Waganda on favourable ground for defence. All Kamrasi was intent on doing was to get to his island sanctuary in the Nile, east of the Falls, without a fight. Not even Baker could put courage into him; Kisoona was burnt down, and Baker and the Turks left to fend for themselves.

The situation became extremely confused, but Baker, as one would expect, remained calm and made his plans. He sent four men off to Shooa, some eighty miles north, to contact Ibrahim and get him to rendezvous at the Karuma Falls; then he got his twenty-odd men to march north-east in open order, protecting the expedition. Mtesa's army was a few miles from them; Kamrasi and his non-combatant army were scampering along, with their women, children and herds trying to keep up, a few miles ahead of Baker. His expedition formed a small but strong rearguard. Baker had decided, however, not to fight Mtesa unless attacked. Disgusted with Kamrasi's headlong flight and the total disorder around him, he felt he no longer had any obligation to help the cowardly King. It was anyway becoming impossible to know where Kamrasi's horde was—or where it was going.

For days the fog of a chaotic withdrawal closed in on Baker. It was often quite impossible to find the right path, and they were forced to stay put until guides could be found or the route worked out by trial and error. On one occasion the stalwart Richarn was lost, believed killed, whilst trying to discover where they were; he turned up a week later, having been wandering towards the Nile, more or less blind among the tall grass.

By the time Richarn came back from the dead and found Baker the expedition was completely divorced from Kamrasi, and settled in another deserted village called Foweera, a few miles from the Karuma Falls. Mtesa was about three miles away, and Baker was prepared for an attack. He had twenty-odd guns, Mtesa had three or four guns but no bullets, only powder. (Kamrasi's brother was in the same position, and Baker had been told of a skirmish between the Wunyoro and the Waganda where the guns were aimed and the result was a lot of smoke but no fire). Nevertheless, it was not a very pleasant situation, and Mtesa's reputation as a bloodthirsty monster was well known to Baker—whatever Speke may have told him suggesting the contrary. Possibly Mtesa's intentions were more mercenary than warlike, and that Baker considered to be a frightful thought.

It would mean being Mtesa's "guest", as Speke and Grant were, for as long as the Uganda King felt like playing the host.

They were saved from this ominous predicament by Ibrahim and his hundred thieves arriving at the Karuma Falls. Mtesa's spies got wind of this, and by the time Ibrahim and Baker met, on 20 September, the Uganda army had retreated twenty miles, and was obviously going back to their own country as fast as they could. The meeting with Ibrahim was poignant in more ways than one. It marked the beginning of the end of the Bakers' exploration, and it brought them the first contact they had had with England for over two years, in the form of letters sent on from Khartoum. In the mail bag was a letter from Speke, sending cuttings, about his discovery of the Nile at Lake Victoria from the *Illustrated London News* and *Punch*. "For a whole day," Baker wrote, "I revelled in the luxury of letters and newspaper."

Ibrahim had also given the Bakers up for dead at one time, now he ". . . was astounded at our success, but rather shocked at our personal appearance". Baker says that Florence and he were thin and haggard; so much so that the few clothes they had left hung on them like on scarecrows, and Baker had to vie with Speke and hold his trousers up with string. (Speke always used tape, he never trusted belts or braces.) But things were now turning for the better; Ibrahim had brought cloth for clothes for both of them, as well as honey, rice and coffee. After a couple of days they moved camp to a healthier spot nearer the river; and, of course, they were visited by a grateful, warlike Kamrasi. Ibrahim was presented with an immense quantity of ivory, and his men hired to make war on another of Kamrasi's many enemies.

It was here that, whilst these little wars were going on, Baker started the "Central African Unyoro Potato-Whisky Company, Unlimited", cured himself of the fever for good by drinking hot toddy, and quite accidentally got Kamrasi addicted to the drink. The King was also delighted with the Paris fashions in the *Illustrated London News*, which were cut out and given him as pin-ups. It is not recorded if he became addicted to these also and tried to dress his twenty-stone-plus wives in a like manner.

With Ibrahim's guns added to his strength, the fair-weather warrior King was doing very well in the wars, and had decided to make his capital at Baker and Ibrahim's camp, where he strutted around in great style, liberally served by newly captured slaves. Now and again one of the slaves attempted to escape, and when caught was promptly executed and the body strung up on a tall tree for all to see, the slaves being driven to the spot as a warning of what would happen to them should they try to run away. It was not exactly a happy idea but, as Baker acknowledges, his own countrymen did not behave so differently. "Superlatively brutal as this appeared, I could not help reflecting that our public executions in England convey a similar moral; the only difference being in the conduct of the women; the savages having to be driven to the sight as witnesses, while European females throng curiously to such disgusting exhibitions."

By the middle of November both Ibrahim and Baker had had enough of Kamrasi; Ibrahim had also collected more ivory than he had porters to carry. They decided to leave for Shooa, much to the King's anguish, an anguish that did not overpower his avariciousness, however. Once again he begged of Baker: ". . . as you are going home where you can obtain all you require . . . give me before you leave the little double-barrelled rifle that you PROMISED ME . . .", and just as firmly once again Baker refused. It was Kamrasi's last fling; upon being refused he went into the sulks, tried to hinder Ibrahim obtaining enough porters, and would have nothing more to do with anybody.

On 17 November 1863 the explorers and the trader moved off. King Kamrasi and his subjects ignored their going, a feat of some difficulty, considering that the combined expeditions now numbered a thousand people. A brightly coloured column spread out over five hundred yards when the going was smooth, elongating to almost a mile when hills were being climbed. Ibrahim led, the Bakers brought up the rear. In between them were porters carrying vast burdens on their heads, sometimes three or four heads sharing a long and heavy collection of ivory tusks. The women, carrying their smallest offspring, drifted up and down the line of march, accompanied by the children who could walk holding on to each other in an unruly crocodile. The servants and what can be best described as camp followers, loaded with household impedimenta, always fell to the back, where they were constantly harried by Baker—a necessary operation, as otherwise this group would lose the column, owing to its propensity for short, unofficial halts. The armed irregulars formed a thin black line on either side of the column, their guns carried at every conceivable angle. There was a great deal of noise. Conversations were generally shouting matches, the singing of songs was rampant, never in unison and often to the accompaniment of the available pots and pans. Quarrels singed up and down the line, those that developed into fights being put down by the irregulars with the ferocity of modern riot police.

For five days they marched in this manner until they reached their main station at Shooa. Here they stayed until the next February, doing very little. Baker describes his activities as ". . . rambling about the neighbourhood, ascending the mountain, making duplicates of my maps, and getting information". Ibrahim's activities were not so peaceful, however. With Mahommed, De Bono's leader, who was stationed about twenty-five miles away, he raided and pillaged. "For many miles circuit from Shooa the blackened ruins of villages and deserted fields bore witness to the devastation committed." There was nothing Baker could do to stop this rape of a country, although he resolved to get the British Government interested once he arrived home. The only hopeful sign was the fact that some African chiefs were beginning to be able to take care of their tribes, and by retreating into the mountains with their cattle, so that the Turks followed, proved themselves superior on ground of their own choosing. One such chief, called Werdella, gave the traders a really bloody nose. When Baker was told of the fight by Ibrahim he reacted in his usual hearty, if rather tactless, manner. "'Bravo Werdella!' I exclaimed. He deserved the Victoria Cross."

Whilst all this was going on, Mrs Baker made a home and became a foster parent to six small African slave children. It was an idyllic time, with Sam making bows and arrows for the boys and teaching them to shoot straight. Florence lavished a maternal affection upon her charges; they were scrubbed clean, dressed and decorated with red ochre, fed regularly and put to bed after an evening's games and dances. When the time came to leave them behind the scene was heartbreaking, with the youngest crying: "Where are you going?" and: "Take me with you, Lady."

The Bakers' expedition, with some of Ibrahim's party, turned their backs on the south and firmly struck out for Gondokoro. Within a day they were at the place where the Italian, Miani, had carved his name on a tree. From here they followed the route which Speke and Grant had taken just over two years earlier, following the course of the Nile, and like the two other explorers marvelling at the beauty of the countryside. Within a couple of marches of Gondokoro they were attacked by a group of Bari. "It was child's play," writes Baker. The Bari, although looking extremely dangerous, never really got to grips with their objective, preferring to dart back and forth, firing badly aimed and slow flying arrows. A number of the Bari were killed, but Baker and Ibarhim suffered no casualties.

On or about 21 March 1865 they entered the slave station of Gondokoro. It was quite an occasion, with Baker giving three cheers for old England and three more for the Sources of the Nile, whilst his men fired into the air—sometimes more horizontally than vertically—and the traders in the station marching out to greet them firing with reckless abandon into the ground. Nobody was hurt, by some miracle. Once this celebration was over the Bakers set out in search for their boats and their letters, their newspapers and their supplies. They found nothing. "We had long since been given up as dead by the inhabitants of Khartoum, and by all those who understood the difficulties and danger of the country. We were told that some people had suggested that we might possibly have gone to Zanzibar, but the general opinion was that we had all been killed. At this cold and barren reply I felt almost choked."

Baker, as we have seen, was not the man to remain sunk in despair for any length of time. By the next day he had pounced on a boat about to return empty to Khartoum. The reason why a boat was preparing to return to Khartoum empty comprised the snag in his arrangements. The plague had struck Khartoum, and naturally nobody much wanted to go there at that moment. The boat itself had carried men down from the stricken city, men who had died on the way. Baker knew, however, that he must take the risk: there was no point in remaining in the awfulness of Gondokoro. He had the boat scrubbed out with boiling water and sand, and fumigated with tobacco burnt within the cabin. When they left Gondokoro the plague had started there also.

As they sailed away from the slave station, the Union Jack flying from the masthead, crowds lined the Nile's banks to wave them farewell. It was a royal departure, the end of a remarkable journey, a triumph of courage and perseverance. Baker wrote of it with quiet humility.

"What were our feelings at that moment? Overflowing with gratitude to a Divine Providence that had supported us in sickness, and guided us through all dangers. . . . I felt no triumph, but with a feeling of calm contentment and satisfaction we floated down the Nile. My great joy was in the meeting that I had contemplated with Speke in England . . ."

*   *   *

The voyage on the Nile to Khartoum was a bitter one. After a week's sailing the plague broke out amongst the few remaining irregulars on the boat. Two men died, others were ill but recovered, and then, just when the disease seemed to have run its course, the much loved boy, Saat, became ill. There was nothing the Bakers could do but watch him die. They buried him on the shore by a group of mimosa trees.

They reached Khartoum on 5 May 1865, where they were given a splendid reception. It all turned to ashes when Baker heard of the death of Speke. He made up his mind to leave the place as soon as possible. Khartoum was in a chaotic state, but somehow he managed to get the wheels moving and, taking Richarn and his wife with them, the Bakers left the plague-ridden city within a week. By the beginning of June they were in Suez, where they found an English hotel, and in it ". . . a bar for refreshments with Allsopps Pale Ale on draught with an ice accompaniment. What an Elysium! The beds had *sheets* and *pillow cases*! neither of which I had possessed for years."

From Suez they went to Cairo, where the Richarns were found a situation which could not have been more appropriate: as servants to the manager of the already famous Shepheard's Hotel. They said goodbye and caught the boat train.

"I had left Richarn and none remained of my people. The past appeared like a dream. . . . Had I really come from the Nile Sources? It was no dream. A witness sat before me; a face still young, but bronzed like an Arab with years of exposure to a burning sun; the devoted companion of my pilgrimage to whom I owed success and life—my wife."

SAMUEL WHITE BAKER

from

The Albert N'yanza Great basin of the Nile
(1866)

THERE IS A rule to be observed in hunting the giraffe on horse-back: the instant he starts, he must be pressed—it is the speed that tells upon him, and the spurs must be at work at the very commencement of the hunt, and the horse pressed along at his best pace; it must be a race at top speed from the start, but, should the giraffe be allowed the slightest advantage for the first five minutes, the race will be against the horse.

I was riding "Filfil", my best horse for speed, but utterly useless for the gun. I had a common regulation sword hanging on my saddle in lieu of the long Arab broadsword that I had lost at Obbo, and starting at full gallop at the same instant as the giraffes, away we went over the beautiful park. Unfortunately Richarn was a bad rider, and I, being encumbered with a rifle, had no power to use the sword. I accordingly trusted to ride them down and to get a shot, but I felt that the unsteadiness of my horse would render it very uncertain. The wind whistled in my ears as we flew along over the open plain. The grass was not more than a foot high, and the ground hard;—the giraffes about four hundred yards distant steaming along, and raising a cloud of dust from the dry earth, as on this side of the mountains there had been no rain. Filfil was a contradiction; he loved a hunt and had no fear of wild animals, but he went mad at the sound of a gun. Seeing the magnificent herd of about fifteen giraffes before him, the horse entered into the excitement and needed no spur—down a slight hollow, flying over the dry buffalo holes, now over a dry watercourse and up the incline on the other side—then again on the level, and the dust in my eyes from the cloud raised by the giraffes showed that we were gaining in the race; *miseri-*

cordia!—low jungle lay before us—the giraffes gained it, and spurring forward through a perfect cloud of dust now within a hundred yards of the game we shot through the thorny bushes. In another minute or two I was close up, and a splendid bull giraffe was crashing before me like a locomotive obelisk through the mimosas, bending the elastic boughs before him in his irresistible rush, which sprang back with a force that would have upset both horse and rider had I not carefully kept my distance. The jungle seemed alive with the crowd of orange red, the herd was now on every side, as I pressed the great bull before me. Oh for an open plain! I was helpless to attack, and it required the greatest attention to keep up the pace through the thick mimosas without dashing against their stems and branches. The jungle became thicker, and although I was in the middle of the herd and within ten yards of several giraffes, I could do nothing. A mass of thick and tangled thorns now received them, and closed over the hardly contested race—I was beaten.

Never mind, it was a good hunt—first-rate—but where was my camp? It was nearly dark, and I could just distinguish the pass in the distance, by which we had descended the mountain; thus I knew the direction, but I had ridden about three miles, and it would be dark before I could return. However, I followed the heel tracks of the herd of giraffes. Richarn was nowhere. Although I had lost the race, and was disappointed, I now consoled myself that it was all for the best; had I killed a giraffe at that hour and distance from camp, what good would it have been? I was quite alone, thus who could have found it during the night? and before morning it would have been devoured by lions and hyenas;—in-offensive and beautiful creatures, what a sin it appeared to destroy them uselessly! With these consoling and practical reflections I continued my way, until a branch of hooked thorn fixing in my nose disturbed the train of ideas and persuaded me that it was very dark, and that I had lost my way, as I could no longer distinguish either the tracks of the giraffes or the position of the mountains. Accordingly I fired my rifle as a signal, and soon after I heard a distant report in reply, and the blaze of a fire shot up suddenly in the distance on the side of the mountain.

With the help of this beacon I reached the spot where our people were bivouacked; they had lighted the beacon on a rock about fifty feet above the level, as although some twenty or thirty fires were blazing, they had been obscured by the intervening jungle I found both my wife and my men in an argumentative state as to the propriety of my remaining alone so late in the jungle; however, I also found dinner ready; the angareps (stretcher bedsteads) arranged by a most comfortable blazing fire, and a glance at the star-lit heavens assured me of a fine night—what more can man wish for?—wife, welcome, food, fire, and fine weather?

★   ★   ★

On the 18th January, 1864, we left Shooa. The pure air of that country had invigorated us, and I was so improved in strength, that I enjoyed the excitement of the launch into unknown lands. The Turks knew nothing of the route south, and I accordingly took the lead of the entire party. I had come to a distinct understanding with Ibrahim that Kamrasi's country should belong to *me*; not an act of felony would be permitted; all were to be under my government, and I would insure him at least 100 cantars of tusks.

Eight miles of agreeable march through the usual park-like country brought us to the village of Fatiko, situated upon a splendid plateau of rock upon elevated ground, with beautiful granite cliffs, bordering a level tableland of fine grass that would have formed a race-course. The high rocks were covered with natives, perched upon the outline like a flock of ravens.

We halted to rest under some fine trees growing among large isolated blocks of granite and gneiss.

In a short time the natives assembled around us: they were wonderfully friendly, and insisted upon a personal introduction to both myself and Mrs Baker. We were thus compelled to hold a levee; not the passive and cold ceremony of Europe, but a most active undertaking, as each native that was introduced performed the salaam of his country, by seizing both my hands and raising my arms three times to their full stretch above my head. After about one hundred Fatikos had been thus gratified by our submission to this infliction, and our arms had been subjected to at least three hundred stretches each, I gave the order to saddle the oxen immediately, and we escaped a further proof of Fatiko affection that was already preparing, as masses of natives were streaming down the rocks hurrying to be introduced. Notwithstanding the fatigue of the ceremony, I took a great fancy to these poor people; they had prepared a quantity of merissa and a sheep for our lunch, which they begged us to remain and enjoy before we started; but the pumping action of half a village not yet gratified by a presentation was too much; and mounting our oxen, with aching shoulders we bade adieu to Fatiko.

*   *   *

After some hours passed in rambling over the black ashes of several villages that had been burnt, they discovered a hollow place, by sounding the earth with a stick, and, upon digging, they arrived at a granary of the seed known as "tullaboon"; this was a great prize, as, although mouldy and bitter, it would keep us from starving. The women of the party were soon hard at work grinding, as many of the necessary stones had been found among the ruins.

Fortunately there were three varieties of plants growing wild in great profusion, that, when boiled, were a good substitute for spinach; thus we were rich in vegetables, although without a morsel of fat or animal food. Our dinner consisted daily of a mess of black porridge of bitter mouldy flour, that no English pig would condescend to notice, and a large dish of spinach. "Better a dinner of herbs where love is," &c. often occurred to me; but I am not sure that I was quite of that opinion after a fortnight's grazing upon spinach.

Tea and coffee were things of the past, the very idea of which made our mouths water; but I found a species of wild thyme growing in the jungles, and this, when boiled, formed a tolerable substitute for tea; sometimes our men procured a little wild honey, which, added to the thyme tea, we considered a great luxury.

This wretched fare, in our exhausted state from fever and

general effects of climate, so completely disabled us, that for nearly two months my wife lay helpless on one angarep, and I upon the other; neither of us could walk. The hut was like all in Kamrasi's country, a perfect forest of thick poles to support the roof (I counted thirty-two); thus, although it was tolerably large, there was but little accommodation. These poles we now found very convenient, as we were so weak, that we could not rise from bed without hauling by one of the supports.

We were very nearly dead, and our amusement was a childish conversation about the good things in England, and my idea of perfect happiness was an English beef-steak and a bottle of pale ale; for such a luxury I would most willingly have sold my birth-right at that hungry moment. We were perfect skeletons; and it was annoying to see how we suffered upon the bad fare, while our men apparently throve. There were plenty of wild red peppers, and the men seemed to enjoy a mixture of porridge and *legumes a la sauce piquante*. They were astonished at my falling away on this food, but they yielded to my argument when I suggested that a "lion would starve where a donkey grew fat". I must confess that this state of existence did not improve my temper, which, I fear, became nearly as bitter as the porridge. My people had a windfall of luck, as Saat's ox, that had lingered for a long time, lay down to die, and stretching himself out, commenced kicking his last kick; the men immediately assisted him by cutting his throat, and this supply of beef was a luxury which, even in my hungry state, was not the English beefsteak for which I sighed; and I declined the diseased bull.

The men made several long excursions through the country to endeavour to purchase provisions, but in two months they pro-cured only two kids; the entire country was deserted, owing to the war between Kamrasi and Fowooka. Every day the boy Saat and the woman Bacheeta sallied out and conversed with the inhabitants of the different islands on the river; sometimes, but very rarely, they returned with a fowl; such an event caused great rejoicing.

We had now given up all hope of Gondokoro, and were per-fectly resigned to our fate; this, we felt sure, was to be buried in

Chopi. I wrote instructions in my journal in case of death, and told my headman to be sure to deliver my maps, observations, and papers to the English Consul at Khartoum; this was my only care, as I feared that all my labour might be lost should I die. I had no fear for my wife, as she was quite as bad as I, and if one should die, the other would certainly follow; in fact, this had been agreed upon lest she should fall into the hands of Kamrasi at my death. We had struggled to win, and I thanked God that we had won; if death were to be the price, at all events we were at the goal, and we both looked upon death rather as a pleasure, as affording *rest*; there would be no more suffering; no fever; no long journey before us, that in our weak state was an infliction; the only wish was to lay down the burthen.

Curious is the warfare between the animal instincts and the mind! Death would have been a release that I would have courted, but I should have liked that one "English beefsteak and pale ale" before I died!

*   *   *

At the hour appointed M'Gambi appeared, with a great crowd of natives. My clothes were in rags,—and as personal appearance has a certain effect, even in Central Africa, I determined to present myself to the king in as favourable a light as possible. I happened to possess a full-dress Highland suit that I had worn when I lived in Perthshire many years ago; this I had treasured as serviceable upon an occasion like the present;—accordingly I was quickly attired in kilt, sporran, and Glengarry bonnet, and to the utter amazement of the crowd, the ragged-looking object that had arrived in Kisoona now issued from the obscure hut, with plaid and kilt of Athole tartan. A general shout of exclamation arose from the assembled crowd; and taking my seat upon an angarep, I was immediately shouldered by a number of men, and attended by ten of my people as escort, I was carried towards the camp of the great Kamrasi.

In about half an hour we arrived. The camp composed of grass huts extended over a large extent of ground, and the approach was perfectly black with the throng that crowded to meet me.

Women, children, dogs, and men all thronged at the entrance
of the street that led to Kamrasi's residence. Pushing our way
through this inquisitive multitude, we continued through the
camp until at length we reached the dwelling of the king. Halting
for the moment, a message was immediately received that we
should proceed; we accordingly entered through a narrow
passage between high reed fences, and I found myself in the
presence of the actual king of Unyoro, Kamrasi. He was sitting
in a kind of porch in front of a hut, and upon seeing me he
hardly condescended to look at me for more than a moment; he
then turned to his attendants and made some remark that appeared
to amuse them, as they all grinned as little men are wont to do
when a great man makes a bad joke.

UPON my arrival at Gondokoro I was looked upon by all these
parties as a spy sent by the British Government. Whenever I
approached the encampments of the various traders, I heard the
clanking of fetters before I reached the station, as the slaves were
being quickly driven into hiding-places to avoid inspection. They
were chained by two rings secured round the ankles, and connected by three or four links. One of these traders was a Copt, the
father of the American Consul at Khartoum; and, to my surprise, I saw the vessel full of brigands arrive at Gondokoro, with
the American flag flying at the mast-head.

Gondokoro was a perfect hell. It is utterly ignored by the
Egyptian authorities, although well known to be a colony of cut-
throats. Nothing would be easier than to send a few officers and
two hundred men from Khartoum to form a military government, and thus impede the slave-trade; but a bribe from the
traders to the authorities is sufficient to insure an uninterrupted
asylum for any amount of villainy. The camps were full of
slaves, and the Bari natives assured me that there were large depots
of slaves in the interior belonging to the traders that would be
marched to Gondokoro for shipment to the Soudan a few hours

after my departure. I was the great stumbling-block to the trade, and my presence at Gondokoro was considered as an unwarrantable intrusion upon a locality sacred to slavery and iniquity. There were about six hundred of the traders' people at Gondokoro, whose time was passed in drinking, quarrelling, and ill-treating the slaves. The greater number were in a constant state of intoxication, and when in such a state, it was their invariable custom to fire off their guns in the first direction prompted by their drunken instincts; thus, from morning till night, guns were popping in all quarters, and the bullets humming through the air sometimes close to our ears, and on more than one occasion they struck up the dust at my feet. Nothing was more probable than a ball through the head by *accident*, which might have had the beneficial effect of ridding the traders from a spy. A boy was sitting upon the gunwale of one of the boats, when a bullet suddenly struck him in the head, shattering the skull to atoms. *No one had done it.* The body fell into the water, and the fragments of the skull were scattered on the deck.

After a few days' detention at Gondokoro, I saw unmistakable signs of discontent among my men, who had evidently been tampered with by the different traders' parties. One evening several of the most disaffected came to me with a complaint that they had not enough meat, and that they must be allowed to make a razzia upon the cattle of the natives to procure some oxen. This demand being of course refused, they retired, muttering in an insolent manner their determination of stealing cattle with or without my permission. I said nothing at the time, but early on the following morning I ordered the drum to beat, and the men to fall in. I made them a short address, reminding them of the agreement made at Khartoum to follow me faithfully, and of the compact that had been entered into, that they were neither to indulge in slave-hunting nor in cattle-stealing. The only effect of my address was a great outbreak of insolence on the part of the ringleader of the previous evening. This fellow, named Eesur, was an Arab, and his impertinence was so violent, that I immediately ordered him twenty-five lashes, as an example to the others.

I

Upon the vakeel (Saati) advancing to seize him, there was a
general mutiny. Many of the men threw down their guns and
seized sticks, and rushed to the rescue of their tall ringleader.
Saati was a little man, and was perfectly helpless. Here was an
escort! these were the men upon whom I was to depend in hours
of difficulty and danger on an expedition in unknown regions;
these were the fellows that I had considered to be reduced "from
wolves to lambs!"

I was determined not to be done, and to insist upon the punishment of the ringleader. I accordingly went towards him with
the intention of seizing him; but he, being backed by upwards
of forty men, had the impertinence to attack me, rushing forward
with a fury that was ridiculous. To stop his blow, and to knock
him into the middle of the crowd, was not difficult; and after a
rapid repetition of the dose, I disabled him, and seizing him by
the throat, I called to my vakeel Saati for a rope to bind him,
but in an instant I had a crowd of men upon me to rescue their
leader. How the affair would have ended I cannot say; but as the
scene lay within ten yards of my boat, my wife, who was ill
with fever in the cabin, witnessed the whole affray, and seeing
me surrounded, she rushed out, and in a few moments she was in
the middle of the crowd, who at that time were endeavouring to
rescue my prisoner. Her sudden appearance had a curious effect,
and calling upon several of the least mutinous to assist, she very
pluckily made her way up to me. Seizing the opportunity of an
indecision that was for the moment evinced by the crowd, I
shouted to the drummer-boy to beat the drum. In an instant the
drum beat, and at the top of my voice I ordered the men to
"fall in". It is curious how mechanically an order is obeyed if
given at the right moment, even in the midst of mutiny. Two-
thirds of the men fell in, and formed in line, while the remainder
retreated with the ringleader, Eesur, whom they led away,
declaring that he was badly hurt. The affair ended in my insisting
upon all forming in line, and upon the ringleader being brought
forward. In this critical moment Mrs Baker, with great tact,
came forward and implored me to forgive him if he kissed my
hand and begged for pardon. This compromise completely won

the men, who, although a few minutes before in open mutiny, now called upon their ringleader Eesur to apologise, and that all would be right. I made them rather a bitter speech, and dismissed them.

*   *   *

My vakeel was not to be found; my men were lying idly in the positions where they had slept; and not a man obeyed when I gave the order to prepare to start—except Richarn and Sali. I saw that the moment had arrived. Again I gave the order to the men, to get up and load the animals; . . . not a man would move, except three or four who slowly rose from the ground, and stood resting on their guns. In the meantime Richarn and Sali were bringing the camels and making them kneel by the luggage. The boy Saat was evidently expecting a row, and although engaged with the black women in packing, he kept his eyes constantly upon me.

I now observed that Bellaal was standing very near me on my right, in advance of the men who had risen from the ground, and employed himself in eyeing me from head to foot with the most determined insolence. The fellow had his gun in his hand, and he was telegraphing by looks with those who were standing near him, while not one of the others rose from the ground, although close to me. Pretending not to notice Bellaal, who was now as I had expected once more the ringleader, for the third time I ordered the men to rise immediately, and to load the camels. Not a man moved, but the fellow Bellaal marched up to me, and looking me straight in the face dashed the butt-end of his gun in defiance on the ground, and led the mutiny. "Not a man shall go with you!—go where you like with Ibrahim, but we won't follow you, nor move a step farther. The men shall not load the camels; you may employ the 'niggers' to do it, but not us."

I looked at this mutinous rascal for a moment; this was the burst of the conspiracy, and the threats and insolence that I had been forced to pass over for the sake of the expedition all rushed before me. "Lay down your gun!" I thundered, "and load the camels!" . . . "I won't"—was his reply. "Then stop here!"

I answered; at the same time lashing out as quick as lightning with my right hand upon his jaw.

He rolled over in a heap, his gun flying some yards from his hand; and the late ringleader lay apparently insensible among the luggage, while several of his friends ran to him, and did the good Samaritan. Following up on the moment the advantage I had gained by establishing a panic, I seized my rifle and rushed into the midst of the wavering men, catching first one by the throat, and then another, and dragging them to the camels, which I insisted upon their immediately loading. All except three, who attended to the ruined ringleader, mechanically obeyed. Richarn and Sali both shouted to them to "hurry"; and the vakeel arriving at this moment and seeing how matters stood, himself assisted, and urged the men to obey.

Ibrahim's party had started. The animals were soon loaded, and leaving the vakeel to take them in charge, we cantered on to overtake Ibrahim, having crushed the mutiny, and given such an example, that in the event of future conspiracies my men would find it difficult to obtain a ringleader. So ended the famous conspiracy that had been reported to me by both Saat and Richarn before we left Gondokoro;—and so much for the threat of "firing simultaneously at me and deserting my wife in the jungle." In those savage countries success frequently depends upon one particular moment; you may lose or win according to your action at that critical instant. We congratulated ourselves upon the termination of this affair, which I trusted would be the last of the mutinies.

THE *sun* is the great arbitrator between the white and the black man. There are productions necessary to civilized countries, that can alone be cultivated in tropical climates, where the white man cannot live if exposed to labour in the sun. Thus, such fertile countries as the West Indies and portions of America being without a native population, the negro was originally imported as a slave to fulfil the conditions of a labourer. In his own country he was a wild savage, and enslaved his brother man; he thus became a victim to his own system; to the institution of slavery that is indigenous to the soil of Africa, and that has *not been taught to the African by the white man*, as is currently reported, but that has ever been the peculiar characteristic of African tribes.

Under peculiar guidance, and subject to a certain restraint, the negro may be an important and most useful being; but if treated as an Englishman, he will affect the vices but none of the virtues of civilization, and his natural good qualities will be lost in his attempts to become a "white man".

It was amusing to watch the change that took place in a slave that had been civilized (?) by the slave-traders. Among their parties, there were many blacks who had been captured, and who enjoyed the life of slave-hunting—nothing appeared so easy as to become professional in cattle razzias and kidnapping human beings, and the first act of a slave *was to procure a slave for himself*! All the best slave-hunters, and the boldest and most energetic scoundrels, were the negroes who had at one time themselves been kidnapped. These fellows aped a great and ridiculous importance. On the march they would seldom condescend to carry their own guns; a little slave boy invariably attended to his master, keeping close to his heels, and trotting along on foot during a long march, carrying a musket much longer than himself; a woman generally carried a basket with a cooking-pot, and a gourd of water and provisions, while a hired native carried the soldier's change of clothes and ox-hide upon which he slept. Thus the man who had been kidnapped became the kidnapper, and the slave became the master, the only difference between him and the Arab being an absurd notion of his own dignity. It was in vain that I attempted to reason with them against the principles of slavery; they thought it wrong when they were themselves the sufferers, but were always ready to indulge in it when the preponderance of power lay upon their side.

HARDLY had the few boatmen departed, than some one shouted suddenly, and the entire crowd sprang to their feet and rushed towards the hut where I had left Mrs Baker. For the moment I thought that the hut was on fire, and I joined the crowd and arrived at the doorway, where I found a tremendous press to see some extraordinary sight. Every one was squeezing for the best place; and, driving them on one side, I found the wonder that had excited their curiosity. The hut being very dark, my wife had employed her solitude during my conference with the natives in dressing her hair at the doorway, which, being very long and blonde, was suddenly noticed by some native—a shout was given, the rush described had taken place, and the hut was literally mobbed by the crowd of savages eager to see the extraordinary novelty.

*   *   *

On the following morning we had the usual difficulty in collecting porters, those of the preceding day having absconded, and others were recruited from distant villages by the native escort, who enjoyed the excuse of hunting for porters, as it gave them an opportunity of foraging throughout the neighbourhood. During this time we had to wait until the sun was high; and we thus lost the cool hours of morning and increased our fatigue. Having at length started, we arrived in the afternoon at the Kafoor river, at a bend from the south where it was necessary to cross over in our westerly course. The stream was in the centre of a marsh, and although deep, it was so covered with thickly-matted water-grass and other aquatic plants, that a natural floating-bridge was established by a carpet of weeds about two feet thick: upon this waving and unsteady surface the men ran quickly across, sinking merely to the ankles, although beneath the tough vegetation there was deep water. It was equally impossible to ride or to be carried over this treacherous surface; thus I led the way, and begged Mrs Baker to follow me on foot as quickly as possible, precisely in my track. The river was about eighty yards wide, and I had scarcely completed a fourth of the distance and looked back to see if my wife followed close to me, when I was horrified to see her standing in one spot, and sinking gradually through the weeds, while her face was distorted and perfectly purple. Almost as soon as I perceived her, she fell, as though shot dead. In an instant I was by her side; and with the assistance of eight or ten of my men, who were fortunately close to me, I dragged her like a corpse through the yielding vegetation, and up to our waists we scrambled across to the other side, just keeping her head above the water: to have carried her would have been impossible, as we should all have sunk together through the weeds. I laid her under a tree, and bathed her head and face with water, as for the moment I thought she had fainted; but she lay perfectly insensible as though dead, with teeth and hands firmly clenched, and her eyes open, but fixed. It was a *coup de soleil*.

Many of the porters had gone on ahead with the baggage; and I started off a man in haste to recall an angarep upon which to carry her, and also for a bag with a change of clothes, as we had dragged her through the river. It was in vain that I rubbed her heart, and the black women rubbed her feet, to endeavour to restore animation. At length the litter came, and after changing her clothes, she was carried mournfully forward as a corpse. Constantly we had to halt and support her head, as a painful rattling in the throat betokened suffocation. At length we reached a village, and halted for the night.

I laid her carefully in a miserable hut, and watched beside her. I opened her clenched teeth with a small wooden wedge, and inserted a wet rag, upon which I dropped water to moisten her tongue, which was dry as fur. The unfeeling brutes that composed the native escort were yelling and dancing as though all were well; and I ordered their chief at once to return with them to Kamrasi, as I would travel with them no longer. At first they refused to return; until at length I vowed that I would fire into them should they accompany us on the following morning. Day broke, and it was a relief to have got rid of the brutal escort. They had departed, and I had now my own men, and the guides supplied by Kamrasi.

There was nothing to eat in this spot. My wife had never

stirred since she fell by the *coup de soleil*, and merely respired about five times in a minute. It was impossible to remain; the people would have starved. She was laid gently upon her litter, and we started forward on our funeral course. I was ill and broken-hearted, and I followed by her side through the long day's march over wild park-lands and streams, with thick forest and deep marshy bottoms; over undulating hills, and through valleys of tall papyrus rushes, which, as we brushed through them on our melancholy way, waved over the litter like the black plumes of a hearse. We halted at a village, and again the night was passed in watching. I was wet, and coated with mud from the swampy marsh, and shivered with ague; but the cold within was greater than all. No change had taken place; she had never moved. I had plenty of fat, and I made four balls of about half a pound, each of which would burn for three hours. A piece of a broken water-jar formed a lamp, several pieces of rag serving for wicks. So in solitude the still calm night passed away as I sat by her side and watched. In the drawn and distorted features that lay before me I could hardly trace the same face that for years had been my comfort through all the difficulties and dangers of my path. Was she to die? Was so terrible a sacrifice to be the result of my selfish exile?

Again the night passed away. Once more the march. Though weak and ill, and for two nights without a moment's sleep, I felt no fatigue, but mechanically followed by the side of the litter as though in a dream. The same wild country diversified with marsh and forest. Again we halted. The night came, and I sat by her side in a miserable hut, with the feeble lamp flickering while she lay, as in death. She had never moved a muscle since she fell. My people slept. I was alone, and no sound broke the stillness of the night. The ears ached at the utter silence, till the sudden wild cry of a hyena made me shudder as the horrible thought rushed through my brain, that, should she be buried in this lonely spot, the hyena would . . . disturb her rest.

The morning was not far distant; it was past four o'clock. I had passed the night in replacing wet cloths upon her head and moistening her lips, as she lay apparently lifeless on her litter.

I could do nothing more; in solitude and abject misery in that dark hour, in a country of savage heathens, thousands of miles away from a Christian land, I beseeched an aid above all human, trusting alone to Him.

The morning broke; my lamp had just burnt out, and, cramped with the night's watching, I rose from my low seat, and seeing that she lay in the same unaltered state, I went to the door of the hut to breathe one gasp of the fresh morning air. I was watching the first red streak that heralded the rising sun, when I was startled by the words, "Thank God," faintly uttered behind me. Suddenly she had awoke from her torpor, and with a heart overflowing I went to her bedside. Her eyes were full of madness! She spoke, but the brain was gone!

I will not inflict a description of the terrible trial of seven days of brain fever, with its attendant horrors. The rain poured in torrents, and day after day we were forced to travel for want of provisions, not being able to remain in one position. Every now and then we shot a few guinea-fowl, but rarely; there was no game, although the country was most favourable. In the forests we procured wild honey, but the deserted villages contained no supplies, as we were on the frontier of Uganda, and M'tese's people had plundered the district. For seven nights I had not slept, and although as weak as a reed, I had marched by the side of her litter. Nature could resist no longer. We reached a village one evening; she had been in violent convulsions successively—it was all but over. I laid her down on her litter within a hut; covered her with a Scotch plaid, and I fell upon my mat insensible, worn out with sorrow and fatigue. My men put a new handle to the pickaxe that evening, and sought for a dry spot to dig her grave!

The sun had risen when I woke. I had slept, and, horrified as the idea flashed upon me that she must be dead, and that I had not been with her, I started up. She lay upon her bed, pale as marble, and with that calm serenity that the features assume when the cares of life no longer act upon the mind, and the body rests in death. The dreadful thought bowed me down; but as I gazed upon her in fear, her chest gently heaved, not with the convulsive throbs of fever, but naturally. She was asleep; and when at a sudden noise she opened her eyes, they were calm and clear. She was saved! When not a ray of hope remained, God alone knows what helped us. The gratitude of that moment I will not attempt to describe.

* * *

In our present weak state another year of Central Africa without quinine appeared to warrant death; it was a race against time, all was untrodden ground before us, and the distance quite uncertain. I trembled for my wife, and weighed the risk of another year in this horrible country should we lose the boats. With the self-sacrificing devotion that she had shown in every trial, she implored me not to think of any risks on her account, but to push forward and discover the lake—that she had determined not to return until she had herself reached the "M'wootan N'zige".

I now requested Kamrasi to allow us to take leave, as we had not an hour to lose. In the coolest manner he replied, "I will send you to the lake and to Shooa, as I have promised; but, *you must leave your wife with me!*"

At that moment we were surrounded by a great number of natives, and my suspicions of treachery at having been led across the Kafoor river appeared confirmed by this insolent demand. If this were to be the end of the expedition I resolved that it should also be the end of Kamrasi, and, drawing my revolver quietly, I held it within two feet of his chest, and looking at him with undisguised contempt, I told him, that if I touched the trigger, not all his men could save him: and that if he dared to repeat the insult I would shoot him on the spot. At the same time I explained to him that in my country such insolence would entail bloodshed, and that I looked upon him as an ignorant ox who knew no better, and that this excuse alone could save him. My wife, naturally indignant, had risen from her seat, and maddened with the excitement of the moment, she made him a little speech in Arabic (not a word of which he understood), with a countenance almost as amiable as the head of Medusa. Altogether the *mise en scène* utterly astonished him; the woman Bacheeta, although a savage, had appropriated the insult to her mistress, and she also fearlessly let fly at Kamrasi, translating as nearly as she could the complimentary address that "Medusa" had just delivered.

Whether this little *coup de théâtre* had so impressed Kamrasi with British female independence that he wished to be off his bargain, I cannot say, but with an air of complete astonishment, he said, "Don't be angry! I had no intention of offending you by asking for your wife; I will give you a wife, if you want one, and I thought you might have no objection to give me yours; it is my custom to give my visitors pretty wives, and I thought you might exchange. Don't make a fuss about it; if you don't like it, there's an end of it; I will never mention it again." This very practical apology I received very sternly, and merely insisted upon starting. He seemed rather confused at having committed himself, and to make amends he called his people and ordered them to carry our loads. His men ordered a number of women who had assembled out of curiosity, to shoulder the luggage and to carry it to the next village where they would be relieved. I assisted my wife upon her ox, and with a very cold adieu to Kamrasi, I turned my back most gladly on M'rooli.

AMONG my people were two blacks: one, "Richarn", already described as having been brought up by the Austrian Mission at Khartoum; the other, a boy of twelve years old, "Saat". As these were the only really faithful members of the expedition, it is my duty to describe them. Richarn was an habitual drunkard, but he had his good points; he was honest, and much attached to both master and mistress. He had been with me for some months, and was a fair sportsman, and being an entirely different race to the Arabs, he kept himself apart from them, and fraternised with the boy Saat.

Saat was a boy that would do no evil; he was honest to a superlative degree, and a great exception to the natives of this

wretched country. He was a native of "Fertit", and was minding
his father's goats, when a child of about six years old, at the time
of his capture by the Baggara Arabs. He described vividly how
men on camels suddenly appeared while he was in the wilderness
with his flock, and how he was forcibly seized and thrust into a
large gum sack, and slung upon the back of a camel. Upon
screaming for help, the sack was opened, and an Arab threatened
him with a knife should he make the slightest noise. Thus quieted,
he was carried hundreds of miles through Korodofan to Dongola
on the Nile, at which place he was sold to slave-dealers, and taken
to Cairo to be sold to the Egyptian government as a drummer-
boy. Being too young he was rejected, and while in the dealer's
hands he heard from another slave, of the Austrian Mission at
Cairo, that it would protect him could he only reach their asylum.
With extraordinary energy for a child of six years old, he escaped
from his master, and made his way to the Mission, where he was
well received, and to a certain extent disciplined and taught as
much of the Christian religion as he could understand. In company with a branch establishment of the Mission, he was subsequently located at Khartoum, and from thence was sent up the
White Nile to a Mission-station in the Shillook country. The
climate of the White Nile destroyed thirteen missionaries in
the short space of six months, and the boy Saat returned with the
remnant of the party to Khartoum, and was readmitted into the
Mission. The establishment was at that time swarming with little
black boys from the various White Nile tribes, who repaid the
kindness of the missionaries by stealing everything they could
lay their hands upon. At length the utter worthlessness of the
boys, their moral obtuseness, and the apparent impossibility of
improving them, determined the chief of the Mission to purge
his establishment from such imps, and they were accordingly
turned out. Poor little Saat, the one grain of gold amidst the
mire, shared the same fate.

It was about a week before our departure from Khartoum that
Mrs Baker and I were at tea in the middle of the court-yard, when
a miserable boy about twelve years old came uninvited to her
side, and knelt down in the dust at her feet. There was something

so irresistibly supplicating in the attitude of the child, that the first impulse was to give him something from the table. This was declined, and he merely begged to be allowed to live with us, and to be our boy. He said that he had been turned out of the Mission, merely because the Bari boys of the establishment were thieves, and thus he suffered for their sins. I could not believe it possible that the child had been actually turned out into the streets, and believing that the fault must lay in the boy, I told him I would inquire. In the meantime he was given in charge of the cook.

It happened that, on the following day, I was so much occupied that I forgot to inquire at the Mission; and once more the cool hour of evening arrived when, after the intense heat of the day, we sat at table in the open court-yard; it was refreshed by being plentifully watered. Hardly were we seated, when again the boy appeared, kneeling in the dust, with his head lowered at my wife's feet, and imploring to be allowed to follow us. It was in vain that I explained that we had a boy, and did not require another; that the journey was long and difficult, and that he might perhaps die. The boy feared nothing, and craved simply that he might belong to us. He had no place of shelter, no food; had been stolen from his parents, and was a helpless outcast.

The next morning, accompanied by Mrs Baker, I went to the Mission and heard that the boy had borne an excellent character, and that it must have been *by mistake* that he had been turned out with the others. This being conclusive, Saat was immediately adopted. Mrs Baker was shortly at work making him some useful clothes, and in an incredibly short time a great change was effected. As he came from the hands of the cook—after a liberal use of soap and water, and attired in trousers, blouse, and belt— the new boy appeared in a new character.

From that time he considered himself as belonging absolutely to his mistress. He was taught by her to sew; Richarn instructed him in the mysteries of waiting at table, and washing plates, &c.; while I taught him to shoot, and gave him a light double-barrelled gun. This was his greatest pride.

In the evening, when the day's work was done, Saat was

allowed to sit near his mistress; and he was at times amused and instructed by stories of Europe and Europeans, and anecdotes from the Bible adapted to his understanding, combined with the first principles of Christianity. He was very ignorant, notwithstanding his advantages in the Mission, but he possessed the first grand rudiments of all religion—honesty of purpose. Although a child of only twelve years old, he was so perfectly trustworthy that, at the period of our arrival at Gondokoro, he was more to be depended upon than my vakeel, and nothing could occur among my mutinous escort without the boy's knowledge: thus he reported the intended mutiny of the people when there was no other means of discovering it, and without Saat I should have had no information of their plots.

Not only was the boy trustworthy, but he had an extraordinary amount of moral in addition to physical courage. If any complaint were made, and Saat was called as a witness—far from the shyness too often evinced when the accuser is brought face to face with the accused—such was Saat's proudest moment; and, no matter who the man might be, the boy would challenge him, regardless of all consequences.

We were very fond of this boy; he was thoroughly good; and in that land of iniquity, thousands of miles away from all except what was evil, there was a comfort in having some one innocent and faithful, in whom to trust.

*   *   *

One morning the boy Saat came to me with his head bound up, and complained of severe pain in the back and limbs, with all the usual symptoms of plague: in the afternoon I saw him leaning over the ship's side; his nose was bleeding violently! At night he was delirious. On the following morning he was raving, and on the vessel stopping to collect firewood he threw himself into the river to cool the burning fever that consumed him. His eyes were suffused with blood, which, blended with a yellow as deep as the yolk of egg, gave a horrible appearance to his face, that was already so drawn and changed as to be hardly recognised. Poor Saat! the faithful boy that we had adopted, and who had formed so bright an exception to the dark character of his race, was now a victim to this horrible disease. He was a fine strong lad of nearly fifteen, and he now lay helplessly on his mat, and cast wistful glances at the face of his mistress as she gave him a cup of cold water mixed with a few lumps of sugar that we had obtained from the traders at Gondokoro.

Saat grew worse and worse: nothing would relieve the unfortunate boy from the burning torture of that frightful disease. He never slept, but night and day he muttered in delirium, breaking the monotony of his malady by occasionally howling like a wild animal. Richarn won my heart by his careful nursing of the boy, who had been his companion through years of hardship. We arrived at the village of Wat Shely, only three days from Khartoum. Saat was dying. The night passed, and I expected that all would be over before sunrise; but as morning dawned a change had taken place,—the burning fever had left him, and although raised blotches had broken out upon his chest and various parts of his body, he appeared much better. We now gave him stimulants; a tea-spoonful of araki that we had bought at Fashoder was administered every ten minutes on a lump of sugar. This he crunched in his mouth, while he gazed at my wife with an expression of affection, but he could not speak. I had him well washed, and dressed in clean clothes, that had been kept most carefully during the voyage, to be worn on our *entree* to Khartoum. He was laid down to sleep upon a clean mat, and my wife gave him a lump of sugar to moisten his mouth and to relieve his thickly-furred tongue. His pulse was very weak, and his skin cold. "Poor Saat," said my wife, "his life hangs upon a thread. We must nurse him most carefully; should he have a relapse, nothing will save him." An hour passed, and he slept. Karka, the fat, good-natured slave woman, quietly went to his side: gently taking him by the ankles and knees, she stretched his legs into a straight position, and laid his arms parallel with his sides. She then covered his face with a cloth, one of the few rags that we still possessed. "Does he sleep still?" we asked. The tears ran down the cheeks of the savage but good-hearted Karka, as she sobbed, "He is dead!"

We stopped the boat. It was a sandy shore; the banks were high, and a clump of mimosas grew above high water-mark. It was there that we dug his grave. My men worked silently and sadly, for all loved Saat: he had been so good and true, that even their hard hearts had learnt to respect his honesty. We laid him in his grave on the desert shore, beneath the grove of trees. Again the sail was set, and, filled by the breeze, it carried us away from the dreary spot where we had sorrowfully left all that was good and faithful. It was a happy end—most merciful, as he had been taken from a land of iniquity in all the purity of a child converted from Paganism to Christianity. He had lived and died in our service a good Christian. Our voyage was nearly over, and we looked forward to home and friends, but we had still fatigues before us: poor Saat had reached his home and rest.

AT about 9 p.m. one night we were suddenly disturbed by a tremendous din—hundreds of nogaras were beating, horns blowing, and natives screaming in all directions. I immediately jumped out of bed, and buckling on my belt I took my rifle and left the hut. The village was alive with people all dressed for war, and bearded with cows' tails, dancing and rushing about with shields and spears, attacking imaginary enemies. Bacheeta informed me that Fowooka's people had crossed the Nile and were within three hours' march of Kisoona, accompanied by *a hundred and fifty* of Debono's trading party, the same that had formerly attacked Kamrasi in the preceding year in company with Rionga's people. It was reported, that having crossed the Nile they were marching direct on Kisoona with the intention of attacking the country and of killing Kamrasi. M'Gambi, the brother of Kamrasi, whose hut was only twenty yards distant, immediately came to me with the news: he was in a great state of alarm, and was determined to run off to the king immediately to recommend his flight. After some time I succeeded in convincing him that this was unnecessary, and that I might be of great service in this dilemma if Kamrasi would come personally to me early on the following morning.

The sun had just risen, when the king unceremoniously marched into my hut;—he was no longer the dignified monarch of Kitwara clothed in a beautiful mantle of fine skins, but he wore nothing but a short kilt of blue baize that Speke had given him, and a scarf thrown across his shoulders. He was dreadfully alarmed, and could hardly be persuaded to leave his weapons outside the door, according to the custom of the country—these were three lances and a double-barrelled rifle that had been given him by Speke. I was much amused at his trepidation, and observing the curious change in his costume, I complimented him upon the practical cut of his dress, that was better adapted for fighting than the long and cumbrous mantle. "*Fighting*," he exclaimed, with the horror of "Bob Acres," "I am not going to fight! I have dressed lightly to be able to run quickly. I mean to run away! Who can fight against guns? Those people have one hundred and fifty guns; you must run with me; we can do nothing against them; you have only thirteen men; Eddrees has only ten; what can twenty-three do against *a hundred and fifty*? Pack up your things and run; we must be off into the high grass and hide, at once; the enemy is expected every moment!"

I never saw a man in such a deplorable state of abject fright, and I could not help laughing aloud at the miserable coward who represented a kingdom. Calling my headman, I ordered him to hoist the English ensign on my tall flag-staff in the courtyard. In a few moments the old flag was waving in a brisk breeze and floating over my little hut. There is something that warms the heart in the sight of the Union Jack when thousands of miles away from the old country. I now explained to Kamrasi that both he and his country were under the protection of that flag, which was the emblem of England; and that so long as he trusted to me, although I had refused to join him in attacking Fowooka, he should see that I was his true ally, as I would defend him against all attacks. I told him to send a large quantity of supplies into my camp, and to procure guides immediately, as I should send some of my men without delay to the enemy's camp with a message to the vakeel of Debono's party. Slightly reassured by this arrangement, he called Quonga, and ordered him to procure two of his chiefs to accompany my men. In half an hour from the receipt of my order, the party started;—eight well-armed men accompanied by about twenty natives of Kamrasi's with two days' provisions. Kisoona was about ten miles from the Victoria Nile.

At about 5 p.m. on the following day my men returned, accompanied by ten men and a choush, or sergeant, of Debono's party;—they had determined to prove whether I was actually in the country, as they had received a report some months ago that both my wife and I were dead;—they imagined that the men that I had sent to their camp were those of the rival party belonging to Ibrahim, who wished to drive them out of Kamrasi's country by using my name. However, they were now undeceived, as the first object that met their view was the English flag on the high flagstaff, and they were shortly led into my court-yard, where they were introduced to me in person. They sat in a half-circle around me.

Assuming great authority, I asked them how they could presume to attack a country under the protection of the British flag? I informed them that Unyoro belonged to me by right of discovery, and that I had given Ibrahim the exclusive right to the produce of that country on the condition that he should do nothing contrary to the will of the reigning king, Kamrasi; that Ibrahim had behaved well; that I had been guided to the lake and had returned, and that we were now actually fed by the king; and we were suddenly invaded by Turkish subjects in connexion with a hostile tribe who thus insulted the English flag. I explained to them that I should not only resist any attack that might be made upon Kamrasi, but that I should report the whole affair to the Turkish authorities upon my return to Khartoum; and that, should a shot be fired or a slave be stolen in Kamrasi's country, the leader of their party, Mahommed Watel-Mek, would be hanged.

They replied that they were not aware that I was in the country; that they were allies of Fowooka, Rionga, and Owine, the three hostile chiefs; that they had received both ivory and slaves from them on condition that they should kill Kamrasi; and that, according to the custom of the White Nile trade, they had agreed to these conditions. They complained that it was very hard upon them to march six days through an uninhabited wilderness between their station at Faloro and Fowooka's islands and to return empty handed. In reply I told them, that they should carry a letter from me to their vakeel Mahommed, in which I should give him twelve hours from the receipt of my order to recross the river with his entire party and their allies and quit Kamrasi's country.

They demurred to this alternative; but I shortly settled their objections, by ordering my vakeel to write the necessary letter, and desiring them to start before sunrise on the following morning. Kamrasi had been suspicious that I had sent for Mahommed's party to invade him because he had kept me starving at Shooa Moru instead of forwarding me to Shooa as he had promised. This suspicion placed me in an awkward position; I therefore called M'Gambi (his brother) in presence of the Turks, and explained the whole affair face to face, desiring Mahommed's people themselves to explain to him that they would retire from the country simply because I commanded them to do so, but that, had I not been there, they would have attacked him. This they repeated with a very bad grace, boasting, at the completion, that, were it not for me, they would shoot M'Gambi where he stood at that moment. The latter, fully aware of their good intentions, suddenly disappeared. . . . My letter to Mahommed was delivered to Suleiman Choush, the leader of his party, and I ordered a sheep to be killed for their supper. . . . At sunrise on the following morning they all departed, accompanied by six of my men, who were to bring a reply to my letter. These people had two donkeys, and just as they were starting, a crowd of natives made a rush to gather a heap of dung that lay beneath the animals; a great fight and tussle took place for the possession of this valuable medicine, in the midst of which the donkey lifted up his voice and brayed so lustily that the crowd rushed away with more eagerness than they had exhibited on arriving, alarmed at the savage voice of the unknown animal. It appeared that the dung of the donkey rubbed upon the skin was supposed to be a cure for rheumatism, and that this rare specific was brought from a distant country in the East where such animals existed.

THE woman Bacheeta knew the country, as she had formerly been to Magungo when in the service of Sali, who had been subsequently murdered by Kamrasi; she now informed me that we should terminate our canoe voyage on that day, as we should arrive at the great waterfall of which she had often spoken. As we proceeded, the river gradually narrowed to about 180 yards, and when the paddles ceased working we could distinctly hear the roar of water. I had heard this on waking in the morning, but at the time I had imagined it to proceed from distant thunder. By ten o'clock the current had so increased as we proceeded, that it was distinctly perceptible, although weak. The roar of the waterfall was extremely loud, and after sharp pulling for a couple of hours, during which time the stream increased, we arrived at a few deserted fishing-huts, at a point where the river made a slight turn. I never saw such an extraordinary show of crocodiles as were exposed on every sandbank on the sides of the river; they lay like logs of timber close together, and upon one bank we counted twenty-seven, of large size; every basking place was crowded in a similar manner. From the time we had fairly entered the river, it had been confined by heights somewhat precipitous on either side, rising to about 180 feet. At this point the cliffs were still higher, and exceedingly abrupt. From the roar of the water, I was sure that the fall would be in sight if we turned the corner at the bend of the river; accordingly I ordered the boatmen to row as far as they could: to this they at first objected, as they wished to stop at the deserted fishing village, which they explained was to be the limit of the journey, further progress being impossible.

However, I explained that I merely wished to see the fall, and they rowed immediately up the stream, which was now strong against us. Upon rounding the corner, a magnificent sight burst suddenly upon us. On either side the river were beautifully wooded cliffs rising abruptly to a height of about 300 feet; rocks were jutting out from the intensely green foliage; and rushing through a gap that cleft the rock exactly before us, the river, contracted from a grand stream, was pent up in a narrow gorge of scarcely fifty yards in width; roaring furiously through the rock-bound pass, it plunged in one leap of about 120 feet perpendicular into a dark abyss below.

The fall of water was snow-white, which had a superb effect as it contrasted with the dark cliffs that walled the river, while the graceful palms of the tropics and wild plaintains perfected the beauty of the view. This was the greatest waterfall of the Nile and, in honour of the distinguished President of the Royal Geographical Society, I named it the Murchison Falls, as the most important object throughout the entire course of the river.

The boatmen, having been promised a present of beads to induce them to approach the fall as close as possible succeeded in bringing the canoe within about 300 yards of the base, but the power of the current and the whirlpools in the river rendered it impossible to proceed farther. There was a sandbank on our left which was literally covered with crocodiles lying parallel to each other like trunks of trees prepared for shipment; they had no fear of the canoe until we approached within about twenty yards of them, when they slowly crept into the water; all excepting one, an immense fellow who lazily lagged behind, and immediately dropped dead as a bullet from the little Fletcher No. 24 struck him in the brain.

So alarmed were the boatmen at the unexpected report of the rifle that they immediately dropped into the body of the canoe, one of them losing his paddle. Nothing would induce them to attend to the boat, as I had fired a second shot at the crocodile as a "quietus", and the natives did not know how often the alarming noise would be repeated. Accordingly we were at the mercy of the powerful stream, and the canoe was whisked round by the eddy and carried against a thick bank of high reeds;—hardly had we touched this obstruction when a tremendous commotion took place in the rushes, and in an instant a great bull hippopotamus charged the canoe, and with a severe shock striking the bottom he lifted us half out of the water. The natives who were in the bottom of the boat positively yelled with terror, not knowing whether the shock was in any way connected with the dreaded report of the rifle; the black women screamed; and the boy Saat handing me a spare rifle, and Richarn being ready likewise, we looked out for a shot should the angry hippo again attack us.

A few kicks bestowed by my angry men upon the recumbent boatmen restored them to the perpendicular. The first thing necessary was to hunt for the lost paddle that was floating down the rapid current. The hippopotamus, proud of having disturbed us, but doubtless thinking us rather hard of texture, raised his head to take a last view of his enemy, but sank too rapidly to permit a shot. Crocodile heads of enormous size were on all sides, appearing and vanishing rapidly as they rose to survey us; at one time we counted eighteen upon the surface. Fine fun it would have been for these monsters had the bull hippo been successful in his attempt to capsize us; the fat black woman, Karka, would have been a dainty morsel. Having recovered the lost paddle, I prevailed upon the boatmen to keep the canoe steady while I made a sketch of the Murchison Falls, which being completed, we drifted rapidly down to the landing-place at the deserted fishing-village, and bade adieu to the navigation of the lake and river of Central Africa.

THE name of this village was Parkani. For several days past our guides had told us that we were very near to the lake, and we were now assured that we should reach it on the morrow. I had noticed a lofty range of mountains at an immense distance west, and I had imagined that the lake lay on the other side of this chain; but I was now informed that those mountains formed the western frontier of the M'wootan N'zige, and that the lake was actually within a march of Parkani. I could not believe it possible that we were so near the object of our search. The guide Rabonga now appeared, and declared that if we started early on the following morning we should be able to wash in the lake by noon!

That night I hardly slept. For years I had striven to reach the "sources of the Nile". In my nightly dreams during that arduous voyage I had always failed, but after so much hard work and perseverance the cup was at my very lips, and I was to *drink* at the mysterious fountain before another sun should set—at that great reservoir of Nature that ever since creation had baffled all discovery.

I had hoped, and prayed, and striven through all kinds of difficulties, in sickness, starvation, and fatigue, to reach that hidden source; and when it had appeared impossible, we had both determined to die upon the road rather than return defeated. Was it possible that it was so near, and that to-morrow we could say, "the work is accomplished?"

The 14th March—The sun had not risen when I was spurring my ox after the guide, who, having been promised a double handful of beads on arrival at the lake, had caught the enthusiasm of the moment. The day broke beautifully clear, and having crossed a deep valley between the hills, we toiled up the opposite slope. I hurried to the summit. The glory of our prize burst suddenly upon me! There, like a sea of quicksilver, lay far beneath the grand expanse of water,—a boundless sea horizon on the south and south-west, glittering in the noon-day sun; and on the west, at fifty or sixty miles' distance, blue mountains rose from the bosom of the lake to a height of about 7,000 feet above its level.

It is impossible to describe the triumph of that moment;—here was the reward for all our labour—for the years of tenacity with which we had toiled through Africa. England had won the sources of the Nile! Long before I reached this spot, I had arranged to give three cheers with all our men in English style in honour of the discovery, but now that I looked down upon the great inland sea lying nestled in the very heart of Africa, and thought how vainly mankind had sought these sources throughout so many ages, and reflected that I had been the humble instrument permitted to unravel this portion of the great mystery when so many greater than I had failed, I felt too serious to vent my feelings in vain cheers for victory, and I sincerely thanked God for having guided and supported us through all dangers to the good end. I was about 1,500 feet above the lake, and I looked down from the steep granite cliff upon those welcome waters—upon that vast reservoir which nourished Egypt and brought fertility where all was wilderness—upon that great source so long hidden from mankind; that source of bounty and of blessings to millions of human beings; and as one of the greatest objects in nature, I determined to honour it with a great name. As an imperishable memorial of one loved and mourned by our gracious Queen and whose death was deplored by every Englishman, I called this great lake "the Albert N'yanza". The Victoria and the Albert lakes are the two sources of the Nile.

The zigzag path to descend to the lake was so steep and dangerous that we were forced to leave our oxen with a guide, who was to take them to Magungo and wait for our arrival. We commenced the descent of the steep pass on foot. I led the way, grasping a stout bamboo. My wife in extreme weakness tottered down the pass, supporting herself upon my shoulder, and stopping to rest every twenty paces. After a toilsome descent of about two hours, weak with years of fever, but for the moment strengthened by success, we gained the level plain below the cliff. A walk of about a mile through flat sandy meadows of fine turf interspersed with trees and bush, brought us to the water's edge. The waves were rolling upon a white pebbly beach: I rushed into the lake, and thirsty with heat and fatigue, with a heart full of gratitude, I drank deeply from the Sources of the Nile.

THAT night we were full of speculations. Would a boat be waiting for us with supplies and letters? The morning anxiously looked forward to at length arrived. We started;—the English flag had been mounted on a fine straight bamboo with a new lancehead specially arranged for the arrival at Gondokoro. My men felt proud, as they would march in as conquerors;—according to White Nile ideas such a journey could not have been accomplished with so small a party. Long before Ibrahim's men were ready to start, our oxen were saddled and we were off, longing to hasten into Gondokoro and to find a comfortable vessel with a few luxuries, and the post from England. Never had the oxen travelled so fast as on that morning;—the flag led the way, and the men in excellent spirits followed at double quick pace. "I see the masts of the vessels!" exclaimed the boy Saat. "El hambd el Illah!" (Thank God!) shouted the men. "Hurrah!" said I—"Three cheers for old England and the Sources of the Nile! Hurrah!" and my men joined me in the wild, and to their ears savage, English yell. "Now for a salute! Fire away all your powder if you like, my lads, and let the people know that we're alive!" This was all that was required to complete the happiness of my people, and loading and firing as fast as possible, we approached near to Gondokoro. Presently we saw the Turkish flag emerge from Gondokoro, at about a quarter of a mile distant, followed by a number of the traders' people, who waited to receive us. On our arrival, they immediately approached and fired salutes with ball cartridge, as usual advancing close to us and discharging their guns into the ground at our feet. One of my servants, Mahomet, was riding an ox, and an old friend of his in the crowd happening to recognise him, immediately advanced and saluted him by firing his gun into the earth directly beneath the belly of the ox he was riding;—the effect produced made the crowd and ourselves explode with laughter. The nervous ox, terrified at the sudden discharge between his legs, gave a tremendous kick, and continued madly kicking and plunging, until Mahomet was pitched over his head, and lay sprawling on the ground;—this scene terminated the expedition.

Dismounting from our tired oxen, our first inquiry was concerning boats and letters. What was the reply? Neither boats, letters, supplies, nor any intelligence of friends or the civilized world! We had long since been given up as dead by the inhabitants of Khartoum, and by all those who understood the difficulties and dangers of the country. We were told that some people had suggested that we might possibly have gone to Zanzibar, but the general opinion was that we had all been killed. At this cold and barren reply, I felt almost choked. We had looked forward to arriving at Gondokoro as to a home; we had expected that a boat would have been sent on the chance of finding us, as I had left money in the hands of an agent in Khartoum—but there was literally nothing to receive us, and we were helpless to return. We had worked for years in misery, such as I have but faintly described, to overcome the difficulties of this hitherto unconquerable exploration; we had succeeded—and what was the result? Not even a letter from home to welcome us if alive! As I sat beneath a tree and looked down upon the glorious Nile that flowed a few yards beneath my feet, I pondered upon the value of my toil. I had traced the river to its great Albert source, and as the mighty stream glided before me, the mystery that had ever shrouded its origin was dissolved. I no longer looked upon its waters with a feeling approaching to awe, for I knew its home, and had visited its cradle. Had I overrated the importance of the discovery? and had I wasted some of the best years of my life to obtain a shadow? I recalled to recollection the practical question of Commoro, the chief of Latooka,—"Suppose you get to the great lake, what will you do with it? What will be the good of it? If you find that the large river does flow from it, what then?"

INDEX

Albert N'yanza, Lake, 17, 210, 217–19, 262–4

Al-Idrisi (Arab cartographer), 18

Arabs, 37–9, 49, 57–8, 68, 72–4, 76, 80–1

Asua river, 203–4, 209–10

Baker, Florence, 116, 118–19; her background, 184–5; joins her husband's expedition (*see* Baker, Samuel White)

Baker, Samuel White, 101, 107; theory of Central African man, 22; makes potato-whisky, 25–6, 228; *The Albert N'yanza, Great Basin of the Nile and Explorations of the Nile*, 28–9, 183, 208, quoted 234*ff*.; meets Speke and Grant at Gondokoro, 116–19, 148, 183, 189–90; his earlier life, 183–4; sets out on Nile expedition, 185; at Khartoum, 185–7; journey to Gondokoro, 187–90; opinion of missionaries, 187–8; plots against, and difficulties in getting away from Gondokora, 190–4, 243–4; Mrs Baker's pet monkey, 194; Ibrahim's caravan joins the Bakers, 195–7; in the Latuka capital, 197–202; hunting activities, 199–201, 203, 205, 234–6; in the Obbo country, 202–3; exploration of the Asua crossing, and return to Tarrangolle, 203–5; return to the Obbo country, 206–9; journey into Unyoro, 209–12; negotiations with King Karamsi, 212–16; allowed to proceed, 216–17; Mrs Baker's severe illness, 216, 246–50; discovers Lake Albert N'yanza, 217–18, 262–4; sets out for Gondokoro, 218–20; explores the Somerset river, and discovers Murchison Falls, 220–1, 260–2; on island town of Patooan, 221–2; at Kamrasi's capital, 22–3; "protects" Kamrasi, 223–5, 256–60; the power behind Kamrasi, 225–7; at Foweera, and meets Ibrahim at Karuma Falls, 227–8; at Shooa, 229–30; Mrs Baker fosters African slave children, 230–1; return of the expedition, 231–3

Bari people, 107, 111, 115, 240

Belaal (the Bakers' headsman), 196, 243

Berbera, 33, 34

Black magic, 82, 156

Bombay, Seedy Mubarak (leader

Bombay–cont.
of men on Burton-Speke and Speke-Grant expeditions), 41, 48, 57–8, 65, 91, 104, 106–10, 128, 134, 145, 153, 173, 179
Budja (Mtesa's Minister of Affairs), 103–5, 109
Burial customs, 78
Burton, Richard Francis, 95; *The Lake Regions of Central Africa*, 28, 44, 48*ff*.; Somali expedition, 33–4; accuses Speke of cowardice, 34; character with Speke's, 34–5; attacks Speke, 120, 121
See also Burton-Speke Expedition
Burton-Speke Expedition (1857–59); Burton's directives from Royal Geographical Society, 35; Speke joins Burton, 35; at Zanzibar, and organization of the expedition, 36–7; they set out, and reach Ugogi, 37–9; accompanied by Arab caravan, 39–40; at Kazeh, 40–2; reaches Lake Tanganyika, 42; Kannena's extortions, 42–3; Speke searches for canoes, and gets a beetle in his ear, 43, 85–6; sets out for Uvira, and returns to Ujiji, 43–4; in Kazeh again, 44; Speke discovers source of the Nile (and Burton's reactions), 44–7, 56–8; Burton's *Lake Regions of Central Africa*, quoted 48*ff*.; Speke's *What Led to the Discovery of the Source of the Nile*, quoted 84–6

Cairo, 233
Capellan, Baroness Miss A. van, 118, 148
Chopi tribe, 107, 109, 111
Crocodiles, 220–1, 262

De Bono (Maltese trader), 112, 113, 116, 147, 176, 213, 224, 230, 256, 258
Diogenes, 17
Disease, 24–5, 38, 70, 150, 157–8, 188, 214, 232
Dwellings, of the Wanyamwezi, 78–9

Eesa tribe, 33
Ellyria country, 194; the people, 195

Faloro, trading station of, 108, 110–14, 176–80, 259
Fatiko, village of, 236–7
Fauna, 123; of Unyamwezi, 70–3
Food, of the Wanyamwezi, 80–1
Foweera, 227
Fowooka (chief), 224, 226, 258, 259
Fundikira, chief of Unyamwezi, 81–2

Gondokoro, 18, 26–7, 108, 115–19, 147, 186, 189–93, 225, 240–1, 250–1, 265
Grant, James Augustus: *A Walk Across Africa*, 27–8, 121, quoted 150*ff*.; appearance and character, 89–90
See also Speke-Grant Expedition

Hamerton, Lt.-Col. (British Consul at Zanzibar), 37–8
Harar, ancient walled city of, 33, 36

Herne, Lieutenant, 33

Hottentots, 90

Ibrahim (ivory trader and guide to the Baker expedition), 195–9, 201, 204–12, 214, 222, 225, 227–9, 236, 243–4

Illegitimate children, inheritance by, 77

Isamba Rapids, 104, 123

Kamrasi, king of Unyoro, 93, 190–1, 207, 221–2, 228, 247, 256–60; and Speke and Grant, 105–11, 211–13, 215, 257; and Baker, 212–16, 222–3, 239–40; "protected" by Baker, 223–7; refused a rifle by Baker, 229

Kannena, an extortionate chief, 42–3

Karague, kingdom of, 83, 92–5, 162–7

Karuma Falls, 210, 227, 228

Katchiba, chief of the Obbo, 203–4, 208–9

Kazeh, capital of Arab ivory and slave traders, 40–2, 57, 92–3

Khartoum, 119, 120, 185–7, 232

Kisoona, capital of Unyoro, 225–7

Konduchi, 47

Koorshid Aga (Circassian trader), 191–4

Latuka country, 195–202; the people of, 197, 205, 206

Livingstone, Dr, 67, 71

McQueen (geographer), 120

Madi tribe, 107, 111

Mahommed ('also Mahamed'), see p. 112, Wat-el-Mek (agent of De Bono), 112–16, 147, 177, 190–2, 210, 224, 230, 258–9

Mahommed Her (leader of a caravan), 193, 195–6, 198

Maizan (Frenchman murdered by slavers), 20

Missionaries, 18, 187–8

Mombasa, 18

Mtesa, king of Uganda, 93, 96–103, 107, 110, 120, 125–38, 139, 167–71, 173, 176, 224, 227–8

Murchison, Sir Roderick, 89, 148

Murchison Falls, 220–1, 260–2

Musa (Indian merchant), 93

Napoleon Channel, 104–5, 125

Nyassa, Lake of, 35, 37–8

Obbo tribe, 201–2, 207

Patooan, island town of, 221, 222

Petherick (British Vice-Consul at Khartoum), 108–17, 120, 132, 147–9, 176, 208

Plague, 232

Polygamy, 197

Ptolemaeus, Claudius (Ptolemy; geographer), 18

Queen Mother, of Uganda, 97, 101, 140–7

Richarn, Corporal (one of Baker's "irregulars"), 187–8, 190, 192, 212, 217, 219, 227, 232–3, 243, 251, 253

Rimbaud, 36

Rionga (chief), 211, 224, 258

Ripon Falls, 104–5, 124–5, 210

Roscher, Dr, 150

Royal Geographical Society, 35, 38, 46

Rumanika, king of Karague, 92, 93, 109, 120, 131, 138, 164

Saat (the Bakers' servant boy), 190, 193, 207, 212, 217, 232, 243, 251–6

Schmidt, Johann, 186, 187

Shooa country, 210, 227, 229–30

Slavery, slave trade, 18–20, 91, 92, 185, 240–1, 245

Snay, Sheikh, 41, 93

Somali country, 33

Sorcery, 202

Speke, John Hanning, 228; *Journal of a Cruise on the Tanganyika Lake*, 28; *What Led to the Discovery of the Source of the Nile*, 28, quoted 84–6; *Journal of the Discovery of the Source of the Nile*, 28, quoted 123*ff.*; with Burton on Somali expedition, 33; captured by Somali Nomads, 33–4; his character contrasted with Burton's, 34–5; at the Royal Geographical Society, 89; attacked by Burton and others, 120–1; death, 121, 232; Grant's tribute to, 121–2; Burton's opinion of, 122

See also Burton-Speke Expedition; Speke-Grant Expedition

Speke-Grant Expedition (1860–63): Speke and the Royal Geographical Society, 89; Grant joins Speke, 89–90; sets out for Zanzibar, 90; organisation, 91;

the attempt to capture a slave ship, 91–2; reaches Kazeh, 92–3, 152–5; in Karague, and relations with King Rumanika, 93–5, 162–7; Speke sets out alone for Uganda, and his dealings with King Mtesa, 95–103, 125*ff.*; Grant arrives in Uganda, 97, 167–76; Speke reaches the Nile, and Grant reaches Unyoro, 103–5, 123–5; the repulse by King Kamrasi, 105–6; invited into Unyoro, and relations with the king, 106–11, 211–13, 215; Seedy Bombay sent to find Petherick, 108–17, 147–9; reaches Faloro, 111–15, 176–80; at Gondokoro, and meeting with Baker, 116–19, 147–9, 189–90; returns to England, 119

Stanley, H. M., 40

Stocks, Assistant Surgeon, 33

Stroyan, Lieutenant, 33

Tabora, 40 (*see also* Kazeh)

Tamarind, 49

Tanganyika, Lake, 17, 24, 42, 58–60, 72, 85

Tarrangole, capital of Latuka, 197–202, 204–6

Tinne, Mrs and Miss, 118, 148

Uganda, kingdom of, 21–2, 83, 93, 95–103, 130, 167–76

Ugogi, 39

Ugogoland, 40

Ujiji, 37, 42, 83

Ukerewe lake, 41, 44

Unyamwezi, land of, 40, 42, 66–70; the Mukunguru (fever) of,

Uyamwezsi–*cont.*
70; fauna, 70–3; the Wakimbu
people, 73–4; the Wanyam-
wezi people, 74–81; government of, 81–3
Unmarried girls of Wanyamwezi
people, their community life,
77
Unyanyembe, 41, 57, 92
Unyoro, kingdom of, 83, 93, 98,
105–11, 207, 210*ff.*
Usukuma, 76
Uvira, on Lake Tanganyika, 43–4

Victoria N'yanza, Lake, 17, 45,
46, 84–5, 89, 96, 104, 120, 125,
210, 264

Villages, of the Wanyamwezi,
79–80

Wabisa people, 67
Waganda people, 98, 100, 102,
110, 124–5, 128, 143, 146, 163,
227
Wagogo people, 40
Wakalaganza people, 68
Wakimbu people, 73–4
Wanyamwezi people, 26, 73–81
Wasawahili people, 38
Women, 51–2, 159–62

Zanzibar, 17, 18, 19, 26, 36, 91
Zungomero, slave-trading town
of, 38